Personal~Passionate~ Participatory Inquiry Into Social Justice in Education

A volume in
Research for Social Justice:
Personal~Passionate~Participatory Inquiry

Series Editors:
Ming Fang He, *Georgia Southern University*
JoAnn Phillion, *Purdue University*

Research for Social Justice: Personal~Passionate~ Participatory Inquiry

Ming Fang He and JoAnn Phillion, Series Editors

Personal~Passionate~Participatory Inquiry Into
Social Justice in Education (2008)
edited by Ming Fang He and JoAnn Phillion

Personal~Passionate~ Participatory Inquiry Into Social Justice in Education

edited by

Ming Fang He
Georgia Southern University

and

JoAnn Phillion
Purdue University

Information Age Publishing, Inc.
Charlotte, North Carolina • www.infoagepub.com

Library of Congress Cataloging-in-Publication Data

Personal, passionate, participatory inquiry into social justice in education / edited by Ming Fang He and JoAnn Phillion.
  p. cm. -- (Research for social justice: personal, passionate, participatory inquiry)
Includes bibliographical references.
ISBN 978-1-59311-975-1 (pbk.) -- ISBN 978-1-59311-976-8 (hardcover)
I. He, Ming Fang. II. Phillion, JoAnn.
LC191.4.P47 2008
303.3'72--dc
                    2008027250

Printed in the United States of America

CONTENTS

Acknowledgments   *vii*

Foreword
  William Ayers   *ix*

1. Personal~Passionate~Participatory Inquiry:
Research For Social Justice
Ming Fang He and JoAnn Phillion   *1*

2. Stitched From the Soul:
An Auto/Biographical Inquiry of a Black Woman Principal
Sonya D. Jefferson   *23*

3. Teen Mom: A Black Feminist Inquiry
Advis Dell Wilkerson   *37*

4. Resilient Lives: African American Women Scholars
Paula Booker Baker   *53*

5. Self, Others, and Jump Rope Communities:
An Oral History of the Triumphs of
African American Women
Wynnetta Scott-Simmons   *71*

6. Using Multicultural Literature to Develop Empathy and
Compassion inPreservice Teachers: A First Step in
Preparing Culturally Responsive Teachers
Lyndall Muschell   *93*

7. A Curriculum of Imagination in an Era of Standardization
   Robert Lake   *109*

8. A Quiet Awakening: Spinning Yarns From Granny's
   Table in the New Rural South
   Angela Haynes   *127*

9. African American Students With Reading Disabilities:
   A Critical Race Inquiry
   Margie Wiggins Sweatman   *145*

10. Language, Culture, and Identity:
    Immigrant Female Students in U.S. High Schools
    Joanna Stoughton Cavan   *161*

11. Reading Through Brown Eyes:
    Toward Developing a Culturally Congruent Reading Curriculum
    Clara Taylor   *177*

12. Dalton's Suicide: Dealing With Student Death in Education
    Teresa J. Rishel   *199*

13. Fostering Justice in an Unjust World: Stories of
    Successful Native American Women in Academia
    Angela M. Jaime   ,   *217*

14. It Starts at Home: The Familial Relationship of
    Scholarship, Education, and Advocacy
    Tammy A. Turner-Vorbeck   *233*

15. Becoming an Agent of Social Change:
    Stories of Sweatshops, Sweetshops, and
    Women's Social Activism
    Betty Christine Eng   *247*

16. Conclusion: Personal~Passionate~Participatory Inquiry: Potentials,
    Contributions, Concerns, and Future Directions
    JoAnn Phillion and Ming Fang He   *267*

Epilogue: A Love Letter to the Personal~Passionate~
           Participatory Research Group
    Bill Ayers   *275*

About the Authors   *277*

ACKNOWLEDGMENTS

Personal~Passionate~Participatory Inquiry Into Social Justice in Education, the first book in the series, *Research for Social Justice: Personal~Passionate~Participatory Inquiry,* is dedicated to all the people who have engaged in personal~passionate~participatory inquiry with us over the years—students, parents, teachers, educators, administrators, and community workers in various contexts. We deeply appreciate the experience and knowledge of the researchers featured in the book and their participants; their concerns for people who are marginalized and disfranchised; their long-term and heart-felt engagement in schools, families, and communities; their shared efforts driven by commitment to social justice; and their unfaltering stance on equity, equality, social justice, freedom, and human possibility.

FOREWORD

William Ayers

[handwritten margin notes: Paulo Freire — we have to continue to reinvent ourselves]

History charges forward—gyrating, wobbling, crashing, careening, drifting, stampeding, advancing. There is no stopping it—history is always on the move, always on the make.

People are on the move and on the make as well—we slouch toward the next point on our journey, we arrive and just as quickly we stumble or dash from there to the next. We are, each of us, unfinished, incomplete, works-in-progress.

"The streets are narrow and so are the minds," Galileo announced as he prepared to overthrow the dogma of an orthodox church and state. His discovery that the planets and the stars were not—as had been thought—fixed to a crystal vault, but rather that they were spinning through space without visible support—like us, who are also on an immense journey, also free and without support—brought him into direct and fatal conflict with authority. Forced to denounce his discovery and betray his principles, Galileo's last words nonetheless stood up for truth: "Still, it moves," he said.

Even the most casual glance backward offers a big-letter lesson: all that is solid melts into air; the center cannot hold; the way things are is not, can never be, the way things will always be. The dance of the dialectic is underway and ongoing.

History moves. We are led to believe—by authority, by common sense, by existential experience—that we are living somehow at a point of arrival, the end-point of history: all that has occurred until now brings us inevitably to this time, this place. And pretty much this is simply the way it is, the way it must be. We retract into passivity, cynicism: What can I do about it? we ask with a resigned shrug. Whatever, we sigh.

But it's a choice. We can note that the current moment is neither inevitable nor stable, that its imperfections—the unnecessary suffering, the undeserved pain—might be cause for alarm. Our situations are neither fixed nor entirely determined, and history has not stood still for us—another world is both possible and inevitable: Get up, get up, get moving. We can choose to resist passivity and cynicism, to plant the seeds of a world in-the-making. We can learn to create—right here, right now—a bit of the world we want to inhabit.

Ming Fang He and JoAnn Phillion with this book provide a map into a new territory of inquiry: personal~passionate~participatory. The rhythm is intentional, for they intend to break old barriers and break new ground. Here they overthrow the current orthodoxy of "what counts" as research, and provide guideposts into a dazzling terrain overflowing with life. Their instruction for approaching research echo Mary Oliver's (2008) "Instructions for living a life" from her poem "Sometimes":

Pay attention.
Be astonished.
Tell about it. (p. 37)

Teachers, students, and researchers often feel themselves shackled, bound, and gagged. He and Phillion urge us to begin by noticing things as they are: pay attention. If we hope to ease the pain of living for ourselves, for our students and families, for our communities, we need to pinch ourselves awake and blink our eyes open. Not once or twice, but everyday and forever. It will not be easy, never easy, because we must then confront the horrors, as well as the delights, the ecstasies. How should we act? What is to be done? We stir ourselves, a bit uncertainly perhaps, but we then take a step forward. Be astonished. We take another step. And another.

We can, of course, choose to keep our eyes firmly shut against injustice. We may not be able to claim much in terms of moral action or useful inquiry, but it is a choice. We might also choose to anesthetize ourselves with bread and circuses, coke and speed, the drunken puppet show of a simple existence. We might seek rewards, advancement, recognition. The unexamined life may not be worth living, but the examined life is marked with anguish as well as ecstasy. We might also open to feeling the joys of life intensely, exquisitely balanced with the pain. We may try with others to forge ourselves into artisans of a new humanity. What might that entail? What are our wildest dreams? Tell about it.

All of us live in the midst of fear and pressure. If I were not afraid, what might I do? If I act, what do I risk? If I do not act, then what do I risk? What do I need in order to find the courage to get started?

These questions beckon us. If we want to live in a fully human world, a world of mutual recognition, if we want to develop a richer and deeper vision of justice, and a pedagogy and inquiry of justice as well—a pedagogy and research of activism perhaps—something that tries to tell the truth, tries to stand against violence and war and exploitation and oppression, tries to act for love and fairness and balance and peace, how will we proceed?

We see in these pages research and inquiry overflowing with love, and we get a taste of the power of love that does justice. We see researchers who have the courage to get close—to let compassion and, yes, intimacy guide their steps. How do you know a whirlpool, a cyclone, a human life? We see research that is proudly partisan—not neutral—and that intends to challenge existing social forces that hurt or hinder people's full development. We see researchers spending their intellectual and physical energy in solidarity with—not service to—their communities. We see a faith in people to name their own predicaments, to tell their own stories, to ask questions of the universe, fighting to make sense of it all as they construct their own lives. These researchers understand that to alienate people from their own judgment is to turn them into objects, to prevent people from naming their situations and entanglements and predicaments is a form of violence.

Research for these authors is an activity of discovery and surprise, a form of reinventing, recreating, rewriting in dialogue with participants. They understand that every question worth asking is a question you do not know the answer to—so much of research is a theory of the obvious, a trivial pursuit that delivers no new knowledge.

Ming Fang He and JoAnn Phillion offer here a guide to democratic research, pedagogy, and life. The key is faith in people: the best authority and the finest measure of anyone's hurt and desire is the individual herself; life, as anyone has lived it, is part of the massive reservoir of knowledge and feeling that justice demands. Here researchers leave the default of narcissism and, in relation to others, take the full measure of another point of view.

This is a brilliant and necessary contribution to our ongoing journey as teachers and researchers. It invites us to choose love: all kinds of love for all kinds of people in all kinds of circumstances and situations. Choose love.

REFERENCE

Oliver, M. (2008). Sometimes. In *Red bird* (pp. 35–38). Boston: Beacon.

CHAPTER 1

PERSONAL~PASSIONATE~ PARTICIPATORY INQUIRY

Research for Social Justice

Ming Fang He and JoAnn Phillion

INTRODUCTION

Personal~Passionate~Participatory Inquiry Into Social Justice in Education, the first book in the series, *Research for Social Justice: Personal~Passionate~Participatory Inquiry,* features 14 programs of social justice oriented research on life in schools, families, and communities. This work, done by a diverse group of practitioner researchers, educators, and scholars, connects the personal with the political, the theoretical with the practical, and research with social and educational change. The principal aspect of this work that distinguishes it from other work is that the researcher is not separate from the sociopolitical and cultural phenomena of the inquiry, the data collected, findings, interpretations, or writing.

This book draws together work which demonstrates three distinct and interconnected qualities: *personal~passionate~participatory.* Each is

Personal~Passionate~Participatory Inquiry Into Social Justice in Education, pp. 1–21
Copyright © 2008 by Information Age Publishing

1

personal, compelled by values and experiences researchers bring to the work. Each is passionate, grounded in a commitment to social justice concerns of people and places under consideration. Each is participatory, built on long term, heart-felt engagement, and shared efforts. Self, others, and inquiry become interrelated in complex and dialogical relationships over time and place as researchers develop and refine questions, perspectives, and methods by drawing upon passions and commitments. Researchers have explicit research agendas that focus on equity, equality, and social justice. They are not detached observers, nor putatively objective recorders, but active participants in schools, families, and communities. Researchers are immersed in lives, take on the concerns of people who are marginalized and disfranchised, and act upon those concerns. Rather than aiming solely at traditional academic outcomes, positive social and educational change is the focal outcome of inquiry.

Researchers featured in this book

> recognize the necessity of opening spaces to raise embarrassing questions, to confront orthodoxy and dogma (rather than to produce them), to be someone who cannot easily be co-opted by governments or corporations, and whose *raison d'être* is to represent all those people and issues that are routinely forgotten or swept under the rug. (Saïd, 1994, p. 12, as cited in Ayers, 2006, p. 85)

Further, they

> draw sustenance and perspective from the humanities in order to better see the world as it is. Whatever [they] find that is out-of-balance must be challenged, the devastating taken-for-granted dissected, exposed, illuminated.... [The] core of all our work must be human knowledge and human freedom, both enlightenment and emancipation. (Ayers, 2006, p. 87)

They "join one another to imagine and build a participatory movement for justice, a public space for the enactment of democratic dreams" (p. 96).

With equity, equality, social justice, and human freedom as explicit goals of the inquiries, the following guiding questions suggested by Ayers (2006) are illuminated in these inquiries:

1. What are the issues that marginalized or disadvantaged people speak of with excitement, anger, fear, or hope?

2. How can I enter a dialogue in which I will learn from a specific community itself about problems and obstacles they face?

3. What endogenous experiences do people already have that can point the way toward solutions?

4. What is missing from the "official story" that will make the problems of the oppressed more understandable?

5. What current proposed policies serve the privileged and the powerful, and how are they made to appear inevitable?

6. How can the public space for discussion, problem posing, and problem solving be expanded? (p. 88)

The work featured in this book, embedded in lives and communities on the one hand, and powerful ideas of being human with strong commitment to a just society on the other hand, are at the heart of social justice oriented work. These researchers are not only collecting, but also living in, the stories of people with whom they engage in inquiry. These researchers position stories collected in sociopolitical, economic, linguistic, and cultural contexts to pose questions with an "epistemological curiosity—a curiosity that is often missing in dialogue as conversation" (Freire & Macedo, 1995, p. 382). These inquirers are able to connect the practical with the theoretical, and the personal with the political, through passionate participation in, and critical reflection upon inquiry and life. As Freire and Macedo strongly argued:

> We must not negate practice for the sake of theory. To do so would reduce theory to a pure verbalism or intellectualism. By the same token, to negate theory for the sake of practice, as in the use of dialogue as conversation, is to run the risk of losing oneself in the disconnectedness of practice. It is for this reason that I never advocate either a theoretic elitism or a practice ungrounded in theory, but the unity between theory and practice. In order to achieve this unity, one must have an epistemological curiosity. (p. 382)

Researchers featured in this book cultivate this epistemological curiosity in inquiry and life to foster critical consciousness to comprehend and act upon the often contradictory and contested real life world. These researchers thrive on passionate involvement and commitment, advocate for disenfranchised, underrepresented, and invisible groups and individuals, and unite with allies to build communities of researchers and practitioners with shared concerns to foster social justice for educational and social change.

STRUCTURE OF THE BOOK

The book consists of a preface, introduction (chapter 1), 14 additional chapters, and a conclusion (chapter 16). Each chapter features one program of research. Each author begins with an autobiographical account of the origin of passion for the inquiry, describes the participatory research process, and discusses outcomes and changes engendered by the inquiry.

In chapter 2, "Stitched From the Soul: An Auto/Biographical Inquiry of a Black Woman Principal," Sonya D. Jefferson explores the lives of four generations of Black women in her family and how their experiences have impacted her voice and vision as a principal in a Title I elementary school. Sonya's grandmother, her mother, herself, and her daughter have studied and/or taught in public schools in the U.S. South. Sonya discusses how her family narrative parallels and contests community and historical narratives. She explores these narratives through the lens of critical race theory to illustrate how their experiences of an endemically racist educational system have impacted her leadership. She passionately advocates for children living in poverty and works closely with teachers and parents in the school community. Drawing on knowledge she has gained from her participants and the inquiry, Sonya has developed an ethic of care-and-justice as a framework for transforming schools, such as the one she leads, into spaces where all children can reach their highest potential.

In chapter 3, "Teen Mom: A Black Feminist Inquiry," Dell Wilkerson uses feminist thought as the theoretical framework and autobiographical inquiry as methodology. She examines her experience as a Black teenage mother and how she has become successful in spite of difficult circumstances such as poverty, a single-parent household, racism, societal rejection, and other adversities. She explores factors that created adverse conditions or fostered resiliency. Hostile environments, unsupportive schools, feelings of depression and rejection, frequent unemployment, increased homelessness, declining health, and increasing hunger within Black communities due to racism are shown as adverse conditions. Dell has found that factors fostering resiliency in herself and others include personal characteristics, a close bond with a supportive adult, a close-knit community, supportive school environments, and racial awareness. Dell works with policymakers, social service agencies, school administrators, educators, teachers, and parents to promote a strong focal point of Black feminist education as a means to secure quality jobs, housing, and healthcare for teenage mothers and their children in Black communities.

In chapter 4, "Resilient Lives: African American Women Scholars," Paula Booker Baker delves into the lives and experiences of five African American scholars in the field of education and how these women meet challenges, are rejuvenated, and rise above harsh and unyielding obstacles. She asks poignant questions about the conflict between her African American culture, values, beliefs, and personal experiences, and what is expected of her from the viewpoint of the dominant culture. Her passion for the inquiry has strengthened as she teaches young African American girls who are led to believe they are doomed to follow a path to failure.

Using Black feminist thought and critical race theory as a theoretical framework, and critical narrative inquiry as research methodology, Paula explores the challenges, strategies, and accomplishments of these Black women who strive to succeed in predominantly White colleges and universities to provide role models for African American girls. Paula also interrogates the impact of classism, racism, and sexism on African American women's careers. By investigating and participating in a dialogue about educational struggle and academic achievement, she recognizes her own and other Black women's challenges and the ways they work to support and transform one another. Drawing on the knowledge derived from her participants and her inquiry, Paula calls for a revolutionary movement from rhetoric to practice in education to be committed to Black feminism that has been absent in the mentoring experience of Black girls and women.

In chapter 5, "Self, Others, and Jump Rope Communities: An Oral History of the Triumphs of African American Women," Wynnetta Scott-Simmons uses critical race theory, critical literacy, and Black feminist thought as a theoretical framework and oral history as research methodology. She explores the lives of four young African American women as they left their culturally insular surroundings, which she terms "Jump Rope Communities," to seek access to the codes of power and registers of language in an all-White, all-girl, elite private school during the late 1960s and early 1970s. To capture the memories, perceptions, and lived experiences of these women over 39 years later, Wynnetta collects stories of their journeys into a world of divergences: language codes; social, cultural, and economic stratifications; and linguistic expectations, behaviors, and dispositions. Her work focuses on the motivational factors that prompted attendance at all-White, all-girl, private schools despite feelings of success within culturally segregated Jump Rope Communities. She also explores the resilience of spirit necessary to continue to move the race forward as displayed by African American women. Starting from a historical inquiry into the benefits and challenges of segregation, integration, resegregation, and the impact of the Civil Rights Movement, Wynnetta studies the spirit of togetherness, the establishment of unifying goals, creation, and synergy on which the Jump Rope Community thrives. Recognition of cultural identity, an ongoing effort to build a community, and the preservation of cultural and linguistic heritage are key for the success of African Americans. As a preservice teacher educator, Wynnetta works with African American and other minority students to raise their awareness of the triumphant spirit of hope despite the pull to surrender aspects of self-definition, culture, and community in exchange for codes of power that are provided through educational access.

In chapter 6, "Using Literature to Develop Empathy and Compassion in Preservice Teachers: A First Step in Preparing Culturally Responsive Teachers," Lyndall Muschell narrates how she acts upon a passion that has developed over 20 years as a teacher educator: the importance of respect and equity for all individuals regardless of race, religion, culture, or personal beliefs. She has observed countless lessons in which the cultures, experiences, and interests of children are devalued and ignored. She has watched classrooms become more diverse as the teaching population became less diverse. Lyndall has become increasingly aware of the responsibility of teacher educators in preparing teachers to respond to this phenomenon. Using culturally responsive teaching and literary or narrative imagination as a theoretical framework, and cross-cultural narrative inquiry as research methodology, she explores a group of White, middle class, females enrolled in an early childhood teacher preparation program. She examines their existing stereotypes, privileges, awareness of racism and/or oppression, and possibilities for change in their personal, cultural and/or racial attitudes and beliefs. Lyndall has found the following: critically examining one's autobiographical roots develops empathy toward others; acknowledging and confronting Whiteness is a complicated process involving time and risks; multicultural literature raises difficult questions related to diversity; and cultivating empathy fosters development of culturally responsive pedagogy. She incorporates these reflections and conclusions into the preservice teacher and graduate programs for early childhood education in her university, as well as conducting staff development with public schools.

In chapter 7, "A Curriculum of Imagination in an Era of Standardization," Robert Lake explores how imagination permeates every aspect of life experience, and how it helps develop personal and political awareness in students to question what they take for granted. Imagination can explores how imagination permeates every aspect of life experience, and how it develops various ways of knowing, seeing, feeling, and acting upon positive social and educational change that are frequently excluded in the present climate of standardized practices in education. Starting from his personal experience, Robert examines the effects of standardization and the power of imagination to open spaces of personal discovery and meaning. Using a fictional dialogue between Maxine Greene and Paulo Freire as a theoretical framework and method of inquiry with commentary interspersed in the conversation, he traces the evolution of the concept of imagination and its connections to contemporary curriculum theory through artistic and critical praxis. He describes the roles of imagination in naming, being, and transforming private and public worlds through an exploration of historical and contemporary definitions of imagination and metaphor and how they enable the creation of personal meaning and agency. Applications and connections to practice are described in a variety of settings ranging from the use of multiple forms of literacy in content area studies to the use of literature and media to enhance understanding of the "other." He calls for a curriculum of imagination to counter standardized testing, curriculum, and accountability to act against the unjust and move beyond the taken for granted, and to create equitable opportunities for all to achieve.

In chapter 8, "A Quiet Awakening: Spinning Yarns From Granny's Table in the New Rural South," Angela Haynes explores her lived experience as a first generation doctoral student who negates the truths of a rural Southern upbringing steeped in issues of race, class, and gender. She explores the impact of place, class, race, multiple realities, and contested in-between space on Southern female identities and the education of oppressed and repressed women in the South. Family members are main characters in the stories. Using critical theory as a theoretical framework, and oral history as research methodology, Angela collects generational stories and memories from her Granny's table and fictionalizes characters to better understand complex lives that allow subjugation of, and by, people who cling to family, land and their way of life. She explores life in the South from her vantage point as a lower-class, White female caught between the reality of place and the promise of education. Yarns spun from her Granny's table reveal a contested way of life stifled in an ever-changing new rural South and raise questions about Southern legacy and heritage, one of the most complex, controversial, and significant issues lived by teachers, administrators, parents, and students in the South. Angela calls for an education that evokes an awakening for people in the rural communities to act for change. She joins the efforts of other researchers, teachers, educators, administrators, policymakers, students, parents, and community members to create possibilities for the future of her children and many other people's children who are destined to be locked in the South.

In chapter 9, "African American Students With Reading Disabilities: A Critical Race Inquiry," Margie Sweatman examines perspectives of teachers, students, and parents regarding the use of grade level textbooks for reading instruction of African American students with reading disabilities. She talks with participants about the benefits, or lack thereof, of this practice. She asks participants to share their perceptions of whether the minority status of the school contributes to a lack of adequate educational attainment for students. Using critical race theory as a theoretical framework, and critical narrative inquiry as research methodology, Margie explores ways in which race can be used as a lens for examining issues of literacy for minority students and the interconnectedness of race and socioeconomics in student outcomes. She collects stories from participants in a metro Atlanta middle school which serves a predominantly African American population. She has created school and class portraits and participant profiles through interviews, participant observations, teacher questionnaires, and reflective journals of teachers. She identifies the cultural incongruence in the reading curriculum and how grade level textbooks perpetuate low academic achievement among African American students with reading disabilities. She works with teachers, administrators, and African American parents to develop a culturally responsive pedagogy that meets the needs of all students, particularly those who learn differently.

In chapter 10, "Language, Culture, and Identity: Immigrant Female Students in U.S. High Schools," Joanna Stoughton Cavan, using a cross-cultural narrative inquiry, explores the experience of three female immigrant students as they learn new languages and cultures, and develop new identities in a U.S. public high school. She critically examines how her participants interpret their experience of exclusion, marginalization, and neglect, and the impact of this experience on their school success. Although her participants are from different cultural and linguistic backgrounds, they face similar bias and prejudice. They are ridiculed about their linguistic and cultural heritages and excluded from higher academic courses, clubs, and sports. Their aspirations of continuing education in college are negated and they are relegated to low-paying careers with few opportunities for advancement. As a teacher of foreign language and department chair for world languages in her school, she advocates for immigrant students. She organizes foreign language instruction workshops for her county schools and has established an afterschool club for immigrant students where they share their experience of language, culture, and identity development in their families, communities and schools. She has presented her research findings to the faculty in her school in order to promote a deeper understanding of immigrant students, and has developed a system to mentor and counsel immigrant students and families. She works with colleagues, administrators, and immigrant students and parents to develop a pedagogy which is responsive to the needs and concerns of immigrant students and their families, respectful of cultural and linguistic heritages, and proactive in providing educational opportunities for all students to thrive in their schooling and lives.

In chapter 11, "Reading Through Brown Eyes: A Culturally Congruent Reading Curriculum," as an African American mother, educator, and administrator, Clara Taylor has witnessed firsthand the marginalization of African American males in literacy development in public schools, which can lead to academic and career failure. Using critical race theory as a theoretical framework, and critical narrative inquiry as research methodology, she examines the reading motivations of six African

American middle-grade males and investigates why some are more successful academically in reading than others. She also explores participants' experience of reading in public schools and barriers related to their reading achievement and reading motivation. She has found that their racial and ethnic identities related to their backgrounds and learning styles and their interest in popular culture are motivational factors for engaging them in the reading and learning process. She works with participants to help them understand the importance of self-advocacy as they learn more about their preferred learning and teaching styles. She also works with teachers, principals, and other educators on strategies to create a culturally congruent reading curriculum and positive learning opportunities for African American males. She continues to strive for change in curriculum design and instructional and educational processes for African American males and other minority students in public schools.

In chapter 12, "Dalton's Suicide: Dealing With Student Death in Education," Teresa Rishel explores her son's suicide followed by the suicide of a student with whom she had worked closely as a principal. As researcher and participant, as mother and principal, she explores how the routines of schooling impact students—ultimately having the capacity to influence their life and death decisions. Using various tenets from curriculum theory as a theoretical framework, and critical narrative inquiry as research methodology, she examines factors in her son's life that have contributed to his suicide; his relationships with teachers, peers and family; the impact of his suicide on his former teachers, their perspectives and instructional practices; and concomitant change in policy in his school district. Teresa provides a detailed narrative account of a school community and teachers who have little knowledge of suicide and how the nature and structure of schooling may exacerbate problems for adolescents. Discovering the alienating effects of traditional schooling practices, Teresa's research compels her to instruct preservice and in-service teachers about the role of affect in how youth situate themselves within schooling. She calls for an inclusion of suicidal issues in policy making processes at district and school-wide levels, instructional processes in classrooms, and educational processes in communities.

In chapter 13, "Stories of Successful Native American Women in Academia," Angela Jaime uses post colonial theory as a theoretical framework, and story telling and portraiture as research methodology. She portrays the experience of three Native American women in academia to understand what they feel it means to be successful. Her interest in this inquiry grows from her personal experience as a Native American woman in academia and the lack of literature that documents success rather than failure. Angela wants others to hear Native American women's stories and to acknowledge the struggles these women experience on a daily basis. She has found that for these Native American women, success is not defined in orthodox terms of publications, tenure, and promotion, but rather in terms of giving back to their communities, developing indigenous knowledge, and honoring the struggles of Native Americans who have come before them to address pressing issues of social justice and self-determination. Angela articulates a new Native American perspective, one that moves beyond post colonial perspectives to transcendent perspectives, and calls for the education of Native Americans to be brought to the center of concerns in education.

In chapter 14, "It Starts at Home: The Familial Relationship of Scholarship, Education, and Advocacy," Tammy Turner-Vorbeck explores the relationship between scholarship, education and advocacy in relation to family diversity. As a curriculum researcher, scholar, teacher educator, and a mother of three adopted children, she advocates for an inclusion of family diversity in multicultural education. She embeds her research in her teaching practice and explores the complex relationship between the primary forms of curriculum on family at work in schools in order to fully illuminate the real-life consequences that various curricular messages about the concept of family create for students. She inquires about and advocates for the expansion of multicultural education to include an often neglected, yet common form of diversity—family structure diversity. She works with preservice and in-service teachers and administrators to foster awareness of family diversity and to make curriculum change to meet the challenge of such diversity.

In chapter 15, "Becoming an Agent of Social Change: Women's Stories of Sweatshops and Sweetshops," using Asian American and cross-cultural perspectives as a theoretical framework and autobiographical narrative inquiry as research methodology, Betty Eng explores her personal and family narrative which parallels the historical narrative of Asian Americans who fight for social justice, equality, and human rights in the United States. To search for the origins of her passion for social justice, she reflects upon her experience of being born in a village in People's Republic of China, growing up as an Asian American in California where her parents worked in sweatshops and canneries and where she became an advocate for Asian American rights, and advocating for women's rights in Hong Kong. As she critically examines her personal and family narrative and the historical narrative of Asian Americans, she has recognized that the social activist awareness she grew up with has become the driving force to teach and live for social justice as she continues to work with and advocate for Asian Americans and Asian women in Hong Kong and the United States.

In chapter 16, "Personal~Passionate~Participatory Inquiry: Potentials, Contributions, Concerns, and Future Directions," JoAnn Phillion and Ming Fang He open discussions on potentials, contributions, concerns, and future directions of personal~passionate~participatory inquiry. Issues not explicitly addressed in each individual chapter are also explored.

PERSONAL~PASSIONATE~PARTICIPATORY INQUIRY

Convergence of Diversity and Inquiry

The world landscape is becoming increasingly multicultural and multilingual (United Nations Educational, Scientific and Cultural Organization [UNESCO], 2003). Global diversity permeates life in schools, communities, and societies. In response to the emergence of this cultural and linguistic diversity, there has been a movement toward developing methods appropriate for understanding the complexities and contradictions engendered by this diversity. There is a new wave of thinking in education that challenges traditional ways of engaging in and interpreting research. It has been called the "sixth moment" (Denzin, 1997), a time of questioning whose knowledge should be considered valid, and a time when people have their own ideas on how their experiences are to be interpreted, theorized, and represented. Many researchers, such as those featured in this book, have responded to the sixth moment by developing approaches to diversity issues in education that focus on an in-depth understanding of the complexity of experience of individuals, families, and communities who are often underrepresented or misrepresented in the literature (Carger, 1996; Feuerverger, 2001; Soto, 1997; Valdés, 1996; Valenzuela, 1999). Many of these researchers speak the languages of their participants, hold similar ethnic, cultural, and linguistic heritages, and share similar experiences of injustice.

This new wave of thinking led to "paradigms wars" (Schön, 1991) among positivists, interpretivists, and critical theorists in the field of educational research. The action orientation, reflectiveness and reflexiveness on action, and dialogical relationship between research to practice are alien, or somewhat marginalized, within the above mentioned three paradigms on the one hand; yet, they respond strongly, on the other hand, to the sixth moment. Researchers engaged in personal~passionate~participatory inquiry have not only responded to the sixth moment by questioning whose knowledge should be considered valid and how experience should be interpreted, theorized, and represented, but also have confronted issues of equity, equality, social justice, and societal change through both research and action.

Research Traditions

Personal~passionate~participatory inquiry draws on an array of research traditions: action research, teacher research, self study, life history, teacher lore, participatory inquiry, narrative inquiry, and cross-cultural and multicultural narrative inquiry. Many of these traditions can be traced back to practitioner research, which originated in action research in social sciences such as social psychology (Collier, 1945; Lewin, 1946) to counteract racial prejudice and promote more democratic forms of leadership in the workplace. The scientific study of education movements in the late nineteenth and early twentieth century brought practitioner research to education (Zeichner & Noffke, 2001). It flourished during the progressive movement of John Dewey's era (Dewey, 1938; Schubert & Lopez-Schubert, 1997) to promote the "Democratic Ideal" (Dewey, 1916, pp. 86–88) in education and in many aspects of life (Kemmis, 1980/1988; Zeichner & Noffke, 2001). For Dewey (1938),

> a democratic society repudiates the principle of external authority.... A democracy is more than a form of government; it is primarily a mode of associated living, of conjoint communicated experience ... individuals who participate in an interest so that each has to refer his own action to that of others, and to consider the actions of others to give point and direction to his own. (p. 87)

Parallel with Dewey's democratic ideas, the work of W. E. B. Du Bois (1903/1994), Anna Julia Cooper (1892/1988), and Carter G. Woodson (1933/1977) also greatly influenced practitioner research in terms of perceiving research connected to equity, equality, and social justice. However, action research was ridiculed by traditional educational researchers and theorists for lack of academic rigor and validity. Thus action research almost disappeared in the U.S. educational literature until the late 1970s (Zeichner & Noffke, 2001). In spite of the decline of action research in the United States in the early 1960s, it became prominent in the United Kingdom in the context of school based curriculum development (e.g., Elliot, 1991; Stenhouse, 1968). In Australia "emancipatory action research" (e.g., Carr & Kemmis, 1986; Grundy & Kemmis, 1988) built on Habermas' (1971) critical theory with an emphasis on the participatory and social action orientation of the inquiry.

In the 1980s, new movement for teacher research emerged to "challenge the hegemony of an exclusively university-generated knowledge base for teaching" (Cochran-Smith & Lytle, 1999). Cochran-Smith and Lytle have identified five trends that characterize the teacher research movement in the United States in the past 2 decades (p. 15): (a) "the prominence of teacher research and inquiry communities in preservice teacher education, professional development, and school reform" (e.g., Cochran-Smith & Lytle, 1993; Hollingsworth & Sockett, 1994); (b) "the development of conceptual frameworks for teacher research that may be thought of as social inquiry" (e.g., Anderson, Herr, & Nihlem, 1994), "ways of knowing in communities" (e.g., Hollingsworth, 1994), "practical inquiry" (e.g., Connelly & Clandinin, 1995); (c) "the dissemination of teacher research at and beyond the local level" (e.g., Hollingsworth & Sockett, 1994); (d) "the emergence of critique of the teacher research movement on epistemological" (e.g., Fenstermacher, 1994), "methodological" (e.g., Huberman, 1996), and "critical grounds" (e.g., Anderson, Herr, & Nihlem, 1994); and (e) "the transformative possibilities of teacher research for university cultures" (e.g., Allen, Cary, & Delgado, 1995; Richardson, 1997).

Self study in the teacher research movement parallels the development in life history research (e.g., Cole & Knowles, 2001) and teacher lore (Schubert & Ayers, 1999), in which the teacher is perceived as researcher engaged in deeply reflective practice to change the curriculum and the world (Schön, 1991). Participatory inquiry, another form of practitioner inquiry, originated in Latin America, Africa, and Asia (e.g., Freire, 1970; Hall, 1993). This research tradition has been closely associated with adult education and literacy movements (Freire & Marcedo, 1987). The explicit aim of participatory inquiry is to work with oppressed groups and individuals to empower them so that they take effective actions toward more just and humane conditions (Freire, 1970; hooks, 1994).

A Turn to Narrative

In addition to action research, teacher research, self study, life history, teacher lore, and participatory inquiry, another major response to the sixth moment is a turn to narrative (Clandinin & Connelly, 2000; Phillion, He, & Connelly, 2005; Witherall & Noddings, 1991) in educational research, which Denzin and Lincoln (2003) call the "seventh moment." This turn to narrative, prominent in personal~passionate~participatory inquiry, is in response to recognition of the complexity of human experience in increasingly diversified societies (Coles, 1989). Researchers in different disciplines, responding to the call of the seventh moment, incorporate narrative, story, autobiography, memoir, fiction, oral history, documentary film, painting, and poetry into inquiries in education such

Check this out

as Bell (1997), Carger (1996), and Valdés (1996) in language and culture issues; Carter (1993), Florio-Ruane (2001), Foster (1997), Michie (1999), and Schubert (1991) in teacher narrative; Ayers and Ford (1996), Ayers, Ladson-Billings, Noguera, and Michie (2008) in teacher and student stories and poetry; Ayers (2001), Neumann and Peterson (1997), Hoffman (1989), and Tan (1989) in autobiography, memoir, and fiction; Knowles and Cole (2008) in art including painting and poetry; Feuerverger (2001) and Soto (1997) in family and community narrative; Chan (2006), Elbaz-Luwisch (1997, 2002), Hollingsworth (1994), and Phillion (1999, 2002a, 2002b, 2002c, 2002d) in multicultural teaching and learning; Conle (2000) and He (1999, 2002a, 2002b, 2002c, 2003) in cross-cultural teaching and learning; Gay (2000) in culturally responsive teaching, and hooks (1991) in race, gender, and class.

One quality of narrative inquiry that distinguishes it from other forms of educational research, but similar to personal~passionate~participatory inquiry, lies in understanding experience in its own terms rather than categorizing experience according to predetermined structures and theories (Phillion, 1999). This form of inquiry is "peopled" with characters, rather than filled with categories and labels. In some forms of traditional educational research, experience is seen, shaped, and written about by the researcher using theoretically derived forms; in effect the experience is determined by the theory. In contrast, experience is the starting point of narrative inquiry (Clandinin & Connelly, 2000) and is in the forefront at every stage of research; as such, narrative inquiries, as well as personal~passionate~participatory inquiries, arise from experiences of researchers and participants, rather than being formulated as abstract research questions, and they proceed by continual reference to experience as field texts are collected, analyzed, and interpreted, and as meanings are crafted. Another quality of narrative inquiry is the fluidity of the inquiry. This notion of fluid inquiry is influenced by the work of Schwab (Westbury & Wilkof, 1978):

> There are two kinds of inquiries: stable inquiry and fluid inquiry. Stable inquiry lends itself to fixed research phenomena, questions, purposes, objectives, methodologies and outcomes … ambiguity characterizes fluid inquiry … focused on developing understandings of changing real-life situations and contexts, rather than on the use of pre-established, often unfit, theory. (He, 2003, p. 80)

This fluid quality permeates every aspect of both narrative inquiry and personal~passionate~participatory inquiry.

The inquirers engaged in this form of inquiry, such as the authors featured in this book, explore experience by bringing personal experience to bear on inquiry, seeing research as having autobiographical roots, as connected to, rather than disconnected from life; by thinking narratively, seeing experience as the starting point of inquiry, as fluid and changing rather than fixed, as contextualized rather than decontextualized; by being in the midst of lives, seeing research as long-term, passionate involvement in daily lives of participants, rather than short-term, in and out, detached observation; and by making meaning of experience in relationship, rather than making meaning in isolation (Phillion & He, 2001, 2007). Narrative inquiry and personal~passionate~participatory inquiry, approaches that focus on experience, humanize research.

Cross-Cultural and Multicultural Narrative Inquiry

Within the turn to narrative, there is a significant shift of focus on narrative and contextual qualities of experience to a focus on the complex and untold experience of marginalized and underrepresented groups and individuals played out in contested cultural, linguistic, and sociopolitical milieus. We term this recent, significant shift *cross-cultural and multicultural narrative inquiry* (He, 2002a, 2002b, 2002c, 2003; Phillion, 2002a, 2002b, 2002c, 2002d; Phillion, He, & Connelly, 2005). Cross-cultural and multicultural narrative inquiry (Phillion & He, 2008) builds on Dewey's theory of experience (1938), Schwab's fluid inquiry (Westbury & Wilkof, 1978), Connelly and Clandinin's narrative inquiry (1990; Clandinin & Connelly, 2000), multicultural perspectives (Gay, 1995; Ladson-Billings, 1994; Nieto, 2000; Sleeter & McLaren, 1995), life based literary narratives (Hoffman, 1989; Tan, 1989), ethnographic work (Soto, 1997), and Ayers' (2004, 2006) social justice and activist oriented inquiry. Cross-cultural and multicultural narrative inquiry connects the personal with the political, the theoretical with the practical, and inquiry with social change.

This shift originated in our growing concerns with language, culture, identity and power issues (Cummins, 1989a, 1989b, 2000) in the education of marginalized and disenfranchised individuals and groups. To understand these issues, rather than relying solely on theoretical literature in this area (Banks & Banks, 1989, 2004; Gay, 2000; Nieto, 2000), we turned to life based literary narratives written by immigrant and minorities including memoirs, autobiographies and novels (Hoffman, 1989; Kaplan, 1993; Kingston, 1975; Rodriguez, 1982; Santiago, 1993; Tan, 1989), narrative inquiries (Carger, 1996; He, 2003; Phillion, 2002d), and ethnographies (Feuerverger, 2001; Soto, 1997; Valdés, 1996). These researchers, such as those featured in this book, passionately engage in nuanced, in-depth, explorations of the experience of diverse individuals and groups which are often stereotyped, misrepresented, or dehumanized in research literature (Phillion & He, 2004, 2007).

We also turn to life based literary narratives written by oppressed and underrepresented individuals who narrativize untold stories of experience of injustice which may foster critical consciousness and inspire social action. This work, as well as personal~passionate~participatory inquiry work and some narrative, cross-cultural and multicultural narrative work, brings theoretical literature to life; develops narrative imagination—the ability to reflect on experience, question assumptions, and actively empathize with others; and fosters critical self-examination of who we are as educational researchers, and how we live and relate to others (Greene, 1995; Nussbaum, 1997). Unlike theoretical literature, this work is filled with people with names and faces, experiences and actions, feelings and emotions. It promotes learning not only to listen to, but also to hear, the stories of others, to enter the realities of others' lives different than their own, not through abstract reasoning, but through developing emotions and empathic understanding (Phillion & He, 2004).

Narrative is also becoming prevalent as educational researchers draw on critical race theory (Ladson-Billings, 1998, 2003; Stovall, 2005). These researchers use stories to tell hidden and silenced narratives of suppressed and underrepresented groups to counter the preconceived metanarrative represented in "scientific based research" that has often portrayed these groups as deficient and inferior. By telling counter stories, researchers begin to be aware of the importance of commitment to equity and social justice, and to recognize their obligation to link inquiry to social and educational change.

There is a convergence of research traditions in personal~passionate~participatory inquiry: action research, teacher research, self study, life history, teacher lore, participatory inquiry, narrative inquiry, and cross-cultural and multicultural narrative inquiry. The work featured in this book draws on aspects of these traditions. It is inherently personal, passionate, and participatory. This intrinsic quality politicizes and transforms inquiry. Personal~passionate~participatory inquiry begins with conscious reflection on experience to challenge assumptions and recognize contradictions between theory and practice, and demands an epistemological curiosity (Freire & Macedo, 1995) to critically examine the impact of inquiry on practice and the impact of practice on theory. It builds on long term, heart-felt engagement, and shared efforts driven by commitment to social justice. Researchers engaged in this form of inquiry are not distant observers but active participants in the life of schools, families, and communities. It embodies an unfaltering stance on equity, equality, social justice, freedom, and human possibility. The explicit agendas of the research featured in this book bring inquiry to life and life to inquiry as vulnerable and resilient, and always dynamic, grounded, and incomplete. Researchers join one another and others to move beyond boundaries, to transgress orthodoxies, and to build a participatory movement to promote a more balanced, fair, and equitable human condition in an increasingly diversified world.

REFERENCES

Allen, J, Cary, M., & Delgado, L. (1995). *Exploring blue highway.* New York: Teacher College Press.

Anderson, G., Herr, K., & Nihlem, A. (1994). *Studying your own school: An educator's guide to qualitative practitioner research.* Thousand Oaks, CA: Corwin.

Ayers, W. C. (2001). *To teach: The journey of a teacher.* New York: Teachers College Press.

Ayers, W. C. (2004). *Teaching toward freedom: Moral commitment and ethical action in the classroom.* Boston: Beacon Press.

Ayers, W. C. (2006). Trudge toward freedom: Educational research in the public interest. In G. Ladson-Billings & W. F. Tate (Eds.), *Education research in the public interest: Social justice, action and policy* (pp. 81–97). New York: Teachers College Press.

Ayers, W. C., & Ford, P. (1996). *City kids/city teachers: Reports from the front row.* New York: The New Press.

Ayers, W. C., Ladson-Billings, G., & Noguera, P., & Michie, G. (2008). *City kids/city Teachers: Reports from the front row.* New York: The New Press.

Banks, J. A., & Banks, C. A. M. (Eds.). (2004). *Handbook of research on multicultural education* (2nd ed.). San Francisco: Jossey-Bass.

Banks, J. A., & Banks, C. A. M. (Eds.). (1989). *Multicultural education: Issues and perspectives.* Needham Heights, MA: Simon & Schuster.

Bell, J. S. (1997). *Literacy, culture, and identity.* New York: Peter Lang.

Carger, C. (1996). *Of borders and dreams: A Mexican-American experience of urban education.* New York: Teachers College Press.

Carr, W., & Kemmis, S. (1986). *Becoming critical: Education, knowledge, and action research.* London: Falmer.

Carter, K. (1993). The place of story in the study of teaching and teacher education. *Educational Researcher, 22*(1), 5–12, 18.

Chan, E. (2006). Teacher experiences of culture in the curriculum. *Journal of Curriculum Studies, 38*(2), 161–176.

Clandinin, D. J., & Connelly, F. M. (2000). *Narrative inquiry.* San Francisco: Jossey-Bass.

Cochran-Smith, M., & Lytle, S. L. (1993). *Inside/outside: Teacher research and knowledge.* New York: Teachers College Press.

Cochran-Smith, M., & Lytle, S. L. (1999). The teacher research movement: A decade later. *Educational Researcher, 28*(7), 15–25.

Cole, A. L., & Knowles, J. G. (2001). *Lives in context: The art of life history research.* Lanham, MD: Altamira/Rowman & Littlefield.

Coles, R. (1989). *The call of stories: teaching and the moral imagination.* Boston: Houghton Mifflin.

Collier, J. (1945). United States Indian Administration as a laboratory of ethnic relations. *Social Research, 12*, 265–303.

Conle, C. (2000). Thesis as narrative: What is the inquiry in narrative inquiry? *Curriculum Inquiry, 30*(2), 189–213.

Connelly, F. M., & Clandinin, D. J. (1990). Stories of experience and narrative inquiry. *Educational Researcher, 19*(5), 2–14.

Connelly, F. M., & Clandinin, D. J. (1995). *Teachers' professional knowledge landscapes.* New York: Teachers College Press.

Cooper, A. (1988). *A voice form the South.* New York: Oxford University Press. (Original work published 1892)

Cummins, J. (1989a). *Empowering minority students.* Sacramento, CA: California Association for Bilingual Education.

Cummins, J. (1989b). *Negotiating identities: Education for empowerment in a diverse society.* Sacramento, CA: California Association for Bilingual Education.

Cummins, J. (2000). *Language, power and pedagogy: Bilingual children in the crossfire.* Clevedon: Multilingual Matters.

Denzin, N. K. (1997). *Interpretive ethnography: Ethnographic practices for the 21st century.* Thousand Oaks, CA: SAGE.

Denzin, N., & Lincoln, Y. (2003). *The landscape of qualitative research: Theories and issues* (2nd ed.). Thousand Oaks, CA: SAGE.

Dewey, J. (1916). *Democracy and education: An introduction to the philosophy of education.* New York: Free Press.

Dewey, J. (1938). *Experience and education.* New York: Collier Books.

Du Bois, W. E. B. (1994). *The souls of Black folks.* New York: Fine Creative Media. (Original work published 1903)

Elbaz-Luwisch, F. (1997). Narrative research: Political issues and implications. *Teaching and Teacher Education, 13*(1), 75–83.

Elbaz-Luwisch, F. (2002). Writing as inquiry: Storytelling the teaching self in writing workshops. *Curriculum Inquiry, 32*(4), 403–428.

Elliot, J. (1991). *Action research for educational change.* Philadephia: Open University Press/Milton Keynes.

Fenstermacher, G. (1994). The knower and the known: The nature of knowledge in research on teaching. In L. Darling-Hammond (Ed.), *Review of research in education* (Vol. 20, pp. 3–56). Washington, DC: American Educational Research Association.

Feuerverger, G. (2001). *Oasis of dreams: Teaching and learning peace in a Jewish-Palestinian village in Israel.* New York: Routledge Falmer.

Florio-Ruane, S. (2001) *Teacher education and the cultural imagination: Autobiography, conversation, and narrative.* Mahwah, NJ: Erlbaum.

Foster, M. (1997). *Black teachers on teaching.* New York: The New Press.

Freire, P. (1970). *A pedagogy of the oppressed.* New York: Seabury.

Freire, P., M., & Macedo, D. (1995). A dialogue: Culture, language, and race. *Harvard Educational Reveiew, 65*(3), 379–382.

Gay, G. (1995). Bridging multicultural theory and practice. *Multicultural Education, 3*(1), 4–9.

Gay, G. (2000). *Culturally responsive teaching: Theory, research, and practice.* New York: Teachers College Press.

Greene, M. (1995). *Releasing the imagination: Essays on education, the arts, and social change*. San Francisco: Jossey-Bass.

Grundy, S., & Kemmis, S. (1988). Educational action research in Australia: The State of art (an overview). In S. Kemmis & R. McTagart (Eds.), *The action research reader* (3rd ed., pp. 321–335). Geelong, Australia: Deakin University Press.

Habermas, J. (1971). *Knowledge and human interests* (J. J. Shapiro, Trans.). Boston: Beacon.

Hall, B. L. (1993). Participatory inquiry. In T. Husen & T. N. Postlethwaite (Eds.), *The international encyclopedia of education* (pp. 4330–4336). Oxford, England: Pergamon.

He, M. F. (1999). A life-long inquiry forever flowing between China and Canada: Crafting a composite auto-biographical narrative method to represent three Chinese women teachers' cultural experiences. *Journal of Critical Inquiry into Curriculum and Instruction, 1,* 5–29.

He, M. F. (2002a). A narrative inquiry of cross-cultural lives: Lives in China. *Journal of Curriculum Studies, 34*(3), 301–321.

He, M. F. (2002b). A narrative inquiry of cross-cultural lives: Lives in Canada. *Journal of Curriculum Studies, 34*(3), 323–342.

He, M. F. (2002c). A narrative inquiry of cross-cultural lives: Lives in North American Academe. *Journal of Curriculum Studies, 34*(5), 513–533.

He, M. F. (2003). *A river forever flowing: Cross-cultural lives and identities in the multicultural landscape*. Greenwich, CT: Information Age.

Hoffman, E. (1989). *Lost in translation: A life in a new language*. New York: Penguin Books.

Hollingsworth, S. (1994). *Teacher research and urban literacy education: Lessons and conversations in a feminist key*. New York: Teachers College Press.

Hollingsworth, S., & Sockett, H. (Eds.). (1994). *Teacher research and educational reform*. Chicago, IL: University of Chicago Press.

hooks, b. (1991). Narratives of struggle. In P. Mariani (Ed.), *Critical fictions: The politics of imaginative writing* (pp. 53–61). Seattle, WA: Bay.

hooks, b. (1994). *Teaching to Transgress: Education as the practice of freedom*. New York: Routledge.

Huberman, M. (1996). Focus on research moving on mainstream. Taking a closer look at teacher research. *Language Arts, 73*(2), 124–140.

Kaplan, A. (1993). *French lessons: A memoir*. Chicago: University of Chicago Press.

Kemmis, S. (1988). Action research in retrospect and prospect. In S. Kemmis & R. McTaggart (Eds.), *Action research reader* (3rd ed., pp. 27–39). Geelong, Australia: Deakin University Press. (Original work published 1980)

Kingston, M. H. (1975). *The woman warrior: Memoirs of girlhood among ghosts*. New York: Random House.

Knowles, J. G., & Cole, A. L. (Ed.). (2008). *Handbook of the arts in qualitative research: Perspectives, methodologies, examples, and issues*. Thousand Oaks, CA: SAGE.

Ladson-Billings, G. (1994). *The dreamkeepers*. San Francisco: Jossey-Bass.

Ladson-Billings, G. (1998). Just what is critical race theory and what's it doing in a nice field like education? *International Journal of Qualitative Studies in Education, 11*(1), 7–24.

Ladson-Billings, G. (Eds.). (2003). *Critical race theory perspectives on the social studies: The profession, policies, and curriculum.* Greenwich, CT: Information Age.

Lewin, K. (1946). Action research and minority problem. *Journal of Social Issues, 2*(4), 34–46.

Michie, G. (1999). *Holler if you hear me: The education of a teacher and his students.* New York: Teachers College Press.

Neumann, A., & Peterson, P. L. (Eds.). (1997). *Learning from our lives: Women, research, and autobiography in education.* New York: Teachers College Press.

Nieto, S. (2000). *Affirming diversity: The sociopolitical context of multicultural education.* New York: Longman.

Nussbaum, M. (1997). *Cultivating humanity: A classical defense of reform in liberal education.* Cambridge, MA: Harvard University Press.

Phillion, J. (1999). Narrative and formalistic approaches to the study of multiculturalism. *Curriculum Inquiry, 29*(1), 129–141.

Phillion, J. (2002a). *Narrative inquiry in a multicultural landscape: Multicultural teaching and learning.* Westport, CN: Ablex.

Phillion, J. (2002b). Narrative multiculturalism. *Journal of Curriculum Studies, 34*(3), 265–279.

Phillion, J. (2002c). Classroom stories of multicultural teaching and learning. *Journal of Curriculum Studies, 34*(3), 281–300.

Phillion, J. (2002d). Becoming a narrative inquirer in a multicultural landscape. *Journal of Curriculum Studies, 34*(5), 535–556.

Phillion, J., & He, M. F. (2001). Narrative inquiry in educational research. *Journal of Critical Inquiry into Curriculum and Instruction, 3*(2), 14–20.

Phillion, J., & He, M. F. (2004). Using life based literary narratives in multicultural teacher education. *Multicultural Perspectives, 6*(3), 3–9.

Phillion, J., & He, M. F. (2007). Narrative inquiry in English language teaching: Contributions and future directions. In C. Davison & J. Cummins (Eds.), *International handbook of English language teaching* (Vol. 2, pp. 919–932). Norwell, MA: Springer.

Phillion, J., & He, M. F. (2008). Multicultural and cross-cultural narrative inquiry in educational research. *Thresholds in Education.*

Phillion, J., He, M. F., & Connelly, F. M. (Eds.). (2005). *Narrative and experience in multicultural education.* Thousand Oaks, CA: SAGE.

Richardson, V. (Ed.). (1997). *Constructivist teacher education: Building new understanding.* Washington, DC: The Palmer.

Rodriguez, R. (1982). *Hunger of memory: The education of Richard Rodriguez: An autobiography.* New York: Bantam Books.

Santiago, E. (1993). *When I was Puerto Rican.* New York: Vintage Books.

Schön, D. A. (1991). *The reflective turn: Case studies in reflective practice.* New York: Teachers College Press.

Schubert, W. H. (1991). Teacher lore: A basis for understanding praxis. In C. Witherell & N. Noddings (Eds.), *The stories lives tell: Narrative and dialogue in education* (pp. 207–233). New York: Teachers College Press.

Schubert, W. H., & Ayers, W. C. (Eds.). (1999). *Teacher lore: Learning from our own experience.* Troy, NY: Educators International Press.

Schubert, W. H., & Lopez-Schubert. (1997). Sources of a theory for action research in the United States of America. In R. McTaggart (Ed.), *Participatory action research: International contexts and consequences* (pp. 203–222). Albany, NY: State University of New York Press.

Sleeter, C., & McLaren, P. (1995). (Eds.). *Multicultural education, critical pedagogy, and the politics of difference.* Albany, NY: State University of New York Press.

Soto, L. D. (1997). *Language, culture, and power: Bilingual families and the struggle for quality education.* Albany, NY: State University of New York Press.

Stenhouse, L. (1968). The Humanities Curriculum Project. *Journal of Curriculum Studies, 23*(1), 26–33.

Stovall, D. (2005). A challenge to traditional theory: Critical race theory, African-American community organizers, and education. *Discourse: Studies in the Cultural Politics of Education, 26*(1), 95–108.

Tan, A. (1989). *The joy luck club.* New York: Ballantine Books.

United Nations Educational, Scientific and Cultural Organization. (2003). *Education in a multilingual world.* France: UNESCO.

Valdés, G. (1996). *Con respeto: Bridging the distances between culturally diverse families and schools.* New York: Teachers College Press.

Valenzuela, A. (1999). *Subtractive schooling: U.S.-Mexican youth and the politics of caring.* New York: State University of New York Press.

Westbury, I., & Wilcof, N. J. (Eds.). (1978). *Science, curriculum and liberal education: Selected essays: Joseph J. Schwab.* Chicago: University of Chicago Press.

Witherall, C., & Noddings, N. (1991). *Stories lives tell: Narrative and dialogue in education.* New York: Teachers College Press.

Woodson, C. G. (1977). *The mis-education of the Negro.* Trenton, NJ: Africa World Press. (Original work published 1933)

Zeichner, K. M., & Noffke, S. E. (2001). Practitioner research. In V. Richardson (Ed.), *Handbook of research on teaching* (4th ed., pp. 298–330). Washington, DC: American Educational Research Association.

CHAPTER 2

STITCHED FROM THE SOUL

An Auto/Biographical Inquiry of a Black Woman Principal

Sonya D. Jefferson

AUTO/BIOGRAPHICAL ROOTS

Two friends and I met recently for dinner. As we stood around the kitchen counter one asked, "Who are you today because of your experiences as a child in school?" Three powerful memories began swirling around in my mind. In the first, I am in a classroom alone among strangers. I burn my leg on the wood stove heating the room. I am a big girl now and big girls don't cry. I suffer in silence, not sure I can share my pain without crying. In the second, I sit in a desk talking to another student. An angry teacher slams a ruler across my desk. I come to see speaking as a risky act that can lead to anger and punishment. I sit in a reading group in the third. My White classmates read aloud from a chart, but I am unsure of the words. If I were smart enough for the top group, I would be sure. I choose to remain silent.

Personal~Passionate~Participatory Inquiry Into Social Justice in Education, pp. 23–36
Copyright © 2008 by Information Age Publishing
All rights of reproduction in any form reserved.

Reflecting on those memories I am reminded that we are who we are because of our remembered experiences. Whether we remember school as a joyful haven, a temporary refuge, or a lonely prison, we became educators because of what we experienced in those spaces and how those experiences impacted our daily work in schools. My earliest educational experiences occurred in predominately White schools with White teachers. Roots of the silence and the fear I struggle against as well as my passion for educating Black children run deeply through my memories of feeling alone and afraid in those classrooms. There are also feelings of loss. Perhaps I am not the person I would have been had I shared those classrooms with teachers who viewed teaching and learning as "counter-hegemonic acts" (hooks, 1994, p. 2). It is a loss many Black children attending our public schools today feel.

For those who claim to hold schools accountable for meeting the needs of students (politicians, policy makers, parents, the media), success often means improving standardized test scores and increasing graduation rates. By these standards many of the 36.4 million Blacks living in the United States are not being successful in schools. The fact that Black students, regardless of economic status or education level, tend to lag behind their White counterparts on various indicators of academic achievement has been well documented (Jenks & Phillips, 1998). Nationwide, Black kindergarten students score lower on attitudinal measures including persisting at a task, being eager to learn, and sustaining attention (U.S. Department of Education, 2000). Fewer Black children beginning kindergarten demonstrate proficiency in letter recognition and identification of beginning and ending sounds than White students and most other minorities (U.S. Department of Education, 2000). Eleven percent of all Blacks between the ages of 16 and 19 are not in school and do not hold a high school diploma (Day & Jamieson, 2003). Only 26% of Blacks graduate 5 years after entering college, and Black students post the lowest grade point averages upon entering and leaving college (Williams, 2000).

I grew concerned about these issues when my own child entered middle school and turned her back on school, refusing to do more than was necessary to get by. Education has always been important in our family. I grew up listening to my mother's stories of learning in segregated classrooms. Stories of T. J. Elder High School and teachers like Miss Lena West, Mr. William F. Moses, Miss Eunice Pearson, and Miss Gladys F. Rice are etched in my memory as if I had sat in their classrooms. My mother graduated from high school in 1959. Fifteen years later she returned to school and earned an associates degree. Her great grandfather was a founder of the first school for Blacks in Washington County, Georgia, established in 1889. His daughter was my great grandmother and a teacher for over 30 years. I was the first person in my family to graduate from college. By the time my daughter was in middle school, I had put myself through graduate school. I could not understand why, with such a history as a foundation, my daughter would refuse to fully engage in her education. How could she and so many others reject an opportunity our ancestors had fought and died for?

The resistance I saw in my daughter and other young Black students sent me in search of answers. My search eventually led to the curriculum studies program at Georgia Southern University. It was there, while studying multicultural education, that I became aware of schooling's ability to "serve as well as betray" the interests of Black Americans (Shujaa, 1994, p. 14). The focus of my questions then began to change. Rather than asking what was wrong with Black children, I began to question what was wrong with our schools. More importantly, how might our schools be transformed to better meet the needs of all children in general and Black children in particular? How can principals develop the visionary leadership needed to transform schools? How does my experience of a racist educational system impact my practice as leader of a Title I elementary school?

THEORETICAL ROOTS

My research began as a multicultural exploration miniproject focused on school desegregation. Using narrative inquiry (Clandinin & Connelly, 2000), I explored the legal history of public school desegregation in the United States and the loss of care that followed (Anderson, 1988; Schwarz, 2000; hooks, 1994; Pitts, 1999; Walker, 1993, 1996). I collected stories from my mother who attended segregated schools in Washington County, Georgia and from my husband who lived the transition from segregated to desegregated schools in Richmond, Virginia. Their stories testified to the caring embedded in their segregated schools and lack of care in the desegregated schools I attended as a child. This caring, communicated through high expectations, a refusal to accept failure, and a commitment to doing whatever was necessary to ensure students' success enabled Black children to be successful despite the incredible hardships most segregated Black schools endured. Educators in those schools committed themselves to "teaching as if woods [were] on fire" (Crawford, 1992, p. 87). They envisioned themselves as "fire[men] who would not dream of quitting but just [go] on battling to overcome" (p. 88) ignorance and illiteracy. It is this level of passion and commitment that was missing from my own experiences in desegregated schools. My research uses auto/biographical inquiry to recover that value and apply it to transforming contemporary urban schools.

As a form of curriculum inquiry, auto/biography involves "reflexive analysis" (Grumet, 1999, p. 24) of educational experiences in and out of schools, always with the goal of contributing to the educational experiences of others. Three streams of auto/biographical inquiry can be traced through the field of education (Smith, 1998). Within the first are those who explore teachers' lives (Ball & Goodson, 1985; Goodson, 1992, 1998; He, 2003; Morris, 2001) in order to "change both the teachers themselves and the educational system of which they are a part" (Smith, 1998, p. 215). A second stream includes those with alternative visions of education (Ashton-Warner, 1963; Neill, 1960). A third stream involves teachers using action research to reflect on their own practice (Elliot, 1991). I place my work in an underdeveloped fourth stream which proposes auto/biography as one strategy for "preparing leaders committed to social justice and equity" (Brown, 2004, p. 77).

My work explores the lives of four generations of Black women from my family. Each of these women studied and/or taught in the public schools in the United States. I explore our lives to better understand how our experiences in an endemically racist educational system impact my practice as a school leader. I piece together memories of lived events, memories of stories told, and information gathered from documents to create a narrative of school experiences across four generations. I situate my personal narrative within the context of a historical narrative around the desegregation of schools in the Southern United States and one community's narrative of that experience. I then explore my narrative through the theoretical lenses of critical race theory and Black feminist thought.

A critical race theory of education begins with the recognition of racism as having played a pivotal role in school structures and practices (Solorzano & Yosso, 2001). It "challenges dominant social and cultural assumptions regarding culture and intelligence, language and capability" (p. 4), is committed to a "research agenda that leads toward the elimination of racism, sexism, and poverty and the empowering of underrepresented minority groups" (p. 5), and recognizes the legitimacy of the experiential knowledge of women and men of color. Within a critical race theory of education, storytelling, narratives, chronicles, family histories, biographies, and parables become legitimate forms of inquiry. Finally, a critical race theory of education uses interdisciplinary methods to place race and racism in an historical and contemporary context.

While critical race theory encourages me to question the impact of race and racism, Black feminist thought (Collins, 2000; Frazier, Smith, & Smith, 1977; Guy-Sheftall, 1995) encourages me to question how being a

Black female growing up and living in the United States impacts my experience. Black feminist thought offers insight into how early Black women educators found the courage to challenge prevailing beliefs about themselves as Black women and about their race as a whole.

My work grows out of my passion for providing Black children with an education that empowers them to be successful in a society that is still racist. As a critical race theory educator, I recognize that schools, like the law, produce racial power. I also recognize that multicultural paradigms fail to effectively interrupt this production. Drawing on the lives of Black feminist educators, I further develop my vision for schools that interrupt the production of racial power by educating Black children for critical consciousness.

GENERATIONAL NARRATIVES

In 1914 my great grandmother, Hattie Cummings Wilcher, began her teaching career in a one room schoolhouse in Jenkins County, Georgia. She dedicated 37 years of her life to educating her people. My mother, Connie Wilcher Duggan, began her education in that schoolhouse and went on to graduate from T. J. Elder High School, the first high school for Black students in Washington County, Georgia. My daughter, Danielle, lived the resegregation of American classrooms. She overcame low expectations and negative perceptions to successfully finish high school. Now in college, she struggles to complete her own education as she begins to guide her son's.

My Grandma Lilla's love of quilting inspires me to view our life stories as a collection of quilt squares pieced together from various memories and stories. Each of these women's lives intertwines with my own as a student, teacher, and educational leader. As I share my reflections on this work, I also share moments from our lives. These quilt squares, presented in italics, highlight the impact of racism on our experiences and testify to our struggles and triumphs.

Schools in Lawton were desegregated when I entered Gladys Fullerton's 1st grade class at Eisenhower Elementary School in 1968. My memories of that first year in school are limited ... the teacher slamming a ruler down on my desk because I was talking ... learning to read with Dick and Jane ... an evening spent with my mother trying to learn the difference between a 6 and a 9 ... the scolding Mom received from my teacher because I had not attended kindergarten. I had lived a life full of rich experiences. Unfortunately those experiences did not fit inside Miss Fullerton's curriculum ...

—*Sonya*

When I view our quilt of stories through the lens of critical race theory, the previously hidden role of race and racism becomes visible. The absence of my race and culture in those Dick and Jane stories and in my first grade classroom becomes apparent. My parents could not anticipate the isolation and fear I felt as one of only two Black children in Miss Fullerton's classroom. For them and many others of their generation, school desegregation held the power to liberate their children. They believed the skills and knowledge we gained in White schools would free us to rise above the racism they had experienced. These beliefs from home paired with the White middle class environment I faced in school left me blind to the role race played in my life. Deconstructing my denial required a theory that would open my eyes to race and racism. Critical race theory recognizes racism as endemic to life in The United States and embedded in the stories of the marginalized. It values those stories and shines a light on the impact of race and racism in them. Viewing our stories through critical race theory changes my understanding of our experiences. My new understanding changes me and impacts every colleague, teacher, student, and parent I encounter.

> *I taught school for over 37 years before retiring in 1949. My parents made sure we got an education and I made sure my children … did too. My sons Jack and Remus left the South … and built dry cleaning businesses. Lilla … my youngest daughter … ran a successful business from home.*
>
> —*Hattie*

Through this intergenerational auto/biographical study, I also begin to see through the false images society projects onto the women in my family (Collins, 2000). For years my Grandma Lilla worked as a housekeeper for a White family. After age would not allow her to continue keeping house, she cleaned the law offices of one of the family members. She held this job until her death. After burying her mother, Mom consulted the same lawyer about settling Grandma Lilla's affairs. Initially, he tried to dismiss my mother. My grandmother's holdings, he said, would not be significant enough to involve the courts. I will always remember the look in his eyes when Mom mentioned the properties Grandma Lilla owned. As a White male looking at my Black grandmother, he saw only a servant whose labor could not result in an estate worth settling.

His view of my grandmother differed significantly from how she viewed herself and how I have come to see her. Grandma Lilla, like her mother Hattie, refused to accept the dominant culture's portrait of her as a poor and desperate caregiver. She defined herself as an intelligent, shrewd business woman taking advantage of every opportunity to contribute to the future security of her family. The stories of those who had gone before her gave Grandma Lilla the courage to reject the negative images others were too willing to project on her. Her story and those of other self-defined Black women form counter-narratives that allow Black women to imagine things differently for ourselves.

Popular culture offers few opportunities for us to view empowered Black women like my grandmother and great grandmother. Movies and television bombard us with narrow images of Black women as servers, seducers, and manipulators (Harris, 2003). Popular culture uses these same images to portray Black women educators giving us characters such as *Boston Public's* (Kelly, 2000) sexy music teacher and the professional but insecure principal on *The Steve Harvey Show* (Lathan, 1996).

> Because the authority to define societal values is a major instrument of power, elite groups, in exercising power, manipulate ideas about Black womanhood. They do so by exploiting already existing images, or creating new ones. These controlling images are designed to make racism, sexism, poverty, and other forms of social injustice appear to be natural, normal, and inevitable parts of everyday life. (Collins, 2000, p. 70)

Television and movie characters embody negative images which those in power use to blame Black women for our own victimization (Taylor, 1998). Without stories to contradict such images, we accept them as truth and form our identities around them.

Auto/biography provides counter-stories. Through reading the lives of other Black women and writing my own, I uncovered the falseness of the controlling images I have internalized. I now work to define myself incorporating images of empowered and successful Black women. I reject internalized images of myself as less intelligent, less capable, and less deserving and redefine myself as a competent, capable, and empowered Black woman educator.

> *My mother remembers little reaction to Brown v. Board of Education. She remembers reading about in the paper and doing current events on it but there was no trouble. While the news of the Supreme Court ruling may have passed without incident in Sandersville, the South reacted with massive resistance. Voters approved an amendment to the Georgia constitution allowing the elimination of the public school system.... The Georgia General Assembly made it a felony to allow integration ... Black teachers were ordered to withdraw from the NAACP.... The confederate battle emblem was placed alongside the state seal on the state flag.*
>
> —*Sonya*

The question of whether educational policies and practices should be guided by an ethic of justice or an ethic of care has long been debated (Walker & Snarey, 2004). Absent from the conversation have been the communal experiences of Black Americans who often "see both justice and care as necessary for their children's development" (Walker & Snarey, 2004, p. 6).

> Unlike the either-or construction of care and justice that has polarized the moral education debate, for many in the [Black] community, justice and care are equally yoked and, in effect, form a unified and overarching care-and-justice ethic. (p. 131)

A care-and-justice ethic seeks both equity in the distribution of resources and opportunities and careful attention to the development of the whole child (Walker & Snarey, 2004).

Certainly the most notable example of Black communities' commitment to justice in education lies in the battle to desegregate public schools. The fight waged by litigants in *Brown v. Board of Education* sought equity in the quality of education their children received. They believed admittance into White schools would achieve that goal. A comparison of stories from segregated classrooms with my experiences in desegregated classrooms reveals that *Brown v. Board of Education* failed to deliver what Black communities believed it promised. More than 15 years after the initial ruling, the equity they sought still eludes Black communities. Sharing classrooms with White students does not guarantee that Black children would benefit in the same way. The loss of care many experienced after desegregation guaranteed that they would not benefit. For those of us who were successful, too often the price was loss of our identities as members of Black communities.

These understandings lead to curiosity about the impact my experiences in desegregated classrooms have on my work as an elementary school principal. What lessons could I find in my stories and in the history of Black education? How might those lessons be applied to improving contemporary urban schools? How might we develop leaders needed to guide the changes?

My previous education offered little help in answering these questions. The history of American education I studied as an undergraduate and later in graduate school did not include the stories of Black education. I was ignorant of the harm embedded in White missionaries' attempts to assimilate Blacks into White society and philanthropists' attempts to relegate "Black workers to the lowest forms of labor" (Anderson, 1988, p. 36). I was also ignorant of Black communities' commitment to education as a vehicle for personal and racial uplift and their successes at circumventing the system to achieve their educational goals.

"The history of education ... is concerned with building a full understanding of he current education situation through the study of the evolution of educational practices, ideas, and institutions in social context" (Pulliam & Van Patten, 1995, p. 6). Reaching a full understanding of Black education in The United States requires viewing evolution through a racial context. Through this work, I disrupt the absence of race in my own understanding of the history of education. I develop a fuller understanding of that history through an exploration of the stories of Black education, its founders, and the Black educators who made it work in spite of the many obstacles they encountered.

Black feminist educators like Lucy C. Laney and Mary McLeod Bethune envisioned educated Black women as the key to lifting the burdens of "ignorance ... shame and crime and prejudice" (Laney, 1897/1999, p. 209). Laney's vision led to her founding Haines Normal School in Augusta, Georgia. It was under Laney's leadership that Mary McLeod Bethune developed her vision of educating Black children, a vision that lead to her founding Bethune-Cookman College. Both of these women encountered incredible hardships as they worked to bring their visions to life. They and many others struggled against limited financial resources, poor physical facilities, and other hardships to bring schools to those who would otherwise not have them. Their stories relate a care-and-justice ethic (Walker & Snarey, 2004) which countered many of the negative effects of the racism so endemic to the public education system in the United States.

I remember leaving our home in Wrightsville, Georgia on Sunday evenings and walking the three miles to the school in Donovan. During the week we would room with families in Donovan and after school on Friday walk back to Wrightsville. Mama retired from teaching in 1949. Two years later we moved to Sandersville in Washington County, Georgia and I entered 5th grade at Thomas Jefferson Elder High and Industrial School. I have good memories of my years at Elder. My classes included Algebra, Biology, Oration, Typing, and Home Economics. My teachers cared about us and expected us to do our best.

—Connie

History tends to view Black educational institutions in the same "deficit mindset" (Gay, 2000, p. 24) through which it wrongly views Black children. However,

to remember segregated schools largely by recalling only their poor resources presents a historically incomplete picture. Although black schools were indeed commonly lacking in facilities and funding, some evidence suggests that the environment of the segregated school had affective traits...that helped black children learn in spite of the neglect their schools received from white school boards. (Walker, 1996, p. 3)

Although others suggest that such positions "romanticize the pre-Brown days" (Shaw, 1996, p.11), the point that there were Black schools where climates of interpersonal caring were beneficial to Black students is a valid one.

Teachers like those at T. J. Elder "were committed to nurturing intellect so that [students] could become scholars, thinkers, and cultural workers.... [They] worked with and for [students] to ensure that [they] would fulfill [their] intellectual destiny and by so doing uplift the race" (hooks, 1994 p. 3). They demonstrated caring through their "direct attention ... to [meeting] the psychological, sociological, and academic needs" of their students (Walker, 1993, p. 65). Their caring enabled Black children to be successful learners in spite of the hardships most segregated Black schools endured.

> There were over 1900 students at my high school. It was so overcrowded there were almost as many portables as there were classrooms.... Moving through the halls was a nightmare.... Kids would end up suspended for tardies over and over. Before they knew it they would have so many absences they couldn't earn credit for the semester. Then they would just stop coming at all ...
>
> —Danielle

Gaps in achievement, visible at all levels of education, do not occur by chance. Policies and procedures imposed on public schools ensure their inevitability. My own experiences would have been very different if it was not for a "belief that education makes the difference" (Hrabawski, Maton, Greene, & Greif, 2002, p. 211) that threads through the generations of my family. Granny Hattie in turn passed it to my mother as they walked the miles to and from her one room schoolhouse. I received the message from my mother as she supervised my homework, participated in P. T. A., (Parent-Teacher Association) and paid for book club orders. It was a message reinforced as I watched her return to school and be successful. Now after instilling this same belief in my daughter, I watch as she passes it on to her son.

That belief fueled my mother's determination to see that the education I received was just. Her direct involvement ensured that the teachers I encountered knew someone cared for me and was willing to protect and defend me. She and my father were also able and willing to ensure that my appearance and language reflected middle class White values, increasing the likelihood that I would be treated fairly. Not all children enter schools with advocates like my parents standing behind them. For many others, the advocacy of their parents is viewed as threatening and is, therefore, resisted. To close the achievement gaps suffered by minority children, educators must create environments that provide caring-and-just educations for all students. They must be willing to partner with parents and advocate for children.

MY VISION FOR EDUCATIONAL AND SOCIAL CHANGE

Transforming schools to reflect the care-and-justice ethic early Black educators demonstrated requires a change in the mindset of those who lead schools. Programs designed to prepare educational leaders tend to focus on the day to day practice of public school administration. Traditional topics of study including supervision, management, and planning in educational settings are valuable for anyone anticipating school leadership at any level. However, for those of us leading schools and struggling to educate children living on the margins of our society, these traditional topics are not enough.

Urban schools need transformative leaders who see beyond statistics relating race, poverty, and student achievement and envision schools that offer all students the opportunity to achieve. My research demonstrates that writing and reading auto/biographies has the power to create such leaders. Through reflective readings of my own experiences along side the stories of others whose experiences differed from mine, I gained an understanding of how my experiences influence my practice. With that understanding, I become more mindful in my vision for the school I now lead and how my practices support that vision.

Transforming schools to reflect a care-and-justice ethic requires teachers who believe in their abilities to guide all children in becoming successful learners (Ladson-Billings, 1994). Teachers accept responsibility for student success, view content critically, and understand the importance of community and relationships. They explicitly communicate high standards, believe in their students' abilities to meet those standards, and then "teach as if the woods were on fire" to ensure they do (Crawford, 1992, p. 88).

Caring-and-just schools provide students with exposure to new ideas, career opportunities, cultural experiences, and motivational role models. Segregated schools such as Carswell County Training Center accomplished this through assembly programs which "gave students the opportunity to demonstrate their interests and exercise their talents before other students" and "serve[d] as a teaching situation" (Walker, 1996, p. 109–110). Such school-wide meetings provide an opportunity for building a sense of school identity, offer an opportunity to teach group behavior expected by larger society, and expose students "to ideas they might not otherwise hear" (p. 112).

A final aspect of urban school transformation involves partnering with communities to pursue equity in resources. School councils comprised of educators, parents, researchers from local colleges and universities, and business/community representatives offer ideal settings for engaging in "participatory social inquiry" (Oakes, Rogers, & Lipton, 2006, p. 35). Members would work together to "shape policy through information gathering, exchange, interpretation, and debate" (p. 39). Out of this collaboration would come mutual goals for educational change.

For Black Americans, completing high school and being prepared to succeed in college are imperatives. Of the 36 million Blacks living in the United States, 9 million live in poverty (McKinnon, 2001). Thirty-six percent of the 9 million are children. Children living in poverty are more likely to suffer from developmental delays and learning disabilities; more likely to be retained, expelled, or suspended from school; and more likely to dropout of high school (Wood, 2003). The median income for Black 18- year-olds who do not graduate from high school is less than $11,000 per year.

We can break this cycle by providing Black children with an empowering education that prepares them to be successful beyond high school. Creating such schools requires visionary leaders who "look at things as if they could be otherwise" (Greene, 1995, p. 19).

> The view from a bureaucratic ... distance makes us see in terms of trends, tendencies, and theoretically predictable events. Whenever we are shown a report or a statistical account of what is happening within a school district or the system as a whole, this becomes evident. It is as if automatic processes were at work; it seems impossible to look at things as if they could be otherwise. When, however, a person chooses to view herself or himself in the midst of things, as beginner or learner or explorer, and has the imagination to envisage new things emerging, more and more begins to seem possible.... Imagining things being otherwise may be a first step toward acting on the belief that they can be changed. (p. 22)

The public education system was designed "to perpetuate and maintain the society's existing power relations and the institutional structures that support those arrangements" (Shujaa, 1994, p. 15). Early Black educators circumvented and appropriated the system to ensure that their students were educated. Those of us leading twenty-first century urban schools should strive for this common goal. While the phrase school reform is routinely used as code for improving the performance of minority children, the voices of minority educators are too often absent from the discussion. Stories from the history of Black education testify to the ability of early Black educators to reach and teach Black children. If we are willing to listen, they have so much to tell us.

REFERENCES

Anderson, J. (1988). *The education of Blacks in the South, 1860–1935*. Chapel Hill: The University of North Carolina Press.

Ashton-Warner, S. (1963). *Letters from Jenny*. New York: Harcourt, Brace & World.

Ball, S., & Goodson, I. (Eds.). (1985). *Teachers' lives and careers*. London: Falmer.

Brown, K. M. (2004). Leadership for social justice and equity: Weaving a transformative framework and pedagogy. *Educational Administration Quarterly, 40*, 77–107.

Clandinin, D. J., & Connelly, F. M. (2000). *Narrative inquiry: Experience and story inqualitative research*. San Francisco: Jossey-Bass.

Collins, P. (2000). *Black feminist thought: Knowledge, consciousness, and the politics of empowerment*. New York: Routledge.

Crawford, R. B. (1992). *The woods afire: The memoir of a Georgia teacher before and after desegregation*. Oakland, CA: Regent Press.

Day, J. C., & Jamisen, A. (2003). *School enrollment: 2000*. Retrieved October 5, 2005, from http://www.census.gov/population/www/cen2000/briefs.html

Elliot, J. (1991). *Action research for educational change*. Milton Keynes, England: Open University Press.

Frazier, D., Smith, B., & Smith, B. (1977). A Black feminist statement. In B. Guy-Sheftall (Ed.), *Words of fire: An anthology of African American feminist thought* (pp. 232–240). New York: The New Press.

Gay, G. (2000). *Culturally responsive teaching: Theory, research, and practice*. New York: Teachers College.

Goodson, I. (Ed.). (1992). *Studying teachers' lives*. London: Toutledge.

Goodson, I. (1998). Storying the self: Life politics and the study of the teacher's life and work. In W. F. Pinar (Ed.), *Curriculum: Toward new identities* (pp. 3–20). New York: Garland.

Greene, M. (1995). *Releasing the imagination*. San Francisco: Jossey-Bass.

Grumet, M. R. (1999). Autobiography and reconceptualization. In W. F. Pinar (Ed.), *Contemporary curriculum discourses: Twenty years of JCT* (pp. 24–30). New York: Peter Lang.

Guy-Sheftall, B. (Ed.) (1995). *Words of fire: An anthology of African America feminist thought*. New York: The New Press.

Harris, M. Y. (2003). *Black women writing autobiography: Marginalisation, migration, and self-identity*. Unpublished doctoral dissertation, The University of Manchester, England.

He, M. F. (2003). *River forever flowing: Cross-cultural lives and identities in the multicultural landscape*. Greenwich, CT: Information Age.

hooks, b. (1994). *Teaching to transgress: Education as the practice of freedom*. New York: Routledge

Hrabowski, F. A., Maton, K. I., Greene, M. L., & Greif, G. L. (2002). *Overcoming the odds: Raising academically successful African American women*. New York: Oxford University.

Jenks, C., & Phillips, M. (1998). *The black-white test score gap*. Washington, DC: Brookings Institution.

Kelly, D. (Producer). (2000). *Boston Public* [Television Series]. New York: Fox Broadcasting Company.

Ladson-Billings, G. (1994). *The Dreamkeepers: Successful teachers of African American children*. San Francisco: Jossey-Bass.

Laney, L. (1999). Address before the women's meeting. In S. W. Logan (Ed.), *"Weare coming": The persuasive discourse of nineteenth-century Black women* (pp. 208–210). Carbondale: Southern Illinois University Press. (Original work published 1897)

Lathan, S. (Director). (1996). *The Steve Harvey Show* [Television Series]. Los Angeles: Columbia Broadcasting System.

McKinnon, J. (2001). *The Black population: 2000*. Retrieved October 5, 2005, from http://www.census.gov/population/www.cen2000/briefs.html

Morris, M. (2001). *Curriculum and the Holocaust: Competing sites of memory and representation*. Mahwah, NJ: Erlbaum.

Neill, A. S. (1960). *Summerhill: A radical approach to child rearing*. New York: Hart.

Oakes, J., Rogers, J., & Lipton, M. (2006). *Learning power: Organizing for education and justice*. New York: Teachers College.

Pulliam, J. D., & Van Patten, J. (1995). *History of education in America*. Englewood Cliffs, NJ: Prentice-Hall.

Shaw, T. (1996). Brown was bigger than test scores. *Education Week, 15*, 42–44. Retrieved July 8, 2002, from http://ehostvgw6.epnet.com

Shujaa, M. J. (Ed.). (1994). *Too much schooling too little education: A paradox of black life in White school*. Trenton, NJ: Africa World Press.

Smith, L. M. (1998). Biographical method. In N. K. Denzin & Y. S. Lincoln (Eds.), *Strategies of qualitative inquiry* (pp. 184–224). Thousand Oaks, CA: SAGE.

Solorzano, D., & Yosso, T. (2001). From racial stereotyping and deficit discourse toward a critical race theory in teacher education. *Multicultural Education, 9*, 2–8

Taylor, U. (1998). Making waves: The theory and practice of Black feminism. *The Black Scholar, 28*(2), 18–27.

U.S. Department of Education (2000). *Office of Educational Research and Improvement, National Center for Education Statistics, National Assessment of Education Progress*. Retrieved June 15, 2002, from http://nces.ed.gov/nationsreportcard/

Walker, E. V. S. (1993). Interpersonal caring in the "good" segregated schooling of African-American children: Evidence from the case of Caswell County Training School. *The Urban Review, 25*(1), 63–77.

Walker, S. V. (1996). *Their highest potential: An African American school community in the segregated south*. Chapel Hill: University of North Carolina Press.

Walker, S. V., & Snarey, J. R. (2004). *Race-ing moral formation: African American perspectives on care and justice*. New York: Teachers College.

Williams, W. (2000). The cult of anti-intellectualism amongst Blacks. *Capitalism Magazine*. Retrieved February 24, 2001, from http://www.capitalismmagazine.com.

Wood, D. (2003). Effect of child and family poverty on child health in the United States. *Pediatrics, 112*, 707–711.

CHAPTER 3

TEEN MOM

A Black Feminist Inquiry

Advis Dell Wilkerson

AUTOBIOGRAPHICAL ORIGINS OF THE INQUIRY

The roots of my personal~passionate~participatory inquiry lie in the fact that when I was 15 years old, I became a teenage mom. Although I do not condone teenage pregnancy, I know from experience what it means to have an opportunity for an education to be literally snatched out of my hands because of such an experience. Consequently, I understand the importance of having sound, supportive networks. I am grateful to have been a teen mom who came from a strong family which instilled in me values for education and hard work. Taking an in-depth look at my own experience as a Black teenage mom through a Black feminist lens, I use autobiography as a methodology to spotlight the little known phenomenon of a successful teen mom—me. Delving into the complexities and processes of my life as a teen mom, the purpose of my inquiry is to heal myself and help other teen moms by uncovering and describing my life and the obstacles I encountered and overcame. My wish is to build better

Personal~Passionate~Participatory Inquiry Into Social Justice in Education, pp. 37–51
Copyright © 2008 by Information Age Publishing

lives for both teen moms and their children by promoting character and education as a means to achieve their goals in life.

Growing up in the Deep South in the 1960s and 1970s, resources and opportunities for Blacks were few because education was somewhat restricted. To have a fair chance at life in those days, Black people, primarily segregated, yearned for an education because they saw it as a way out of poverty. Therefore, as a child, I knew that I had to excel in school. All through grade school I was on the honor roll, and I was often the teacher's pet. When I was in fifth grade, the Black and White schools integrated. In high school we must have been on a tracking system because I can remember being one of only two Black students in my all White classes. I knew that I was going to college. Prior to becoming a teenage mom, I had a reputation throughout the community for being smart and athletic, and everyone expected me to succeed. Coming from an admired, respected, and well-known family in the community, until I made a life-changing decision to have unprotected sex, I was on what seemed like a path of success.

Although opportunities for Black people were mostly restricted to positions of servitude, being the progressive and adventurous woman that she was, my mother sought better opportunities for herself and her children. A divorced, Black female with four children in the Deep South with a limited education herself, my mother saw education as the only way around the jobs that she was often forced to take in local roadside cafes, motels, and restaurants in town such as a dishwasher, a cook, or a maid. Coming from a failed marriage with four, small children, my mother did not want me to make the same choices or mistakes that she did. Since I was my mother's only daughter, I had a reputation to uphold. I was expected to excel in school so that I could fare better in life than she did. Thus, my mother was adamant about me fulfilling my potential and not having babies because they would hinder me from continuing my education. My mother would often say, "Two Bs don't mix; it's either the boys or the books!" She chose the books for me.

In the summer of 1973, prior to my first year of high school, my second oldest brother, Roy, drowned during a function hosted by the local National Association for the Advancement of Colored People (NAACP). His loss devastated both my mother and me. My mother tried to compensate for his loss by loving us even more, allowing me just enough freedom and flexibility to get into mischief. Unbeknownst to my mother, I was primed to date and experiment with sex. As a result, I fumbled through a sexual encounter with a young boy who was 1 year my senior. A virgin, only in the ninth grade, I became a teenage mom during my first year of high school for what seemed like less than 5 minutes of pleasure. I was nearly 5 months pregnant before anyone knew for certain. I recall my grandmother and mother having a conversation about dreaming about fish. In the Black community, dreaming of fish is a sign that someone is expecting a child. Somehow, through divine revelation, my mother and grandmother already knew that I was pregnant.

The minute I started showing, the school stepped in. In the spring of 1974, I was literally kicked out of school. In Folkston, Georgia, girls who became pregnant or married were no longer allowed to attend school. They were considered "grown up." Now, obviously pregnant, so-called friends were no longer friends. The baby's father avoided me. As soon as he heard that I was pregnant, he denied being the father. Suddenly ostracized from the rest of society, my mother and grandmother became my closest confidants. Together, they did everything in their power to teach me the ways of a woman. Unexpectedly, my mother opened up and began to converse with me about sex, birth control, and how boys/men tend to treat women.

Ashamed and afraid of what the future held for me, I felt alone and depressed. I can recall crying and praying for nearly the entire time that I was pregnant. I cried because I was ashamed; I felt cursed. I had made a life changing decision without thinking much about the consequences. I had let my mother, and above all, myself down. I had higher aspirations for my own life. I wanted to live the "American Dream." I wanted a nice family, a nice home, a nice car, a nice job, and so forth. Most of all, I wanted to be educated because I knew that it would be the key to my success. I knew that if I were educated, I stood a better chance of acquiring my dreams.

Before long, reality set in, and I accepted my fate. Later, with the wisdom, knowledge, and care bestowed upon me by my mother and, in her absence, my grandmother, I actually enjoyed the latter months of my pregnancy and learned to appreciate the beauty of being an expectant mother. With their help, I forgot about being kicked out of school for the moment and concentrated on having a healthy baby. My focus was on taking care of me and the little one growing inside of me. As nature would have it, on August 18, 1974, I delivered a healthy, 7 lb, 19 inches long baby girl. The first time that I set eyes on her, I remember feeling so proud to hold "my bundle of joy." She was such a beautiful baby. For that moment, somehow, everything seemed worthwhile. Three days later, my beautiful, baby girl and I left the hospital and returned home, where together we embarked on a lifelong journey.

Shortly after my baby was born, the next school year started. In view of that, my mother did not want to waste any time trying to re-enroll me in school. Although by law, girls in Atlanta, Georgia were permitted to continue school after pregnancy; somehow, in Folkston, Georgia, we were denied that right. Together, my mother and I rallied other Black teen moms in the community who had also been kicked out of school. Before long, we had the entire Black community on our side. Once our case was brought to the attention of the NAACP, lawyers from their headquarters in Atlanta descended on Folkston on our behalf. Although she never received any credit or recognition in the community for the role she played, my mother's social activism is the reason, why to this very day, pregnant or married girls in Charlton County can resume their education after childbirth and/or marriage.

Unlike many of my peers who ended up dropping out of school altogether and having more babies because they had no one at home to watch their children while they resumed their education, I had my maternal grandmother, Gramps, who gladly watched over my baby with tender loving care the first nine months of her life., I was able to resume my education, and my mother worked hard to support us. Even though I was able to continue my education with little or no interruption, when I resumed school, everything changed. I no longer felt like that popular, aspiring, smart girl with potential in her class. Once, very active in sports and extracurricular activities such as basketball, track, cheerleading, and school clubs, I was now relegated to the shadows. Knowing that I had a child waiting for me at home, I no longer had time to participate in extracurricular activities at school or any place else for that matter. All I could do was focus on my baby and my studies.

Envisioning the "American Dream"—a nice family, a nice house, a nice car, and educated with a nice job—my aspirations steered my course. I became even more determined to be self-sufficient and independent because I realized that as a teen mom, I had a responsibility to provide for both my child and myself. Once again, I felt compelled to focus on my education. After 5 years of study, I managed to graduate from Georgia State University (GSU) with a bachelor of business administration in management with a 2.14 grade point average. While a junior in college, I met a man 3 years my senior, who later became my husband for 15 years. Together, we raised my daughter into adulthood in the setting I had so often imagined as a child.

Finally, things were coming together. I felt like I had redeemed myself for that grave mistake that I thought that I had made so early in my life when I became a teen mom. Once again, I felt accepted; once again, I sensed normalcy. As fate would have it, 10 years into our happy marriage, my husband and I both became addicted to crack cocaine. After 6 months of addiction, one day I looked in the mirror and did not like what I saw. I had lost weight from not eating properly. I looked like a zombie. I could only imagine how neglected little Dale must have been. When I realized what I was doing to myself, I stopped smoking without any outside intervention. Unfortunately, my husband either could not or would not give

up his addiction to crack. After years and his repeated attempts at reha-
bilitation, to no avail, in 1991, I finally left my husband and moved back
home to live with my mother and daughter. It was time for a change, in
more ways than one. After 15 years on the job, I was burnt out and
decided to quit my job. With the help of my mother, I pursued my calling
to teach. With an undergraduate grade point average below the state
standard of 2.50, gaining entry into a teacher certification program in
Georgia would prove to be very difficult. Before any university would even
consider my application for entry, I had to redeem myself and, once
again, prove that I was worthy. I turned to education. Subsequently, in
1998, I enrolled and took classes at State University of West Georgia in
Carrollton, Georgia for over a year to pull up my grade point average and
demonstrate that I had what it took to be in their program.

Grateful to be in school again, I excelled in my studies while I substitute taught for experience. My hard work paid off because after several
letters of reference and two appeals, I was finally granted conditional
admission into West Georgia's teacher certification program. Now even
more driven, 1 year later, with the help of a few school administrators and
college professors who vouched for me, I secured a teaching position at
Creekside High School in Fairburn, Georgia. Not long afterward, I was
enrolled in one of Central Michigan University's local master's programs.
Just 2 months after I completed my master's degree, I enrolled in a doctoral program at Georgia Southern University in Statesboro, Georgia.

Although not planned, the birth of Little Dale gave me a reason to continue living even when I tried so desperately not to live. In a twisted way,
my teenage pregnancy turned out to be blessing in disguise. In more ways
than one, my teenage pregnancy helped me to maintain my sanity, which
I came very close to losing for various reasons in my life—my brother's
death, a failed marriage, drugs, alcohol, and so forth. Today, thanks to
that teenage pregnancy, I am the proud mother of one daughter, Ardale
Lavone Wilkerson-Shepherd, who is now 33 years old, married with no
children, and currently pursuing a career and degree in performing arts.
Much like my mother, nothing makes me more proud than to watch my
daughter realize her dreams in drama—singing, dancing, and acting on
stage—through education.

PASSIONATE AND PARTICIPATORY RESEARCH PROCESS

Early on in my graduate studies, I was introduced to a body of literature
comprising the work of Black feminist philosophers such as Anna Julia
Cooper, Alice Walker, Patricia Hill Collins, bell hooks, Beverly Guy
Sheftall, and others, too numerous to mention, who through their

writings, greatly influenced my thoughts. Although I knew what it meant to be Black and female, the notion of learning more about me by way of reading about the experiences of other Black females became intriguing. Reading their works, I gained valuable insight into Black feminism as an ethical framework as well as understanding myself as a Black female.

What I found was worldwide: race, class, and gender continually pose a struggle for the Black female. Unfortunately, the aftermath of slavery has cast the Black female as inferior to all human beings. Despite the fact that "African-American women have rights of formal citizenship," Black women "remain at the bottom of the social hierarchy" (Hill Collins, 1998, p. 33). Consequently, fighting to overcome obstacles would become a socially accepted way of life for me as well as others like me. Since "Afro-centric feminist theory suggests that only Black women can truly know what it is to be a Black woman" (Ladson-Billings, 1994, p. 155), an ethical framework grounded in Black feminism seemed appropriate. Despite being socially constructed as inferior to all mankind, we are continually building coalitions and forming strategies to defy negative portrayals of ourselves such as mammy, matriarch, welfare mother, whore, jezebel, and so forth (Andersen & Hill Collins 2004; Davis 1989; Davis, 1995; Hill Collins, 2000, 1998, 2004). Although some would not agree, Black feminism remains a powerful ideology for Black women.

Studying the work of modern day Black feminists has shown me that "knowledge for knowledge's sake is not enough—Black feminist thought must be tied to Black women's lived experiences and aim to better those experiences in some fashion" (Hill Collins, 2000, p. 31). Since race, class, and gender continually pose struggles for Black women, "therapeutic intervention, whether through literature that teaches and enlightens us, or therapy, [is usually required] before many of us can even begin to critically examine childhood experiences and acknowledge the ways in which they impact our adult behavior" (hooks, 2000a, p. 8). Thanks to their labor, I better understand my role as a Black female educator. Like all Black feminists, it is my belief that by writing about my own personal experience as a Black teen mom in the rural South in the early to mid 1970s, not only will I heal from my own childhood experience in terms of race, class, and gender, but I will also contribute to a body of literature that enlightens and inspires others.

Given that the reconceptualization of curriculum studies (Pinar, 1988) has opened the field to multiple perspectives making it possible for voices that were once silenced to speak with conviction on their own personal experiences, my research embraced autobiography as a methodology via a Black feminist lens to promote "a form of identity politics [and] a worldview that sees lived experiences as important to creating a critical Black consciousness and crafting political strategies" (Hill Collins, 2000,

p. 204). Using this approach, I presented my understanding as a Black female who was once a teen mom by articulating and delineating racist, sexist, and classist aspects of my experience. This type of research not only contributes to the small body of Black feminist literature in existence today, but in the process, gives me a better sense of *self*—of who I am, from whence I came, and, where I am going.

While all "women" share similar experiences, their "racial" experiences are markedly different (Andersen & Hill Collins, 2004; Davis, 1989; Hill Collins, 1998, 2000, 2004; hooks, 2000a, 2000b, 2000c). Astoundingly, even today, "in some situations, gender, age, social class, and education do not matter if you are Black" (Hill Collins, 2004, p. 2). From a Black feminist perspective, one can readily see how, over time, race, class, and gender in particular, have forged an alliance between Black women all over the world (Hill Collins, 2004; hooks, 2000a, 2000b, 2000c). My study rests upon the two overarching Black feminist goals—self-definition and self-determination (Hill Collins, 1998) as means of empowerment in Black communities everywhere.

To articulate how teenage pregnancy affected my life in terms of my race, class, and gender, from a Black feminist standpoint, my autobiography was used to explore my experience as a teen mom in the Southern United States from the mid-1970s to the present. Through my inquiry, I aimed to answer the following two questions: What is the sociocultural context in which teen pregnancy is understood and experienced from both my past and present perspectives? How can my story elaborate and illustrate these sociocultural conditions, and reconceptualize teen pregnancy?

A study on teenage mothers found "more than 50% of high school adolescents are sexually active" (Donohoe, 1996, p. 28), and "nearly 60 percent of pregnancies in the United States are unintended; among teenagers that rate is 82 percent" (Gaskin, 1998, p. 37). As with many social issues, teenage pregnancy is often depicted as a problem unique to Black teens (Abramovitz, 1988; Bromberg Bar-Yam, 2000; Merrick, 2001; Luttrell, 2003; Perrin, 1992). Arguing that dominant discourse on Black teenage pregnancy give yet another picture of the racist society in which we live, like some social construction theorists, my inquiry "highlight[s] the influence of social context and suggests that our current understandings of the 'problem' of adolescent pregnancy are rooted less in 'fact' and more in public sentiment" (Merrick, 2001, p. 2). In the context of a patriarchal society, race, class, and gender remain challenges for Black women, especially Black teen moms, and "in essence, the mass media has generated class-specific images of Black women that help justify and shape the new racism of desegregated, color-blind America" (Hill Collins, 2004, p. 147). I agree with Hill Collins (2004) who posits:

> Rather than looking at a lack of sex education, poverty, sexual assault, and other factors that catalyze high rates of pregnancy among young Black women, researchers and policy makers often blame the women themselves and assume that the women are incapable of making their own decisions. (p. 104)

Nationally, there is a wealth of "information on family planning, adolescent pregnancy, abstinence, adoption, reproductive healthcare, and sexually transmitted diseases, including HIV and AIDS" (Office of Population Affairs, 2005, ¶ 4). Teenage pregnancy is often found to be most prevalent in Black and Hispanic communities (The National Campaign to Prevent Teen Pregnancy, 2002; National Center for Health Statistics, 2000; Planned Parenthood, 2005; U.S. Department of Health and Human Services, 2000). There is a wide array of research on teenage pregnancy and some on Black teens; there are, however, few studies grounded in Black feminism. It was this gap that my inquiry aimed to address. The few studies specific to Black teenage pregnancy revealed the dire or dismal social consequences of Black teenage pregnancy (Luttrell, 2003); a greater risk for sexually transmitted diseases such as HIV and AIDS (Jennings, 2000; Johnson, 1995; Robillard, 2000); race associated differences in health outcomes; and high neonatal and infant mortality rates (Jones, 2000) for Black teenage mothers. In addition, some literature on Black teenage pregnancy focused on personality factors related to Black teenage pregnancy (Falk, 1981), the challenges of teenage pregnancy, and the need for support (Derrickson, 2003).

Unlike the majority of research on Black female adolescents, my research is closely akin to Evans-Winters' (2003) work, *Reconstructing Resilience: Including African American Female Students in Educational Resiliency Research,* which focused on the educational resiliency of Black female students and their ability to adjust to social and economic problems despite the odds against them. Similar to Evans-Winters (2003), Madibbo (2004), and Fall (2002), my goal was to contribute to what Evans-Winters termed, "resiliency literature" by helping to fill the gap in the absence of positive educational literature on African American girls.

Different from the bulk of research that focused primarily on negative issues, my research focused on my resiliency as a Black teen mom and my ability to adjust to the many social and economic problems in my life. Analyzing the sociocultural conditions in which I experienced teen pregnancy, similar to Abramovitz (1988), Evans-Winters (2003), Jefferson (2006), Kaplan (1997), Luttrell (2003), Merrick (2001), and others, my study will demonstrate how through the support of family, community, church, etc., common misconceptions regarding Black teenage motherhood are dispelled as Black feminist themes such as education, feminism, social activism, and spirituality are revealed. My study focuses on my own experience because I believed that by studying my own case, I could work to reconceptualize Black teen pregnancy by providing an analysis for a successful experience. Working with an adult provided an opportunity to study what happened in the life of a successful teen mom over time. Knowing first hand the obstacles that Black teen moms face because they are Black and female, as someone who made it, so to speak, I saw it as my civic duty to give back to my community, a community which greatly contributed to my survival and success today.

METHODOLOGICAL PROCEDURES

To assist in writing about my life, I used autobiographical writings including—memoirs, reflective essays, personal essays, and stories. I wrote my personal story from memory using a Black feminist perspective. I relied on photographs to establish a timeline. I analyzed and reflected on what happened in my life and elaborated on relationships with people, places, and things that impacted my life. I reflected on my life over time—at home, in school, in the community, with my family and friends and recorded my thoughts. Themes that emerged from my reflections were education, spirituality, social activism, and feminism—four key aspects of Black feminism.

To fill in the gaps in my memory, I referenced old music, movies, books, and poetry. Cultural artifacts also helped me to elaborate on my past experiences. Other resources included Black magazines such as *Jet* and *Ebony*. To shape my writing, I focused on the turning point in my life—teenage pregnancy. Focusing on what I learned from that particular experience and what I wanted my audience to understand, I presented my understanding as a Black female who was once a teen mom. Using several events in my life to build on one another, I articulated and delineated racist, sexist, and classist aspects of my life as a Black teen mom in the South from the 1970s to date.

OUTCOMES OF THE INQUIRY

A noted Black feminist, Patricia Hill Collins, praised postmodernism and its use of constructive/deconstructive methodologies for disproving socially accepted myths. In her book, *Fighting Words*, Hill Collins (1998) noted that postmodern tools can be beneficial for oppressed groups. She said that "deconstructive methodologies refute not just the context of scientific knowledge but the very rules used to justify knowledge; in this regard, intellectuals from oppressed groups can put deconstructive tools to good use" (p. 138). I agree with this premise. Realizing that "girls of color ... are far more likely to be victimized by sexism in ways that are irreparable" (hooks, 2000, p. 59); although their comments are not extensive, contemporary Black feminists such as hooks (2000); Abramovitz (1988); Davis (1989); and Hill Collins (2004) have addressed teenage pregnancy in selected texts. These contemporary Black feminists call for a focus on reproductive rights to prevent and control unwanted teen pregnancies, contemporary Black feminists call for preventive strategies such as sex education, healthcare, and easy access to contraceptives (Davis, 1989; Hill Collins, 2004; hooks, 2000a, 2000b, 2000c).

Speaking on class, sexuality, and the social stigma of unmarried motherhood in the Black community, hooks (2000c) posits, "More than class, mama saw sexuality—the threat of unwanted pregnancy—as the path that closed all options for a female" (p. 20). I can definitely relate my experience to what hooks says. I remember it as if it were yesterday—the shame of being pregnant, the feelings of loneliness and depression. I was so psychologically scarred from being a teen mom that to this very day, my daughter is the only child. However, in spite of the difficulties, like so many others before me, I found motherhood to be rewarding (also see Hill Collins, 2004; hooks, 2000a, 2000b, 2000c; Merrick, 2000). "Despite mass media's negative assessment of Black motherhood for poor and working-class Black women, motherhood remains valued by the majority of Black women" (Hill Collins, 2004, p. 208), including me. "Through motherhood, they exercise strength, demonstrate power, and, as a result, often suffer the consequences associated with this commitment" (Hill Collins, 2004, p. 208). Once I got past the initial shock of being pregnant, I became focused and realized that I had to grow up fast. I not only had myself to think about, but a child too. I realized that teen sex and teen pregnancy are directly correlated to socioeconomic status and family status (single-vs.-married) (Planned Parenthood, 2005). Since I grew up without my father, it was imperative to me that my daughter be raised in a traditional household where men and women come together on child rearing. I purposely sought a husband and home to raise my child. Like my mother and her mother, I intended to make sure that my daughter fared better than I did.

One of the more radical and militant Black feminists in the contemporary movement, Angela Davis (1989), cautions us against dominant discourse findings. Davis posits, "Effective strategies for the reduction of teenage pregnancy are needed, but we must beware of succumbing to propagandistic attempts to relegate to young single mothers the responsibility for our community's impoverishment" (p. 13). All Black feminists caution others against misinformation with reference to the Black community. For example, "In prior eras, Black women were encouraged to have many children.... Now Black women are seen as producing too many children who contribute less to society than they take" (Hill Collins, 2004, p. 104). I find it amazing how over time, our thinking is so easily swayed by society. Again, I agree with Patricia Hill Collins (2004) who contends:

> Despite a high adolescent pregnancy rate, worrisome increases in the rate of HIV infection among American adolescents, and emerging research demonstrating that high school students grappling with lesbian, gay, bisexual, and transgendered (LGBT) identities are more prone to depression and suicide, the reluctance to talk openly about human sexuality with United States schools places students at risk. (p. 38)

As an educator, I see youth at risk almost daily. More often than not, I also see how "unregulated sexuality results in unplanned for, unwanted, and poorly raised children" (Hill Collins, 2004, p. 130).

In addition, because I was once one of them, I know from experience that "a sizeable portion of families maintained by Black single women are created by unmarried adolescent mothers" (Hill Collins, 2000, p. 63). When it comes to motherhood, Patricia Hill Collins (2000) sums it up best when she notes:

> African American women encounter differential treatment based on our perceived value as giving birth to the wrong race of children, as unable to socialize them properly because we bring them into bad family structures, and as unworthy symbols for U.S. patriotism. This treatment is based, in part, on ideologies that view U.S. Black women as the Other, the mammies, matriarchs, welfare mothers, and jezebels who mark the boundaries of normality for American women overall. (p. 230)

Unlike Black women, "middle-class [W]hite women are encouraged to increase their fertility, and are assisted by a dazzling array of new reproductive technologies in the quest of a healthy [W]hite baby" (Hartouni in Hill Collins, 2000, p. 231), while Black women and children are suffering worldwide.

EDUCATIONAL AND SOCIAL CHANGES RESULTING FROM THE INQUIRY

In an attempt to better understand how race, class, and gender shape Black women's maternal experiences, I explored my experience as a teenage mother. I investigated the sexism and racism that I encountered, and the few support systems that were in place to help my child and me.

Ironically, the birth of my daughter represented the diminishment of my potential in this world as well as the fulfillment of the best that I can be. My daughter's birth brought reason to celebrate life after the tragic death of my brother. It also brought tremendous struggle against the oppressive forces prevalent in U.S. society. Resting upon the two overarching Black feminist goals—self-definition and self-determination (Hill Collins, 1998), from a Black feminist standpoint, the intent of my inquiry was to share my story and promote education as a tool of empowerment for Black teen moms. I had hoped that this sharing would move toward reconceptualizing the sociocultural context—a context that is racist, sexist, and otherwise harmful to teen mothers and their children.

Over time, autobiography has evolved into an acceptable method of education research (Grumet, 1980; Harris, 2005; Neumann & Peterson, 1997; Pinar, 1994; Roth, 2005). Black women are increasingly writing about their lived experiences; specifically, their oppressions and oppressors. From that perspective, reflecting on my life as a teen mom, not only did I help myself as I got a better sense of *self*—of who I am, from whence I came, and where I may be going; but in the process, I assisted others. Dismissed as stupid, unfit, and shut out because they are Black, there are obvious race associated differences in health outcomes of Black teenage mothers and their children (Jones, 2000). As a result, high neonatal and infant mortality rates are common among Black teenage mothers (Jennings, 2000), which is yet another reason why additional research of this nature is warranted.

Coming from a background largely comprised of obstacles—being African American, female, living in the South, and a teen mom—I realize that had it not been for the undying support of my mother, my grandmother, and others, before, during, and after my teenage pregnancy, returning to school to continue my education would not have been an option for me. I came from a strong family and a small town in the South which included my extended family (my grandparents and the Black community). My behavior was shaped through their behavior, their rules, and their reward/punishment systems. They instilled in me character and values for hard work, education, self-discipline, and honesty. Those values assisted me in my development as a productive citizen whose contributions help maintain a functional society. Not only were those values the values of my family, they were also the common values of the Black community and the entire social system of which I had grown accustomed. Combined, the laws, rules, regulations, principles, policies, and procedures of the social system shaped my philosophy and behavior. Behavior converse to that philosophy was sanctioned with countless examples—coming from the family, the school, the church, and the media—about those whose lives had become a disaster for failing to follow those rules and regulations. Whenever I deviated, what brought me back were my philosophies of life—obey the laws of society, education is the key to success, honesty is the best policy, and hard work pays off.

CONCLUSION

Although in recent years, overall trends in teenage pregnancy have declined in the United States (The National Campaign to Prevent Teen Pregnancy, 2002; National Center for Health Statistics, 2000; Office of Population Affairs, 2005; Planned Parenthood, 2005; U.S. Department of Health and Human Services, 2000); trends in pregnancies remain especially high for Black teens. Studies on teenage pregnancy indicate that teen mothers are nearly twice as likely to be Black than White (National Center for Health Statistics, 2000; Planned Parenthood, 2005; The National Campaign to Prevent Teen Pregnancy, 2002; U.S. Department of Health and Human Services, 2000). While "unplanned pregnancies are common even among the most educated and 'responsible' classes" (Gips, 1996, ¶ 6), a recent study on teenage pregnancy "revealed that [Black] women ... stay fewer years in school, have fewer dollars to spend, and bear more economic burdens than any other group in this country" (Hurtado, 1996, p. 5). Single Black mothers who often lack sufficient resources to provide adequate food, clothing, and shelter for their children head many Black families. Thus, more often than not, Black teenage mothers further relegate themselves and their families into poverty because they lack sufficient education. Consequently, they are unable to obtain jobs to adequately provide for their children. As a result, social perils such as homelessness, hunger, and poor health remain commonplace in Black communities not only nationwide but also worldwide.

While all "women" share similar experiences, their "racial" experiences are markedly different (Andersen & Hill Collins, 2004; Davis, 1989; Hill Collins, 1998, 2000, 2004, 2000; hooks, 2000a, 2000b, 2000c). Astoundingly, even today, "in some situations, gender, age, social class, and education do not matter if you are Black" (Hill Collins, 2004, p. 2). From a Black feminist perspective, one can readily see how, over time, race, class, and gender in particular, have forged an alliance among Black women all over the world (Hill Collins, 2004; hooks, 2000a, 2000b, 2000c). Due to the fact that teenage pregnancy is prevalent in Black communities worldwide, I used Black feminist theory to guide my inquiry to explore my personal experience as a teen mom, to make meaning of my experience to empower myself, and to advocate for other Black teen moms. Sharing my experience and providing a critical analysis of the sociocultural context in which I experienced teen pregnancy, my story has implications not only for my daughter, future grand-daughter, and other African American girls but also for other teens worldwide.

REFERENCES

Abramovitz, M. (1988). *Regulating the lives of women social welfare policy from colonial times to the present*. Boston: South End Press.

Andersen, M., & Hill Collins, P. (Eds.). (2004). *Race, class, and gender: An anthology* (5th ed.). Belmont, CA: Wadsworth/Thomson Learning.

Bromberg Bar-Yam, N. (2000). Teen pregnancy: Reframing the question. *International Journal of Childbirth Education, 15*(2), 26–27.

Davis, A. (1995). Reflections on the Black woman's role in the community of slaves. In B. Guy-Sheftall (Ed.), *Words of fire: An anthology of African-American feminist thought*. New York: The New Press.

Davis, A. (1989). *Women, culture, and politics*. New York: Random House.

Derrickson, T. (2003). *Successfully meeting the challenges of teen pregnancy and motherhood in Sussex County, Delaware*. Unpublished doctoral dissertation, Wilmington College, Ohio.

Donohoe, M. (1996). Adolescent pregnancy. *The Journal of the American Medical Association, 276*(4), 282–283.

Evans-Winters, V. (2003). *Reconstructing resilience: Including African American female students in educational resiliency research*. Unpublished doctoral dissertation, University of Illinois at Urbana-Champaign.

Falk, R. (1981). Personality factors related to black teenage pregnancy and abortion. *Psychology of Women Quarterly, 5*(5), 737.

Fall, T. (2002). *Spirituality and its impact in the lives of Black women: An ethic of resistance and resiliency*. Unpublished doctoral dissertation, Miami University, Florida.

Gaskin, I. (1998). Intentional conception. *Birth Gazette, 14*(4), 37.

Gips, J. (1996). Teen parenting reconsidered. *Birth Gazette, 12*(3), 16-17.

Grumet, M. (1980). Autobiography and reconceptualization. *JCT, 2*(2), 155–158.

Harris, M. (2005). Black women writing autobiography: Autobiography in multicultural education. In J. Phillion, M. F. He, & F. M. Connelly (Eds.), *Narrative and experience in multicultural education* (pp. 36–52). Thousand Oaks, CA: SAGE.

Hill Collins, P. (1998). *Fighting words Black women and the search for justice*. Minneapolis, MN: University of Minnesota Press.

Hill Collins, P. (2000). *Black feminist thought knowledge consciousness and the politics of empowerment*. New York: Routledge.

Hill Collins, P. (2004). *Black sexual politics: African Americans, gender, and the newracism*. New York: Routledge.

hooks, b. (2000a). *Feminism is for everybody: Passionate politics*. Cambridge, MA: South End Press.

hooks, b. (2000b). *Feminist theory: From margin to center* (2nd ed.). Cambridge, MA: South End Press.

hooks, b. (2000c). *Where we stand: Class matters.* New York: Routledge.

Jefferson, S. (2006). *Stitched from the soul an autobiographical inquiry into one Black woman administrator's voice and vision.* Unpublished doctoral dissertation, Georgia Southern University, Statesboro.

Jennings, P. (2000). *Genetic ties and genetic "others:" Race, class, and infertility.* Unpublished doctoral dissertation, University of Kentucky, Lexington.

Johnson, V. (1995). *Holding out for the dream: Black women, substance abuse and HIV/AIDS infection.* Unpublished doctoral dissertation, University of California at Berkeley.

Jones, C. (2000). Levels of racism: a theoretic framework and a gardener's tale. *American Journal of Public Health, 90*(8), 1212–1214.

Kaplan, E. (1997). *Not our kind of girl unraveling the myths of Black teenage motherhood.* Berkeley/Los Angeles: University of California Press.

Ladson-Billings, G. (1994). *The dreamkeepers.* San Francisco: Jossey-Bass.

Luttrell, W. (2003). *Pregnant bodies, fertile minds gender, race, and the schooling of pregnant teens.* New York: Routledge.

Madibbo, A. (2004). *Minority within a minority: Black francophones of Ontario and the dynamics of power and resistance.* Doctoral dissertation, University of Toronto, Canada.

Merrick, E. (2001). *Reconceiving Black adolescent childbearing.* Boulder, CL: Westview.

The National Campaign to Prevent Teen Pregnancy. (2002). Retrieved February 27, 2006, from http://www.teenpregnancy.org/

National Center for Health Statistics (2000). Retrieved February 2, 2006, from http://www.cdc.gov/nchs/

Neumann, A., & Peterson, P. (Eds.). (1997). *Learning from our lives women, research, and autobiography in education.* New York: Teachers College Press.

Office of Population Affairs (2005). Retrieved February 2, 2005, from http://opa.osophs.dhhs.gov/clearinghouse.html

Perrin, K. (1992). The 4Ms of teen pregnancy: Managing, mending, mentoring, and modeling. *International Journal of Childbirth Education, 7*(4), 29–30.

Pinar, W. (1988). The reconceptualization of curriculum studies, 1987: A personalretrospective. *Journal of Curriculum and Supervision, 3*(2), 157–167.

Pinar, W. (1994). *Autobiography, politics and sexuality: Essays in curriculum theory 1972–1992.* New York: Peter Lang.

Planned Parenthood. (2005). Retrieved February 27, 2006 from http://www.plannedparenthood.org/pp2/portal/medicalinfo/birthcontrol/

Robillard, A. (2000). *Examining the relationships between music videos and sexual risk behavior in African-American adolescent females.* Unpublished doctoral dissertation, University of Alabama at Birmingham.

Roth, W. (2005). (Ed.). *Auto/biography and auto/ethnography: Praxis of research method.* The Netherlands: Sense.

U.S. Department of Health and Human Services. (2000). *The National Center for Health Statistics.* Retrieved February 27, 2006, from http://www.hhs.gov/

CHAPTER 4

RESILIENT LIVES

African American Women Scholars

Paula Booker Baker

AUTO/BIOGRAPHICAL ORIGINS OF THE INQUIRY

The origin of my inquisitiveness and passions are as diverse as my culture
and race. One path of questions come from understanding the phrase I
have developed from personal experiences: "Learning while Black." I can
recall hearing my elders, family members, friends, and even strangers
discuss the dangers of driving while Black. I have found through my
school matriculation that learning while Black can be as treacherous as
driving while Black. *You do not understand what I am saying?* Then I dare to
say, you have not have the experiences deemed common for many people
of African decent. I am a Black woman who grew up in Southern Alabama, learning and living while Black.

I am a product of the Civil Rights Era. My life has been sprinkled with
stories that forced me to "see" beyond my experiences—experiences that
link me to unfairness, injustice, and apprehension, yet they prepared me
with resilience, strength, and determination. My mother shares stories of

Personal~Passionate~Participatory Inquiry Into Social Justice in Education, pp. 53–69 not being admitted into the main entrance of Dairy Queen to get a treat for her young daughter and summertime battles with retail stores to guarantee suitable yet beautiful Black dolls for Christmas. My mother, aunts, and grandmother tell of segregated schools and neighborhoods and Black only areas in restaurants, doctors' offices and hospitals. My great aunt tells our extraordinary family tale of how late one summer day, Grandpa Amos walked from the small town of Brundidge, Alabama 30 miles to Ozark, Alabama, another town farther south. Grandpa Amos began his walking travels to find a town that allowed African American men to be compensated for their work. From this journey Grandpa Amos found employment and earned enough money to bring his family to Ozark and establish a new legacy. He taught his sons his trade and the value of education. His daughters learned of strength and perseverance as well as self reliance. From there, two of his sons formed the first Black contracting company in the area. This family history survived time through storytelling and provides reminders as the actual houses and businesses they built still stand today, 150 years after construction. As I drive through Ozark and tell my child about his ancestry, I continue the tradition and introduce facets of racism that failed against our family's strength and perseverance.

None of my relatives wrote their stories but made conscious efforts to share their experiences. These tales interwove instances of perseverance, triumph, and success. It is my belief that they hoped the future generations would hear about their struggles but never understand them through actions and life. These tales included life stories of people who fought to learn reading, writing, and arithmetic while struggling against the dominant culture's control to find and maintain a positive sense of self. Even in these treacherous times the older generations carried an understanding that cultural, societal, and global issues were necessary components to education.

I recall stories of life at D. A. Smith High School, a segregated school for Black children in Ozark, Alabama. The schooling of many African Americans began with substandard schools, overcrowded classrooms, outdated texts, and limited materials (Willie, Garibaldi, & Reed, 1991). While I faced these obstacles, there were also caring teachers, challenging curriculum, advanced academics, diverse extracurricular activities, and student success. The environments that were created and maintained by the dominant culture to oppress a people produced doctors, entrepreneurs, lawyers, professors—strong and proud people of color. Why is there a collapse in success for our children now that we have access to greater educational resources? What is happening to our young children when education is supposedly improved and more readily available?

Hearing the stories of my family members and others strengthens my resiliency. As I reflect on my life and education, I must assert that I was not denied entry into places although at times I felt unwanted. Education was always afforded me although I remember classrooms where the "best" was not provided to me. My schools had extracurricular activities designed to develop the whole student; however, my presence was at times shunned in these activities and organizations. I was never beaten or verbally abused although I have on many occasions had to do twice what was required in order to prove my worthiness. Is this how life should be when so many people have marched, struggled, and died so that all children could experience a just life? I find myself reaping the rewards of my ancestors and wanting to educate the younger generations on our cultural prowess and history of perseverance and strength. I join my ancestors in dreaming of a day when children will only know about learning while Black, driving while Black, or living while Black through history.

While living as a girl of color, defining and redefining my identity, and working through my struggles and uncertainties, I found support in my family—their songs, poetry, conversations, and stories. These communicative customs were designed to comfort me while they taught me to resist the racist stereotypes in the schools, refuse the humiliations, and stand up against a society that created experiences that seemed to predestine me for failure. Maya Angelou in 1978 composed the poem, *Still I Rise*. I found that the words in this poem echo the personal conflict, resiliency, and experiences I see when I think of African American women. This poem speaks to my soul and strengthens my resolve to succeed as I peer into the lives of Black women who dreamed, persevered, and succeeded.

Through my life filled with storytelling and support, I learned to except and maneuver through this position of double marginalization. I learned that optimism prevails over obstacles. I believe that Black women who choose to accept this unique position and function in a positive manner become more than just women with labels but agents of change who search out opportunities to experience, learn, and grow. I realize that I *am* more than a label created by others. How can I use this knowledge to teach young girls that they are more than labels, especially when the school systems tell them that they are subgroups within the standardized schooling arena?

As an African American woman, a mother, a mentor, an educator, and a scholar, I have different opportunities to observe Black girls in academic and extracurricular settings. These girls seem to believe the only way to succeed is to become something new, someone new. Many of the students cross the threshold of the school and immediately become defeated because they realize—once Black, always Black. Instead of this being a realization of pride, these girls find they carry two strikes. These girls are members of two subgroups within a standardized world created for and by White men.

I found that I was not alone in my journey of truth but was accompanied by countless passionate advocates—African American women who defend Black womanhood and promote continuation of the stories. My journey led to Patricia Hill Collins (2000) who presented *Black Feminist Thought: Knowledge Consciousness, and the Politics of Empowerment*, in which she discussed the existence of a culture of silence where African American women are seen but not heard. bell hooks (1994) provided additional support to the feminist movement for Black women. In *Teaching to Transgress: Education as the Practice of Freedom*, hooks challenges the preconceptions of education that suppress diversity and the unjust division of power.

As I read through the aforementioned work, I was often reminded of my years as a student in the public education system. I realize that many times I too felt silenced, unworthy, and alone. After years of contemplation, I acknowledged these feelings and created an alternative to the forced positioning of "less than." Others wanted me to be isolated, but through *this* positionality I find more than just a story—I gain a standpoint as well as an inheritance of support.

In conversations with young girls, I realize these students do not have stories, experiences, and thoughts of success. Instead, these students seem to believe they are doomed to follow the path to destruction—a path that has been outlined by the dominant culture. Young girls, our future leaders, are wandering aimlessly through life as they live as pawns in a growing universal phenomenon. Their discussions never include successful women of color or futures full of success. The girls' knowledge of oppression, civil rights, and democracy was one-sided; slavery and repression were center. In order to succeed, appropriate knowledge is vital to building a strong sense of self, one's culture, and a positive future.

PARTICIPATORY RESEARCH PROCESS

My compassion for young girls and desire to help them propels me to act. In my journey I have found I needed to strengthen myself and put order to my interests. My graduate program became that special place that helped me hone my beliefs, emotions, opinions, and perspectives into a tool to impact others. My sometimes muddled thoughts and concerns turned into a methodical collection of questions and scenarios. I found help by combining my stories with those of other women; this provided me the transport to carry tales of hope and healing to my students and other women who needed a broader perspective in order to create a clearer picture of society and develop options for their futures. Instead of worrying about what was missing from society and education and how the students were suffering because of exposures, I decided to focus on how African American women faced obstacles and struggles and became successful. I took on Carter G. Woodson's (1933) definition of education in which he stated, "real education means to inspire people to live more abundantly, to learn to begin with life as they find it and make it better" (p. 29). I chose to meet my students where they were and challenge them to reject stereotypes and to persevere in order to experience success.

The inquiry began many years ago when I began to ask poignant questions about the conflict between my culture, values, beliefs, and personal experiences and what was expected of me from the viewpoint of the dominant culture in the academic setting. The inconsistencies grew as I saw the conflict play out on television and in different educational settings. My passion for my inquiry strengthened. As I worked as a teacher and watched young African American girls stroll aimlessly through the halls of elementary and middle schools, my focus broadened to include other girls and women of African decent.

I structured my inquiry to allow the uniqueness of the women's voices and experiences to be brought forward. I hoped everyone who read the work would have their viewpoints challenged in order to discover new realities. Using Black feminist thought and critical race theory as a theoretical framework, and critical narrative inquiry as research methodology, I am able to connect with and learn from stories of others as well as develop new understandings from the retelling of our own stories. This process is supported by Witherell and Noddings (1991) who believe that "[s]tories invite us to come to know the world and our place in it. Whether narratives of history or the imagination, stories call us to consider what we know, how we know, and what and whom we care about" (p. 13).

Critical race theory focuses on the power of words, the impact of race and racism, and posits that racial background influences perspectives and experiences. This viewpoint supports my claim that each woman's story should be recognized and viewed as unique. Calmore (1992) states that critical race theory supports the idea that race is not a *fixed* term yet is one that oscillates and changes. More important for me, critical race theory calls for deconstruction of the narratives of the dominant culture to change the ideology that all Black women are in one group. In addition, critical race theory takes our knowledge and personal histories and through telling and retelling of the stories forces us to self-reflect (Delgado & Stefancic, 2001). At the same time that critical race theory allows me to understand the power of the stories and racial issues interwoven in the women's lives, Black feminist thought (Collins, 2000; Thompson, 2004) captures the voices and identities of Black women.

According to Collins, Black feminist thought recognizes theoretical interpretations of reality that are presented by all Black women. Moreover, Black feminist thought maintains the conviction of understanding the experiences of Black women individually yet remains aware of the reality that as society changes; the understanding of these experiences must change as well.

"Black feminist thought recognizes the need to look beyond class, age, economics, education, and career positions to understand the perspectives of Black women" (Baker, 2005b, p. 46). Because of this complex identity, I believe it is imperative to incorporate Black feminist thought to connect the experiences, influencers, and perspectives of Black women. The philosophies have compatible viewpoints that look to understand the association of power and various influences and, therefore, work successfully together.

With an understanding of critical race theory and Black feminist thought, I found support for the idea that these narratives could be used to create counter accounts of the existing social realities. I found in my study that the women's lives had similar facets; however; it was important to discern the uniqueness in each. With this in mind I chose critical narrative inquiry to build this study.

When engaging in stories and lives of others, our understanding changes. Through this dialogue and growth, we see our lives through different lenses (Baker, 2005b). Using Black feminist thought and critical race theory, I explored the challenges, strategies, and accomplishments of Black women who attempted and succeeded in diverse settings.

> Two of the theoretical frameworks that offer promise for understanding the intersecting identities of African American women and explaining ways in which [our] needs can be addressed effectively are Black Feminist Thought and Critical Race Theory. (Howard-Hamilton, 2003, p. 20)

To ensure the stories of my participants stand liberated and equal to those of men and White women, Black feminist thought stands equal to critical race theory. Although all Black women may experience racism and oppression, classism and sexism, we must remain cognizant that academic status and social class may impact the type of discrimination experienced. Black feminist thought remains focused on the complexity of identity for Black women and the experiences, influences, and perspectives that impact our stories.

The selection of participants began as a snowball effect as I asked fellow doctoral cohort members, colleagues, and friends if they could recommend women who might be interested in my work. Eleven potential participants were contacted. I was searching for participants who had experience from historically black colleges or universities, predominantly White universities, and work experiences in public and higher education. Drs. Juanita Sims Doty, Fannie Richardson Cooley, Joyce V. Rhoden, Francina L. Williams, and Anna Pearl Atkinson graciously agreed to decline anonymity and allow accurate information to be used from their personal experiences of life from segregation to desegregation and from elementary to post doctoral studies. With a quote in mind and a tape recorder in hand, I set off on a journey of growth, knowledge, and transformation.

My field text included letters, vitas, photographs as shared by the participants, personal data forms, transcripts from interviews, e-mail correspondence, and postal mail used to share edited material. All of the interviews took place in locations specified by the participants. Through one-on-one interviews, I explored the effects of K–12 education, higher education, family, community, and racism on these women and how they overcame obstacles in their paths. The participants were asked structured and unstructured questions about family, educational experiences, life, obstacles, and triumphs. I kept a research journal that detailed my feelings before, during, and after the interviews as well as what I observed during the actual interview process. Audio tapes were transcribed in their entirety and coded manually to reveal primary themes of family, education, friends, spirituality, and the experiences from historically black colleges and universities and predominantly White institutions. Because pseudonyms were not used, transcripts and field notes were presented to participants for verification of facts and clarification.

The participants were allowed to tell their own stories, and the meanings were negotiated between the teller and listener (Casey, 1995-1996; Clandinin & Connelly, 2000). Each time someone hears or reads this work, new meanings will be negotiated. My responsibility with this work was to give resonance to the participants' stories and show connectivity for these women who have beat the odds.

A journey that began with a poem and a story ended with a poem and a vision. Because of this project my passion for continued success and a renewed determination to help others find their futures returned. Dr. Juanita Sims Doty an academician, advocate, entrepreneur, and devoted member of Alpha Kappa Alpha Sorority, Inc. told of a life from humble beginnings to an adulthood of service and excellence. Dr. Fannie Richardson Cooley recalled life from Tunnell Springs, Alabama through international studies to Professor Emeritus of Tuskegee University in Tuskegee Institute, Alabama. Dr. Joyce V. Rhoden opened with a childhood in Jamaica to experiences of learning English and difficult doctoral experiences to her present success as a prominent member of the

Tuskegee University faculty. Dr. Francina L. Williams spoke of early life in Gadsden, Alabama and ended with her second career as the curator of The George Washington Carver Interpretative Museum in Dothan, Alabama. Dr. Anna Pearl Atkinson began with family history and moved through eight prestigious universities to further her education and ended with the desire to author a book to help identify the ill and cure for racism. From these women and their stories, I was able to identify characteristics and dispositions which appear to promote resiliency in lives of Black women.

Dr. Juanita Sims Doty contends that education has always been a priority for her and her family. As the second to youngest daughter in a family of thirteen, family and faith were ever present in her household. Taking from her parents, she believes that we ought to be motivated by seeing others happy because of the services we can provide to assist them. Dr. Sims Doty says we need not focus on our lack but on our options.

Dr. Fannie Richardson Cooley explained that there are always obstacles that must be faced in professional and personal lives. She chooses to take an optimistic approach and search for opportunities. Through our conversations a love of learning, sharing, and helping others was evident. She firmly believes that all things influence who we are and what we become. Dr. Cooley says we do not have to agree with the opinions of others, but we must realize that everyone has something to contribute to the conversation. When you disagree with the opinions of others, you create your individual position.

Throughout our conversations, Dr. Joyce Rhoden maintained that she is a family person who wants to be seen as someone who works hard and wants the best for all people. She believes in the power of optimism, family structure, and education. She believes we as adults short-change the younger generation by not exposing them to diverse activities and providing support. Dr. Rhoden describes herself as a counselor, mentor, parent, grandparent, and friend. These roles are extended to include her students at Tuskegee University. To those who cross her path, she describes a successful person as someone who sets goals, defines them, and strives to accomplish them.

Immediate, extended, and surrogate family was important for Dr. Francina L. Williams. She recalls going to college as her biggest challenge. Her family members were always proponents of education, but finances were the obstacle. She believes that we spend too much time trying to avoid obstacles and they end up stifling our progress. In order to succeed, we need to realize these obstacles as a part of life that helps us to grow. Dr. Williams continues by stating that "in every stage of life there are barriers, hurdles, and obstacles. We must remain optimistic and sacrifice luxuries today for attainment of our goals."

Dr. Anna Pearl Atkinson believes that family expectations and support are keys to survival. Her childhood memories include her family's active role in exposing her to people, places, and things that created experiential knowledge which broadened her perspectives. She believes that if given the opportunity and exposure, children can become or do anything they choose. In order to be successful educators and role models, Dr. Atkinson says we ought to recognize the subtle prejudices that penetrate our educational system. She believes it is not enough to talk about the issues, but we must listen, understand, and act to make positive changes.

The stories of these women bear witness to how lives that are permeated with unjust actions and discriminatory events yet are full of love, support, and understanding that can lead to happiness, fulfillment, and success. Each account of experiences, obstacles, and triumphs was considered individually and then amalgamated to observe common differences and similarities. "The chronicling of stories and counter stories provide spaces where others establish connections with the presented stories and also recognize the differences in their own stories" (Baker, 2005a, p. 88). Dr. Atkinson put it best when she said we must teach our children to be proud and grab hold of their God given power and talent.

Helle (1991) believes the "narrative's power of specifying combines with theory's power of generalizing, ever more inclusive and multiplistic standpoints for knowing become possible" (p. 63). Storytelling allows us to broaden our perspectives to see and even understand these new points of knowing. I believe everyone has a story to tell, and by listening to the stories of others, we not only discover what the teller attempts to portray, we discover different viewpoints and more understandings within ourselves.

Through listening and telling, we gain new experiences—freedom from guilt that allows the mind to critique and dream. This freedom becomes a stop on the path to empowerment. Storytelling is a powerful learning tool that encourages people of all ages and cultures to challenge beliefs and mores and explore personal expressiveness. The process frees us from boundaries and allows us to imagine counter narratives that stand against the oppressive tales that are presented by the dominant culture. Storytellings (narratives) nurture us and teach us to listen, communicate, understand, and grow.

Throughout this process, one concern I remained cognizant of is the creation of dualism, where things are seen in black and white. The focus for many inquiries revolved around rigid theoretical modes with inflexible steps and standard rules. I felt compelled to adopt a fluid line of thinking. In order to incorporate this fluidity, a critical lens was interwoven with the narrative, thus critical narrative inquiry.

ESTABLISHING THE CONSEQUENCES

Through analysis of their stories, I found that resilience for these women was fostered through cultural socialization as well as affirmation individually and culturally. I replayed their stories through the lenses of Black feminism and critical race theory. Just as their experiences created the strong women I interviewed, their stories helped redefine who I am, what I believe, and what I desire. The realization that stands clearest for me is that as life continues—I will live, learn, and change. Ladson-Billings (2005) believes:

> The complexity of Black lives in the midst of overwhelming challenges rarely makes for a rational world. The ability to "make a way out of no way" and to overcome when it seems impossible is regularly and readily attributed to some force beyond individual effort ... Black people throughout history have merged the sacred and the profane as they only way to live mentally, emotionally, and psychically healthy lives. (p. 137)

This study allowed me to explore how five phenomenal African American women defined themselves against the stereotype. The research findings indicated that resilience was fostered through cultural socialization, affirmation individually and culturally, experiential learning, optimism, and faith in God. Many of the participants described resiliency as multifaceted and fluid. These women believed that in order to be resilient one would need to adapt the traits to meet the immediate need.

All five women talked of strong family support, especially their mothers who helped them find their paths and stay focused academically and socially. The family support permeated the walls of the home and encompassed the community and schools. Most of the participants discussed how their families monitored their friendships with playmates as well as the beliefs and values of their friends. Because of this practice, these women were not forced at an early stage to dissociate themselves from children with different mores. This "recognition of obstacles and racism [even within friends] as well as searching for the positive is a tenant of the Black Feminist Thought emphasis" (Collins, 2000, p. 290). Black feminist thought suggests that there is always an option, there is always power to act no matter how dire the situation.

Family and friends became special mentors who also helped the young women find their way academically and career wise. Collins (2000) offers the idea that stories presented by others in the mentorship role present necessary tools to help African American women resist oppression. At some point these mentors helped the participants recognize obstacles and deal with the racism within these obstacles.

A commonality among the experiences of the participants aligns the recognition of racism with the participants' responses to triumph and abilities not to succumb to its presence. Dr. Cooley used her encounters as teachable moments to introduce counter realities to those who carried negative opinions and racist attitudes. Drs. Rhoden, Sims Doty, and Williams used many of their encounters as shots of encouragement and determination to grow, learn, and prove others wrong. Dr. Atkinson took a similar approach as did the aforementioned women; however, she spoke out strongly against the racist actions that provided obstacles to her path. Akin to the others, she remained optimistic, yet she felt that to not recognize this existence in our society short changes those who ought to learn from others. "Only after we acknowledge the presence of racism can we teach others to understand and overcome this intolerance in our society" (Baker, 2005b, p. 171).

Researchers have stated that the avoidance of racism in our stories and our memories is a survival technique. Higginbotham (2001) asserts that "identifying racist comments and individuals is one task; handling such encounters is another" (p. 82). The women who participated in this study agreed that we need to teach our students and our children to handle these encounters. They believe these children need to be equipped with the ideals that empowered many members of Black America to move beyond the dominant culture's status quo and twisted racist environments to grasp an optimistic and positive perspective that allowed them to transform knowledge and persevere. From my exploration, I found that in order to be successful, African Americans need to understand racism and learn not to internalize the attached denigration. This issue is bigger than public education and needs support of family and communities to make the rejection of oppression a reality.

The participants in my exploration agreed that family constructed home environments and community associations support cultural and racial pride, perseverance, and success. Drs. Atkinson, Cooley, Rhoden, Sims Doty, and Williams explained how their families and communities held similar values and goals. The school and church supported the family in teaching the impressionable youth to have internal strength. As Dr. Atkinson believes, "one must know and love ourselves for what we are and recognize what we have to offer."

The family and community connections continued as the women grew and matriculated through K–12 and higher education. Because of family belief systems and values, the study participants had high academic aspirations and found positive spaces in the most negative encounters and experiences. Several of them at the time had no choice other than attend a historically black college and university (HBCU). Whether by choice or influence, these women found additional nurturing and character cultivation within the walls of the HBCUs that provided yet another level of support for academic, emotional, and societal growth. The authoritarian faculty and staff members stepped into the parent/family role and in many instances, acted in the absence of parents (*in loco parentis*). Dr. Atkinson agreed with the support of the HBCU but also brought to mind the false sense of security that was sometimes presented when the prejudices of society did not penetrate the campus border. Dr. Rhoden says in this type of environment, students can focus on becoming agents of change while they gain broader life perspectives.

Whether on the college campus or at community events, the participants recall having had mentors—face-to-face mentors or words-to-experience mentors. They perceive that their mentors are more than nurturing parents or parent figures; they are communicators, counselors, supporters, and understanders. Another characteristic of each of the participants is the realization that they had mentors and in turn now provide mentorship for others. Dr. Rhoden strongly believes that we "short change the younger generation" by not educating them and providing them with nurturing environments to adequately provide what they need to succeed. Dr. Atkinson affectionately known as Momma Pearl has countless children, nieces, nephews, and grandchildren because she believes her purpose in life is to support and nurture those in need. She adds, however, "Our schools and communities no longer carry this same drive to support and nurture others." Because of this, we must consider the question of how do we bring others to understand the very essence of students who are fearful of *the test* and care only about knowledge for the test because the world is now defined by the test?

OUTCOMES RESULTING FROM THE INQUIRY

While growing up, these five African American women had similar experiences in educational settings and in life experiences. This study provided an avenue to explore struggles and successes of African American women with doctoral degrees and career experiences in the field of education. While these women had similar experiences growing up and in academia with challenges of racism and sexism, they were each capable of developing strategies to not only survive but achieve success.

This study reminds me that we ought not attempt to categorize individual stories in simplified charts. Following in the same vein, we must not categorize studies on standardization, African Americans (women and girls) and K–12 education into a descriptor of African Americans. Connections are complex; circumstances, events, and people not only influence but impact our very existence. We need more studies built on stories of Black students at all levels of education from preschool to postsecondary specialized education. However, we must allow the separateness to show through the retellings. These studies should preserve the stories of the contributors to allow their voices to be heard.

This goal of this exploration was to contribute a positive retelling of lived experiences and abilities of five African American women in order to establish a counter narrative to the dominant culture. This work was my attempt to begin to satisfy my charge to make a difference. The study revolved around the essential question of: *How do African American women with doctoral degrees and career experiences in the field of education interpret their experiences in the midst of racial, gender and social oppressions?* Now that I have answers, it becomes my responsibility to connect more success stories with those who want (or need) to connect with resilience or who need direction. Life continues, and we need to prepare our children to expect and work for the best life possible.

I am in agreement with Nobles (1986) that we must know who we are in order to understand where we have been and where we plan to go in life. In these new spaces of knowing, our passion for the journey are re-ignited. Once we teach our children to interweave the stories of their childhoods with their lived experiences and viewpoints, they too will be presented with opportunities to find or create new spaces for resilience and hope. As a public school administrator in today's school, I am first seen as an African American and then as a woman. I am judged by how well I represent the standards that force me to stifle my desire to include cultural connections, personal experiences, mores and values. I deal with being successful while maintaining an individual identity. I realize that I must find the space to remain true to myself, my culture, my gender, and my job responsibilities. How do I protect myself and at the same time teach the children to succeed and not lose self? This dichotomy leads me to think of my years in the public school classroom as a student and then a teacher. I believe the children should see and learn of their past in the classrooms in order to envision better futures. Carter G. Woodson (1933/1999) perceived Black history as necessary to provide a firm foundationfor young Black Americans to build on in order to become productive citizens of our society. I believe that in order to move our children in the right direction we need to instill hope.

EDUCATIONAL AND SOCIAL CHANGES RESULTING FROM THE INQUIRY

I believe if we teach our children to walk with purpose, then we have provided strategies to overcome obstacles. Once we do that we must do something about this subtle racism. We need to find healing for the ill and eradication for racism as a collective purpose. Once we do something about the subtle racism in the schools we will make progress.

Dr. Anna Pearl Atkinson

The time has come to seize the moment and use my voice to spread information. I agree with Dr. Atkinson that in order to see changes we need to provide children with an approach to create change. As a community we need to ensure that our young people realize who they are and where their culture originated.

> We want our children educated.... We want our children trained as intelligent human beings should be and we will fight for all time against any proposal to educate black boys and girls simply as servants and underlings, or simply for the use of other people. They have a right to know, to think, to aspire. (Dubois, 1900)

This statement was made by Dubois over 100 years ago, and we still must fight for our rights. Since this research has been completed, I have worked at three public schools within my system. I would love to say that much has changed, but with standardization, No Child Left Behind, and test prep—this is not true. I have held workshops for teachers and students in my different locations to introduce them to the power of narratives and the inclusion of students' personal experiences in the curriculum. In one location, I gained funding to create a parenting library that included books on various topics as well as computers to introduce parents to the technology that their children are now required to master. When parents visited this library, I would talk with them about helping their children to overcome the obstacles they may face.

I have presented a parenting workshop and use the advice of Nobles (1986) when I try to explain to students and parents that as Black girls, they must know who they are in order to know where their ancestors have been and where they plan to go in life. I propose to workshop participants that traditional conversations in families need to include discussions of history, self confidence, and dreams. My goal is for parents to recognize that children need to be taught the true meaning of perseverance and the power of optimism and education.

This concern travels with me daily as I walk the school's halls and communicate with the students. As I interact with children from 4 to 14 years of age, I think of ways that I can share with them the triumphs and struggles that were shared with me. I initiate conversations to teach them to use the stories of successful African Americans to create their arsenals of hope and strength. As an administrator, I look for ways to include culturally relevant pedagogy into the environment. For teachers and staff I provide written resources and opportunities to learn about other cultures. I meet with students and parents in order to discuss curriculum and school concerns and provide answers to their questions. I have found by including parents more in the education process, we gain support and more connectors.

I believe if circumstances do not change, young Black girls moving through society will one day understand the concepts of driving while Black, learning while Black *and* living while Black. It is my fear that without conversations which are directed to educate and empower, young people will not have the equipment necessary to transcend the ridicule nor the overt and covert obstacles that have been set in order to prevent success. I continue to develop new avenues to successfully pass this rich heritage down to those who *need* to know.

With social justice as the aspiration, I strive to direct others through evolution to a socially just world. Through the sharing of stories and of a cultural legacy I attempt to raise consciousness within the general population and African American community about the prejudices that still exist. According to Delpit (1995) we "must recognize and address the power differential that exists in our society between schools and communities...between poor and well-to-do, between Whites and people of color" (p. 133). I am in a position to help young African American girls recognize this differential and develop internal resilience to succeed despite it. This knowledge will help young women to take charge and interpret their situations for hope and success.

As a public educator in the K–12 arena, I believe more than ever we need to provide for our students a school/home connection to provide emotional support, encouragement, and trust in academia. The current policies of No Child Left Behind seem to push for academics in the event that our children leave themselves behind. We need to allow the stories from the past to resonate through the souls of our future. I envision programs that teach African Americans and others about our culture, history, and customs as well as the culture, history, and customs of others. Through knowledge we develop understanding and acceptance.

We all have a story to tell; we all have experiences to share; we all have something to teach. With our Black girls continually spiraling down in the public education system, we need to become more mindful of our influence. Communication fuels knowledge, and knowledge is power. Once we share our stories and listen to the encounters of others, we create tales to introduce diverse perspectives into the lives of these students. As I have been told most of my life—to whom much is given, much is required. I believe that we ought to share what was learned. Through this broadminded understanding, there is hope for African American girls to recreate themselves in an image of strength and success.

REFERENCES

Angelou, M. (1978). Still I Rise. In *The complete collected poems of Maya Angelou* (pp. 163–164). New York: Random House.

Baker, P. (2005a). The impact of cultural biases on African American students' education: A review of research literature regarding race based schooling. *Education and Urban Society, 37*(3), 243–256.

Baker, P. (2005b). *Resilient lives: A critical narrative inquiry into the triumphs and struggles of five African American women with doctoral degrees.* Unpublished doctoral dissertation, Georgia Southern University, USA.

Calmore, J. O. (1992). Critical race theory, Archie Shepp, and firemusic: Securing an authentic intellectual life in a multicultural world. *Southern California Law Review, 65,* 2129–2230.

Casey, K. (1995–1996). The new narrative research in education. *Review of Research in Education, 21,* 211–253.

Clandinin, D. J., & Connelly, F. M. (2000). *Narrative inquiry: Experience and story in qualitative research.* San Francisco: Jossey-Bass.

Collins, P. H. (2000). *Black feminist thought: Knowledge consciousness and the politics of empowerment* (2nd ed.). New York: Routledge.

Delgado, R., & Stefancic, J. (2001). *Critical race theory: An introduction.* New York: University Press.

Delpit, L. (1995). *Other people's children: Cultural conflict in the classroom.* New York: The New Press.

Dubois, W. E. B. (1900). *Address to the nation. Delivered at the second annual meeting of the Niagara Movement.* Retrieved on September 11, 2007, from http://www.wfu.edu/~zulick/341/niagara.html

Helle, A. P. (1991). Reading women's autobiographies: A map of reconstructed knowing. In C. Witherell & N. Noddings (Eds.) *Stories lives tell: Narrative and dialogue in education,* (pp. 48–66). New York: Teachers College Press.

Higginbotham, E. (2001). *Too much to ask: Black women in the era of integration.* Chapel Hill, NC: The University of North Carolina Press.

hooks, b. (1994). *Teaching to transgress: Education as the practice of freedom.* New York: Routledge.

Howard-Hamilton, M. (2003). Theoretical frameworks for African American women. *New Directions for Student Serivces, 104,* 19–27.

Ladson-Billings, G. (2005). *Beyond the big house: African American educators on teacher education*. New York: Teachers College Press.

Lyles, D.E. (2000). Carter Godwin Woodson: "Father of Black History." *Chicago Public Library*. Retrieved on August 17, 2007, from http://www.chipublib.org/002branches/woodson/woodsonbib.html

Nobles, W. (1986). *African psychology: Towards reclamation, reascension & revitalization*. Oakland, CA: Black Family Institute.

Thompson, G. L. (2004). *Through ebony eyes: What teachers need to know but are afraid to ask about African American students*. San Francisco: Jossey-Bass.

Willie, C. V., Garibaldi, A. M., & Reed, W. L. (Ed.S.) (1991). *The education of Black America*. Westport, CT: Auburn House.

Witherell, C., & Noddings, N. (1991). *Stories lives tell: Narrative and dialogue in education*. New York: Teachers College.

Woodson, C. (1999). *The mis-education of the Negro*. Trenton, NJ: African World Press. (Original work published 1933)

CHAPTER 5

SELF, OTHERS, AND JUMP ROPE COMMUNITY

An Oral History of the Triumphs of African American Women

Wynnetta Scott-Simmons

AUTOBIOGRAPHICAL ORIGINS: INTRODUCTION TO TRIUMPHANT POTENTIAL

Hambone, Hambone where you been?
'Round the world and back again!
Hambone, Hambone where's your wife?
In the kitchen cooking rice.
Hambone, Hambone have you heard?
Papa's gonna buy me a mockingbird.
If that mockingbird don't sing,
Papa's gonna buy me a diamond ring.
If that diamond ring don't shine,
Papa's gonna buy me a fishing line.
Hambone, Hambone where you been?
'Round the world and I'm goin' again!

(Mattox, 1989)

Personal~Passionate~Participatory Inquiry Into Social Justice in Education, pp. 71–91
Copyright © 2008 by Information Age Publishing

One of the great things about jumping (some people say skipping) rope is that there are so many ways to be good at it, and yet there's always some new triumph *to shoot for*. If you can jump 30 times in a row without missing, then you have created a new record just waiting to be broken—by you (Loredo, 1996). Capturing the spirit and determination of strong African American women, along with the synergy and dynamics of a triumphant minority community that developed and shaped them became the something that I chose *to shoot for*. I use the jump rope and the jump rope chant to symbolize the power, rich heritage, and triumph of my segregated community; one that I termed "jump rope community."

The members of my personal jump rope community taught me many ways to be good at the daily theorizing necessary to survive in a world that classifies me as a minority, as other. The Hambone chant symbolizes that heritage, the lessons, and the triumph. The Hambone is a story of community, connection, resistance, and survival. It is a jump rope rhyme that speaks of possibility, of dreams, of hopes, of options presented, of shared struggles, and actions of resistance taken in the face of that struggle.

The Hambone, just as cultural resistance and survival strategies, was passed and shared *Round the world* from pot to pot, neighbor to neighbor to flavor the soup. As it was passed, it picked up new flavors and deposited remnants of previous meals. To serve the needs of the community, to resist, and to provide fuel for the struggle, it would keep *goin' round again*. It is a story of hope and triumph over the daily struggle as a minority comes to life in the relational activity of double dutch as a jump rope chant. It asks the question that prompts the sharing of information through experience—*Hambone, Hambone where you been?*

As African American children, the jump rope and its chants sang for us all, beat for us all, and we all understood the cultural rhythm as we played double dutch on the school playground. Our elementary school served us well until the end of the fifth grade. The sixth grade, however, dawned with a bus ride to "the other side" of our little township, the *White* side. The other world intruded on our reality as we shifted from segregation to desegregation as a result of a bus ride that represented the legal response to a social problem. We boarded the buses of desegregation to follow what we thought would lead to our portion of the American dream in a *better* school across town. Our jump ropes were stilled and with them seemed to go the connective oral links to the rhythms, beats, and encouraging chants of generations past and to the proud educational heritage earned through struggle and sacrifice.

As a result of the shift from segregation to desegregation, I witnessed the relegation to the *less than* classrooms of learning for many of my friends. From shared teachers who presented us with shared lessons and from similar hopes, or common cultural and community memories, we were split into two groups, those who would move on and out and those who would remain behind. The placement of capable friends in "D" classroom sections served as proof of linguistic and cultural disconnect between us and our new teachers. The academic standing of childhood friends switched from ability and aptitude to disability. With new eyes, with new interpretations and with new tools for measuring and being measured, we learned to read the world far more critically and cynically. It was then that we began to question our idyllic segregated existences and common experiences. We saw our world as less than, as "D" for different, "D" for deficient and "D" for diminished. I watched my happy friends, my secure friends, my confident friends, and my successful friends become "D" for defeated. I realized that we were not all expected to succeed outside our jump rope community.

The new looks of defeat on the faces of my friends prompted a series of questions. How had so many gone from self-confident and motivated to insecure and conquered? What magical and mystical event had occurred as we crossed the train tracks? How had our childhood teachers been so unaware of the negative academic transformation and classifications that awaited us in our new school? How had the negative placements been explained to the parents from our jump rope community? What had really happened on that 15 minutes bus ride across the tracks?

That bus ride signaled the end of my segregated existence. I would ride the bus for only 1 school year. That year had exposed, to my mother, the gaps in the separate but equal doctrine. My mother, who saw education as the path out and up, became even more determined to show us the possibilities of a socially just life through the receipt of a quality education. She arranged interviews and drove me to evaluations. In the fall of 1969, I became one of only a handful of African American females to integrate an all-girl, private school located in the suburbs of Philadelphia.

Three other young girls joined me in the search for access through education. Estelle, Joanne, Theresa and I had each jumped rope and sang jump rope chants with friends and neighbors in different jump rope communities in and around Philadelphia during our childhoods in the 1960s. Despite the geographic distinctions and unaware of the other's existence, we found that once united we were connected by knowledge of, and a level of sisterhood borne of, shared cultural experiences. Our integrative experience, coming at a pivotal time during our adolescence, the beginning of seventh grade, changed us individually and collectively. We now share a history that is as unique, interesting, and as complex as the jump rope itself.

The change in academic environment prompted new questions: Why had I become one of the select few to peer through the veil despite the shared experiences begun with childhood friends in our jump rope community? Why had so many been left behind? What had been the motivating factors behind the lifting of the veil on this private world, on the part of trustees and school leaders of our new school? Had our new teachers expected us to thrive? Was there a deliberate and conscientious plan to support and facilitate our success? How would we remain true to our cultural selves in a world and through a curriculum that was so culturally different? What would be the difference between this experience of integration and my earlier experience with desegregation? Would we thrive or merely survive?

The educational requirements of our new school and the desire to *do my family and community proud* managed to temporarily quiet the questioning whispers. It would not be until I had become a teacher myself and witnessed the negative tracking of several of my minority students that the memories of my childhood friends and their negative educational transformation would come rushing back to me. The questions returned again when I became an instructor of preservice teachers. My students, future teachers, were representative of the national statistical percentages in microcosm. Nationally, nearly three out of every four teachers is female, 89% are White. Despite the national growth in ethnic and linguistic diversity among the students in public schools, only 7% of the teaching force is Black, and 2% is Hispanic (National Education Association, 2006). As the diversity among students has increased, is the monocultural teaching force being prepared to connect with the cultural histories, aspirations, and daily challenges faced by their students?

How do I teach to raise the awareness of the lessons of the Hambone while adding the stories of my students to the pot? How do I encourage future educators to develop the necessary tools and strategies to critique negative practices in the institution of education while supporting the educational survival of all children? How do I teach to highlight the commonalities that exist in the stories from various communities? How should teacher education programs be established so as to value and include divergent literacies, divergent communities, and divergent cultural values in the quest to ensure that the *Hambone goes around the world and back again?*

PARTICIPATORY RESEARCH PROCESS

Fortune teller, fortune teller, Please tell me,
What do you think, I'm going to be?
Butcher, baker, undertaker,
Tightwad, tailor, bow-legged sailor,
Rock Star, painter, cowpoke, thief,
Doctor, lawyer, teacher, chief!

(Klutz, 1998)

Jump rope chants exist as the connective link between the physical expression of creative power and the strong oral tradition among the African American community. They are stories of hope, of question, of potential, and of prophecy. They provide the rhythmic backdrop to the jump rope session. As examples of the strong oral tradition and heritage of the African American community, jump rope chants provided oral lessons and warnings of the potential difficulties of life and early academic instruction and opportunities to experiment with the rhythm of the language. The words and beat of a jump rope chant demand involvement, participation, and action while simultaneously offering generational connection, encouragement, and a verbal challenge. They have a home in experience, in the memory of an event, in the living of the life. The rhymes speak of cautions, of wonders, of experience, and of dreams and wishes. In my inquiry, I explored various forms of literacy such as cultural literacy, family literacy, community literacy, music literacy, artistic literacy, historical literacy, and oral literacy. We lived the tenets of critical literacy when we turned the readings into Hop Scotch chants and jump rope rhymes. I explored varied forms of literacy used by members of the African American community to create, define, and display aspects of cultural self, cultural voice, and cultural identity.

Learning to jump double dutch is a process of attempts and successes. There are social structures and social norms to playing double dutch; moves that must be made and things that you must do in order to create a seemingly effortless session—of poetry in motion. You start off as a single jumper as your style is critiqued by a more experienced jumper. Next, you become an *ender*, to increase your comfort and familiarity with the beat of the rope. From the position as *ender*, you are able to watch the footwork, listen to the chants and learn to hold the beat in your head and set the pace and rhythm to suit the jumper. You are an *ender* until you learn how to *get in* to jump double dutch. *Getting in* requires a coordination of self with the movement and pace of the ropes. You must learn to match the beat of the ropes with your own body rhythm, sway back and forth with knees bent and arms pumping, trying to find a moment to enter the twirling ropes (Chambers, 2002). Once in, feet move, arms move, and you continue to build and sustain momentum and pace; you are one with the ropes. At this point, you have become a member of a select group, a member and participant in the life of a game not recognized or known by all.

Double dutch demands participation, connection, and involvement. It is not meant to be a solitary activity. A cross-generational symbol of a proud heritage that spoke to possibility, ability, creativity and endurance, the jump rope represents something not usually viewed as valuable or worthy of what Jane Roland Martin (2002) calls *cultural wealth;* the preservation of, the continuation of, the compilation of all that one generation has to pass onto the next. Girls jumping double dutch and adding their own stylized expressions, techniques, and individual personalities through movement represents the union of the Black Aesthetic (Gayle, 1972) with a form of critical literacy based in cultural and artistic expression. In the tradition of Black feminist thought (Collins, 2000), your personal style, interpretations, and experiences within the ropes help you to create individual and personal theories of triumph and strategies for success with each jump rope session.

There is a sense of pride and recognition of a connection to a unique heritage that comes with jumping double dutch. This is a sisterhood created in a community of cultural isolation and sustained through the strength earned in battles for self awareness, self expression, and self definition; a sisterhood which recognizes the dichotomy created when the body, once used as a tool of oppression and domination, can also be used as a tool of expressional resistance. This is a sisterhood which recognizes the fighting spirit required to define and reconcile multiple consciousnesses, multiple selves that emerge in the spaces constructed by race, gender, and class.

> there is no better symbol of girl power than Double Dutch…. The strength of each girl is not just in her obvious athletic ability as she does hand-spins or spins while still jumping, but also in the support she gives others. No one can get good at Double Dutch working alone. You learn from your sisters, you grow with the help of your sisters, and you teach and encourage your friends. This is a lesson that clearly must remain with each girl in her life beyond the days of Double Dutch. (Chambers, 2002, p. 6)

My research quest was also a process. The passionate participation for my inquiry, evoked by the oral nature of the jump rope chants, is nurtured by the memories of my life as a young member of a segregated community. The participatory process examined the oral histories of four adolescent girls who left the culturally insular surroundings, Jump rope communities, to seek access to the codes of power and registers of language in all-White, all-girl, elite private school. Our identities and the formative steps taken to create the doctor, lawyer, teacher, and chief that we had become was a major part of the research. I focused on the motivational factors that prompted attendance at the private school despite feelings of success within culturally segregated jump rope communities. I took an inside look into the spirit of togetherness, the establishment of unifying goals, the synergy that exists among the jump rope community members and serves as protective factors against a racist society.

Theresa: I remember getting off the bus in the third grade, and there were posters on the gates and on the telephone poles saying they didn't want desegregation. Back then only the Black were bused in. None of the buses took those kids and put them out. And again, we thought that this was White, and rich, so it had to be better, right?

I searched for the need, the desire, and the ability of African Americans, in general, and the African American women in particular, to maintain cultural cohesion and connection through the lessons and strategies learned as a result of struggle in a racist society; to learn and thrive in the face of adverse attacks upon cultural integrity; and to hold onto the ropes in order to continue the session of cultural progression. I examined the ongoing effort to build a cultural community to prevent the loss of cultural and linguistic heritage. He (2003) calls this maintenance of cultural voice, signature, and identity, Nettles (1998, 2001) calls it resilience, Bowers (1995) calls it cultural conservatism, and Jane Roland Martin (2002) calls it cultural wealth.

The inquiry, this jump rope session, began as a search for answers to my childhood, adolescent, and professional questions surrounding the unequal and unjust distribution of educational access and power. Through an inquiry based in the exploration of narratives, I discovered the rich and proud educational heritage of the African American community and the sustaining ethic of care that is rarely discussed and often missing in the public schools of today.

I also explored the impact of African American women as the keepers of the cultural code on the continuation of the educational heritage among Jump Rope Community members, the transference of survival strategies and practical life theories, and the development of positive self-images for their children. The roles of African American women in the early stages of the Civil Rights Movement and the necessary resilience of spirit to continue to move the race forward were also explored. As involved participants in the formation of Native Schools (Anderson, 1988), (a system of common or public schools formed by various freedman educational associations in the South and supported by the determined labor of freed slaves), as teachers in those schools, as writers simultaneously calling for the abolition of slavery and demanding recognition as subjects capable of theorizing, African American women created a rich educational heritage for future members of jump rope communities to follow.

Joanne: My mom used to tell us racial things and as kids we never knew where it was coming from. I do remember thinking, "Okay?" and not understanding what the big deal was. Later when I had my own children and I had to explain the race and history thing to them, I understood a bit better.

In my inquiry, the impact of legal segregation on the creation and continuance of jump rope communities was examined. The impact of desegregation, integration, and currently resegregation on the creation and sustenance of a negative educational legacy that the descendants of the freed slaves have inherited was also explored. I also examined the cultural confusion that ensued as a result of the intersection of integrative experiences with the developmental phase of adolescent identity.

Oral history was used to capture our memories, perceptions, and reflections as lived experiences over 30 years after our arrival at the private school. "Memory is the core of oral history, from which meaning can be extracted and preserved" (Ritchie, 2003, p. 19). It is "the subject as well as the source of oral history" (Perks & Thompson, 1998, p. 211) and is used as a tool of the present to interpret events and experiences from the past. Oral history is a reflective and fluid attempt at creating meaningful accounts through the storied lives of those relating the tales. Our oral histories, our memories, became the threads that tied together the pieces of our lived experiences of segregation and integration.

Using the process of *rememory* (Morrison, 1990), I revisited my childhood and the childhoods of my classmates, in order to stir up old integrative messes. We recreated our educational pasts by looking through yearbooks, saved report cards, and old school programs. The saved mementos of my classmates served as additional pieces of the triumphant puzzle that lay protected in the folds of our memories. Our oral histories examined the concept of community as experienced by African Americans; the commonality of values, of place, of shared history; and the resultant impact on the creation of social identity theory and group orientation theory (Allen, 2001).

We asked questions of each other to discover the common characteristics of players who had been involved in the success of our personal jump rope sessions. We searched for commonalities in our families and communities, the existence of protective factors, and the traits that we each shared that facilitated our ability to minimize risk factors and triumph despite expected odds of failure. Throughout this examination we were each placed at the center of the research process. Our stories, our memories as the subjects of the project determined the pace of the research session as well as the direction. Our stories stand as examples of counter stories to the level of low societal and dominant culture belief in racial achievement. They stand as examples of possibility, of hope, and of triumph over adversity. Black feminist thought (Collins, 2000; Guy-Sheftall, 1995) and critical race theory (Bell, 1995; Crenshaw, Gotanda, Peller, & Thomas, 1995; Delgado & Stefancic, 2001) provided the lenses through which to examine the impact that our experiences as African American adolescent females had upon our private-school experiences. Black feminist thought provided the framework through which I was able to view and position our theories to begin to break the cycle of pain and struggle caused by our existence in the world as examples of double consciousness and double oppression (Collins, 1986, 1998; Du Bois, 1903, hooks, 1981; King, 1988; White, 1999). I was able, through the use of critical literacy theory (Delpit, 1995; Freire, 1987; Heath, 1983; Ong, 2002; Shor, 1992; Shor & Pari, 1999; Tatum, 2007; Wink, 2002), to use jump rope chants as tangible examples of the strong oral tradition of connection, relation, and cultural continuation embedded in the educational heritage of the African American community. Critical literacy involves the use of communicative discourses to disrupt, define, and establish worlds and places in them.

Our stories were just that, *our* stories. They were collected to claim spaces as written examples of triumph on blank and receptive pages of their own accord and in their own style. They touched on issues of race, issues of gender, family, class, education, literacy, and access. The vignettes stand as counter stories to the discourse of racial failure, submission, and inferiority. They also stand as examples of multiple positions of subjectivity in recognition of the fact that "we cannot form an accurate picture of the status of black women by simply focusing on racial hierarchies" (hooks, 1981, p. 12).

As I grew up in a strong segregated African American community, a jump rope community had meant safety, security, solidarity. Membership had shielded my experience and prevented exposure to the negative perceptual existence as an outsider, an *other*. I did not, in my formative years, learn to define myself in relation to what I was not. Instead, my early life experience celebrated all that I was and all that I could become. Through my childhood eyes, my neighborhood held all that was needed. Smitty's was the barbershop where the men gathered to discuss the passing of time, passing of lives, dreams, hopes, and battles won. It was in Couch's Corner Store, our haven of treats and familiar smells, that we purchased Squirrel Nut Zippers, Mary Janes, wax lips, and dill pickles from the barrel while receiving bits of life advice free of charge. Mrs. Sadler, the neighborhood and school music teacher, gave piano lessons in her home and exposed us to the world of culture through song. The volunteer Firehouse No. 8 was the town's social and political center and served as the site of our lessons in civic responsibility as the town's polling place. It was also the site of Friday night dances and Saturday afternoon barbecues. Pam's was the beauty shop that my mother supported. It was here that I was exposed to early theoretical lessons in the *dailiness* in the lives of women of color and listened to real-life, practical applications based in the tenets of the theory of Black feminist thought.

Between my time under the hair dryer and the straightening comb, I learned about the struggles, sacrifices, and strategic expectations of African American women as keepers of the cultural codes seeking to move the race forward. Here the women shared the dreams they held for their children and spoke of strategies for success through observational and subversive resistance, tactics Collins calls (1998) "strategies of everyday resistance" (p. 745). Here I heard stories of the search for potential and possibility, of hope and of dreams; of parental wisdoms and fears; of success in the face of potential failure; of the connectedness of humans in the pains shared and the triumphs enjoyed. Here I was provided with the oral glimpses, traditions, stories, and lived theories of a community of African American families. These are the cultural theories that spring from the daily battles, struggles, and resistances and the *dailiness of women's lives*.

> They form an oral tradition, passed on from one generation to the next. Sometimes they are just seen as anecdotes about family "characters" and their antics. Sometimes they are teaching stories. They are about having respect, about having decent values, about how to live properly, about how to survive. Cultures shape stories in different ways, and stories pass on women's consciousness as it has been shaped by specific cultural, racial, and class experience. (Aptheker, 1989, p. 40)

Surrounded by the stories of the women in the shop and of my own mother, I learned the practice of theorizing and of research through action and reflection by the women in my community. Their theories had practical application and served as responses to the daily dilemmas of facing the world as African American women in the 1960s and 1970s. Their theories provided clarity, direction, strategic support, generational justifications.

My grandmother was well versed in the *dailiness* of theory as a survival technique. As a member of the older generation, she was also aware of the sustaining power of the Hambone. Her cooking and cleaning skills had earned her a position as a domestic in the home of a family on Philadelphia's Main Line. Estelle, one of my participants, and I shared memories of our grandmothers as domestics.

> *Estelle: She had pride in her cleaning ability; she took pride in that life; it was her life. I can clean a house today if I want to. I know how because of her. There was this one time when she was teaching me how to clean the floors and my mom walked by. I just remember my mom saying that cleaning someone else's floors was not in my future.*

I remember questioning, as did many of my friends, our grandmothers' continued service as domestics. My grandmother had simply explained that she "worked at those people's houses so that I would never have to." My grandmother's *dailiness* of theory combined lessons of Black feminist thought, critical race theory, and critical literacy. She explained that she used her position as an invisible, yet subversive, figure in their households to listen and to learn. She learned about china and flatware and crystal and menus as tools of entertainment decorum. She learned about clothing labels and coordinated style and accessories of understatement. She learned about places and people and institutions of access and power. Despite the outwardly negative and pervasive racial social structure of the time, my grandmother, through self-definition and the practical use of her position to suit her needs, and through the use of her cleaning and cooking literacies, had watched, learned and then returned home with her transformative lessons of generational social mobility potentiality. Our grandmothers possessed an ethic of care, of healing, and of generational responsibility.

That ethic was extended to the care that we received as students at the schools in our jump rope communities. Our teachers took up roles as protective figures providing the support and encouragement begun by our families.

Theresa: Even though my mom only had a tenth grade education, she knew an angle when she heard it. She was real crafty when it came to making things happen. My mother with her uneducated self was still very quick learning. And [she] worked in a garment factory, and was sometimes laid off. Half the time my father didn't even work. For many, many years my parents worked sporadically or not at all. But, when it came to education, they made it so that I had what I needed in terms of books and stuff.

Our teachers continued the educational hopes of our parents. They knew our background knowledge, knew where we had been, and framed questions in manners that spoke to those experiences. Our teachers were neighbors, friends and family members. Many had fled to these and other segregated communities to practice their art following the mass dismissals of Negro teachers in the wake of Brown and desegregation. Our segregated school was a second home not only to us as students but also to our teachers. Our teachers spoke the same language and structured "lessons to engage and connect students to their communities and classroom; [our] Black teachers created classroom environments based on mutual respect as a way to acknowledge and validate their students" (Irvine, 2002, p. 43). The ethic of care practiced within served and supported not only our development but also the development of our teachers.

My first grade teacher, Mrs. Ore, possessed a strong awareness of Siddle-Walker's (2004) ethic of care by displaying "a strong emphasis on responsibility, commitment, and a parentlike morality" (p. 16). As my first link between home and school, she was my first encounter with a dreamkeeper (Ladson-Billings, 1994). She openly discussed the pervasiveness of race in America. She exposed and demystified the culture of power through her lessons in racial and cultural expectation as well as racial and cultural strife. As Linda Christensen's (2000) students, we were taught about the differences and the ability to overcome those differences through our teacher's efforts to help us develop a "command of two idioms, their 'home' language and the 'cash' language (Standard English)" (Shor, 1992, p. 53). We learned as Audrey Watkins to be "very well educated on how to speak correctly. We learned to speak incorrectly to survive in the neighborhood" (Watkins in Reynolds & Webber, 2004, p. 161), and to switch over to the language expected during the hours of training and education at school (Hobbs, 2004). In the security of our segregated school, Mrs. Ore told us that "racism is ordinary, not aberrational" (Delgado & Stefancic, 2001, p. 7). She cut through the challenge of political correctness, the semantics of racial vocabulary and directly addressed the problem of the 20th century color line (Du Bois, 1903) by describing for us what it meant to be little Black children in a White man's world. I remember my teacher said: "You'll have to be twice as smart, twice as determined and three times as fast to get half as far. For every one step that they take, you'll have to take three. It ain't fair, but it is what it is. And you will become somebody so long as you remember who you are." We did need to be twice as smart, and our lives as segregated students provided our initial lessons in the mastery of two languages—the language of home and community and the language of the dominant culture.

Critical literacy involves the use of communicative discourses to disrupt, define, and establish worlds and places in them. The disruptive messages of our teachers told us, *"You can do it! You can be anything that you want to be!"* Our teachers, following in the Freireian tradition of education, placed greater emphasis on teaching us to think about and question our existence in the world. In exploring these forms of literacy, I discovered that the teachers of our jump rope community had brought about recognition of cultural self, cultural voice, and cultural identity and an ongoing effort to build a cultural community to prevent the loss of cultural and linguistic heritage.

OUTCOMES RESULTING FROM THE INQUIRY

I visited the "Motor City" for the first time during the month of April to collect from my high school classmate, the third and final verbal vignette of integration *rememory* for my research. We had agreed that the best and easiest place to meet would be at a restaurant inside the city's Wayne

County Airport. As I waited for my classmate's arrival, I listened to the *story du jour* on one of the terminal's suspended TV's tuned to ESPN. The comments of Don Imus had ripped the scab from the ever-present sore that was the nation's color-line. The wound was once again bleeding all over the nation's airwaves. With three words, *Nappy Headed Hos*, this White male had exposed the tenuous, pervasive, and divisive wound that lay just below the outer layer of skin that seemed to always be in a state of sealing and healing the ever present pain of race relations.

At a time that should have been a triumphant celebration, Imus' words had become the focus of the story rather than the athletic accomplishments of a powerful and triumphant group of women. As I listened to the news story, I focused more on what was not being said. Despite this being a sports network and despite the 2007 Rutgers Women's Basketball Team quest for a National Championship, the struggles, the triumphs, and the personal stories of these women were missing. In focusing instead on the insensitive diatribes of this single White male, through their mere existence as women and women of color, they had been forced to suffer the same invisible status and double consciousness as had many of their sisterly ancestors. I was struck by a strange connection of the story to my current research endeavor and the complex omnipresence of race and gender relations in this country.

I traveled to Detroit, just as I had traveled to Philadelphia, to collect the *rememories* of the struggles as well as the integrative triumphs of an African American female almost 40 years after our admittance into a private, all-White, all-girl school. The four of us had traveled far and accomplished much since that September morning in 1969 when we left our segregated communities to catch a peek under the veil of social privilege and academic access. As I waited for my classmate's arrival to the airport lounge, those three little words, *Nappy Headed Hos*, managed to transport me back to a few painful memories of school from my childhood. These were memories of the grand experiment that sought to use the law and the classroom to heal a deeper social wound.

Our integrative experiences, while providing us each with the keys to the educational cave had not happened without the infliction of our own personal wounds. In order to survive in both worlds, our school world and our home world, our collective stories highlighted our experiences with Du Bois' double consciousness.

WYNNETTA

I lived in two different worlds and they collided at the 69th Street train terminal. I was like a Superman figure here. That's where I would change from my street clothes into my uniform on the way out to Irwins and then out of my uniform and back into my street clothes on my way back home. I quickly learned that the uniform was a dead giveaway that I was a preppie and that was a definite invitation for a beat down. The loaded book bag was bad enough but the uniform was a blazing signal of difference.

The collection and examination of our personal vignettes had also opened our old integrative wounds and stirred up old messes. The process of collecting the memories forced us to once again inhabit scenes that had been played out long ago. Despite the pain caused, the collection and examination of our personal vignettes revealed many cultural commonalities. We had each, as a result of our positions of perceived diminished value, sought the codes of power through educational access and through journeys into world of divergences—divergent language codes, divergent social, cultural, and economic stratifications, and divergent linguistic expectations, behaviors, and dispositions.

The four of us had been surviving participants in the grand legal experiment that was academic desegregation. Until this research project our stories too were missing. I had struck up a conversation with a current student of color during a visit to our old alma mater in a reunion year. She had been surprised to learn that I was an alumna of the school. Our histories, our perceptions, our strategies and our fight for tips of success had not been captured and passed on. We had not done our part in transmitting the legacy of educational accomplishment through struggle. The wound of silence and *othering* had occurred and despite our gains and successes through promises of integration, integration had not happened. Reid (1954) describes integration as:

> the mutual appreciation, conservation, and use of all the institutions and values which a society regards as right and just. It is based on two principles: that in a polyglot society men must overcome prejudices and discriminations against races, classes, and religions in order to get along, and; that this ideal can be realized only as it is brought into the experience of living. (p .348)

THERESA

I will always be thankful to Irwins for my life, but I fault them in that way that they handled the whole integration thing. When we were there, the cultural exchange went one way. We were dropped in there to experience their environment, but nothing of our environment was there. There was no Black celebration. We didn't even have Black literature that we studied in English. Well, yeah, we did do Uncle Tom's Cabin, but I mean come on?! It was always the European literature, the Renaissance and Reformation. There was nothing affirming, not in

Music, it was always European. There was nothing that affirmed us culturally. But, not only that, these White girls who were supposed to gain some benefit or experience this cultural exchange got nothing. They didn't get anything because it was all about them. We were expected to come in and absorb it all. They thought that they were helping us by exposing us to their world. And that was good, that was very beneficial to us because that world is the dominant culture. But a lot of interaction that could have been beneficial to everybody was lost, and a lot of the affirmation that could have happened for us as Black girls was lost. We had to go home to get that. Thank goodness we could go home. Imagine if we had gone to Shipley or Baldwin as boarders at the time? We had to go home to be reminded of the fact that we had art, music, literature. They could have at least thrown in Richard Wright.

My goal with this inquiry was to add our voices and our stories based on the impact of integration to the body of research dealing with the achievement of African American students. I sought to add an awareness of the struggle, the searching, the asking, the becoming and also the accomplishments of four African Americans females. We used our individual and subjective voices to tell our stories of self-examination and reenter our distinct, yet connected, pasts with the critical eyes of the present. Through the collection of personal stories of struggle and possibility, I seek to connect the history and lessons of yesterday with the continuing individual stories of resistance and triumph of today. Through the addition of our unique stories, unique experiences, and unique responses to the integrative process, our oral histories add to the body of research dealing with critical race theory, Black feminist thought, and critical literacy.

My personal background and passionate connection to this research and the chosen participants placed me and my interpretation at its center. At the center, as a double dutch diva (Gaunt, 2006), I am in the best position to gaze and reflect outwardly to theorize on the impact of our experiences. From this chosen position of what bell hooks (1994) calls radical black subjectivity, I was able to select theoretical frameworks which allowed me to reclaim "the power imperative to conceive of oneself as a centered, whole entity" (Fuston-White, 2002, p. 462). I chose the position. I choose the platform to relay, express, and establish the metastory of my life that "can't be understood from her friend's frame of reference; instead it must be told within a frame of reference all its own" (Carter, 2001, p. 152). I was able to see that who I am and what I do cannot be separated, nor can it be subjugated based on race, gender, or a whitewashed version of what it is thought that I should be. From the center, amidst the turning ropes, I no longer represent a member holding only double outsider status. From this chosen position, "we looked both from the outside in and the inside out. We focused our attention on the center as well as on the margin. We understood both" (hooks, 1990, p. 341).

From a position of epistemic control, intimate connection and under-standing, I gained the position to decide what counts as theory and the manner in which I choose to theorize. From the position of claimed con-trol and awareness of self, I was in the position to decide upon the voice to be used and the message to be presented. I was able to "show that oral histories are not merely anecdotal tales, but are frames through which Black women develop identities and understand the world" (Fulton, 2006, p. 16). I was able to tell the stories from the margins and use that sense of exclusion as a point of reference, resistance, and strength.

If our stories are our history and our theory, we will tell our stories and leave each as chosen interpretation, chosen possibility, and chosen site for the establishment of existence, knowledge and education. We chose not to, and "we refuse to look at ourselves through the eyes of white America" (Adoff, 1968, p. 159). Rather, we choose to add our perspectives as an attempt to break the "ideological dominance in the canon of Western thought" (Shujaa, 1996, p. 1). Our vignettes presented stories of our per-sonal commitments, expectations, and successes. Estelle persevered to become the first African American female OB/GYN (obstetrics and gynecology) at her hospital. She is most proud of her daughters and of a popular sandwich that carries her name at a deli near the hospital. Joanne, after graduating from Princeton, chose to give back by fighting for the causes of our youngest citizens who experience abuse and neglect. She too is most proud of her children. Theresa extended her Irwins stud-ies by attending Princeton and Columbia Law School. She practiced law in New York before leaving the field to raise her two sons. I graduated, married, and raised two daughters before returning to school seeking my teaching certification and then graduate school to fulfill a doctoral prom-ise made to my mother. I am most proud of the part that I played in the development of my daughters and hope that they recognize the message in the example that I tried to convey. In expecting greatness of yourself learn to self-define and self-describe. Keep moving forward and your feet above the turning ropes.

EDUCATIONAL AND SOCIAL CHANGES RESULTING FROM THE INQUIRY

A cloud, much like the jump ropes, hangs over the educational futures of our African American youth who find themselves in various types of seg-regated existences despite the historic, politically charged ruling that was *Brown v. Board of Education.* In the wake of another political foray into education, No Child Left Behind, growing racial, cultural, class, and social diversity is occurring in our schools. A parallel phenomenon is occurring that relates directly to the educational expectations for those students as we witness the decline in numbers of minority teachers who possess generational pride and cultural expertise as it relates to educational expectations.

Achievement, accomplishment, motivation, and competence are goals listed by those committed to the education of the children in our schools. They are also positive descriptions applied to groups of students, students who are described as self-starters, determined, and having high levels of self-esteem and self-efficacy. These terms are increasingly becoming uncharacteristic descriptions applied to African American students. The labels applied to this group of students often convey deficient or negative connotations: *struggling, at-risk, failing, unmotivated, or incapable.* Forty years after watching the creation of defeat on the faces of my childhood friends, I have returned to the memories of that bus ride across town.

Despite these negative expectations, African American students do succeed, do achieve, and are motivated, competent, and accomplished. There is a growing interest in African American students who not only display positive attitudes but also exhibit high levels of competence and achievement. The body of research reporting on these students who succeed in the face of adversity is also growing (Barbarin, 1993; Masten, Best, & Garmezy, 1990; Miller, 1999; Nettles & Pleck, 1994; Siddle-Walker, 1996). I am as concerned as Gloria Ladson-Billings (1994) with the *way* that we teach the curriculum presented to us as educators. This is the crux of what affects our students, their perceptions of what counts as knowledge, and their beliefs about how they and their lives fit into the realm of valued information. Critical pedagogy seeks to create environments where the question rules. Critical pedagogy seeks to create environments where becoming (Wink, 2000) is just as important as being and knowledge recognized as culturally, socially, and politically framed is valued through these distinct frameworks. The keys to success for all children must be placed in the hands of educators willing to transform the system by asking tough questions of themselves and placing expectations of high achievement on all of their students. As the number of minority educators continues to lag behind the increase in the numbers of minority students, educators who are able to serve as promoters of cultural capital must be created. This responsibility for training teacher as transformative cultural workers will be placed on teacher education programs.

As an educator of preservice teachers, I encourage African American, minority, and White students to bring their personal selves to their teaching, to teach with passion, to participate in their teaching through connection and dialogue. My students are challenged to consider teaching practices that are grounded in cultural sensitivity by discovering and validating the cultural capital that their students bring with them to the classroom. The addition of opportunities for community and cultural involvement, participation, and action to their lessons as a means of fostering social justice is required. Through an examination of issues dealing with race, gender, economics, and class we hold complicated conversations each week during class sessions. I support these future teachers by providing connection to divergent cultures through open and reflective dialogue. We discuss the premise of teaching as political, justice through education and the resultant implications, the recognition of distinct and blended cultures, as well as the redistribution of resources to facilitate change. We talk to discover spaces for connection and change. I challenge my students to teach in a way that is rooted in and accepting of the personal, considerate of conflicting passions, and inviting of divergent participation. Recognizing the political nature of my personal teaching practices, I encourage these educators to accept their political path toward education. They are encouraged to provide their future students with the tools necessary to thrive in a society that expects very little of them yet exacts great payments in terms of cultural integrity and maintenance of cultural practices. I seek to raise their awareness and increase their acceptance of the triumphant spirit of hope and capability existent in the African American jump rope community and the members from those communities. This spirit exists despite the pull to surrender the ever dynamic aspects of cultural heritage, cultural traditions, and self-definition in exchange for access to codes of power and places in a history that is promised through education. This work is in answer to that historical call to represent cultural expectations and obligations. It is as bell hooks (1989) reminds us, "our collective responsibility as individual black women committed to feminist movement to work at making spaces where black women who are just beginning to explore feminist issues can do so without fear of hostile treatment, quick judgments, dismissals, etc" (p. 181).

REFERENCES

Adoff, A. (Ed.). (1968). *Black on Black: Commentaries by Black Americans from Frederick Douglas to Malcolm X*. New York: Macmillan-Collier.

Allen, R. (2001). *The concept of self: A study of black identity and self-esteem*. Detroit: Wayne State University Press.

Anderson, J. (1988). *The education of blacks in the south, 1860-1935*. Chapel Hill, NC: University of North Carolina Press.

Aptheker, B. (1989). *Tapestries of life: Women's work, women's consciousness, and the meaning of daily experience*. Amherst, MA: University of Massachusetts Press.

Barbarin, O. (1993). Coping and resilience: Exploring the inner lives of African American children. *The Journal of Black Psychology, 19*(4), 478–492.

Bell, D. (1995). Serving two masters: Integration ideals and client interests in school desegregation litigation. In R. Delgado (Ed.), *Critical race theory: The cutting edge* (pp. 228–240). Philadelphia: Temple University Press.

Bowers, C.A. (1995). *Educating for an ecologically sustainable culture: Rethinking moral education, creativity and intelligence and other modern orthodoxies.* Albany, NY: SUNY.

Brown v. Board of Education. (1954). *Case number 347 U.S. 483.* Retrieved July 20, 2008 from http://caselaw.lp.findlaw.com/scripts/
getcase.pl?court=US&vol=347&invol=483

Carter, M. (2001). Race, jacks, and jump rope: Theorizing school through personal narratives. In R. Mabokela & A. Green (Eds.), *Sisters of the academy: Emergent black women scholars in higher education* (pp. 151–160). Sterling, VA: Stylus.

Chambers, V. (2002). *Double Dutch: A celebration of jump rope, rhyme and sisterhood.* New York: Hyperion.

Christensen, L. (2000). *Reading, writing, and rising up: Teaching about social justice and the power of the written word.* Milwaukee, WI: Rethinking Schools.

Collins, P. H. (1998). *Fighting words: Black women and the search for justice.* Minneapolis: University of Minnesota Press.

Collins, P. H. (2000). *Black feminist thought: Knowledge, consciousness, and the politics of Empowerment.* New York: Routledge.

Crenshaw, K, Gotanda, N., Peller, G., & Thomas, K. (Eds.). (1995). *Critical race theory: The key writings that formed the movement.* New York: New Press.

Delgado, R., & Stefancic, J. (2000). *Critical race theory: The cutting edge.* Philadelphia: Temple University Press.

Delgado, R., & Stefancic, J. (2001). *Critical race theory: An introduction.* New York: New York University Press.

Delpit, L. (1995). *Other people's children: Cultural conflict in the classroom.* New York: The New Press.

Du Bois, W. E. B. (1903). *The souls of Black folks.* New York: Fine Creative Media.

Freire, P., & Macedo, D. (1987). *Literacy: Reading the word and the world.* Westport, CT: Bergin & Garvey.

Fulton, D. (2006). *Speaking power: Black feminist orality in women's narratives of slavery.* New York: State University of New York Press.

Fuston-White, J. (2002). "From the seen to the told": The construction of subjectivity in Toni Morrison's Beloved. *African American Review, 36*(3), 461–474.

Gaunt, K. (2006). *The games black girls play: Learning the ropes from double-Dutch to hip-hop.* New York: New York University Press.

Gayle, A. (Ed). (1972). *The black aesthetic.* New York: Anchor Books.

Guy-Sheftall, B. (Ed.). (1995). *Words of fire: An anthology of African-American feminist thought.* New York: The New Press.

He, M. F. (2003). *A river forever flowing: Cross-cultural lives and identities in the multicultural landscape.* Greenwich, CT: Information Age.

Heath, S. (1983). *Ways with words: Language, life, and work in communities and classrooms.* New York: Cambridge University Press.

Hobbs, P. (2004). In their own voices: Code switching and code choice in the print and online versions of an African-American women's magazine. *Women and Language, 27*(1), 1–12.

hooks, b. (1981). *Ain't I a woman: Black women and feminism.* Boston, MA: South End.

hooks, b. (1989). *Talking back: Thinking feminist, thinking Black.* Boston, MA: South End.

hooks, b. (1990). Marginality as site of resistance. In R. Ferguson, M. Gever, T. Minh-Ha, & C. West (Eds.), *Out there: Marginalization and contemporary cultures.* New York: New Museum of Contemporary Art and Massachusetts Institute of Technology.

hooks, b. (1994). *Teaching to transgress: Education as a practice of freedom.* New York: Routledge.

Irvine, J. (2003). *Educating teachers for diversity: Seeing with a cultural eye.* New York: Teachers College Press.

King, D. (1988). Multiple jeopardy, multiple consciousness: The context of a Black feminist ideology. *Signs, 14*(1), 42–72.

Klutz. (1998). *Jump rope rhymes.* Palo Alto, CA: Author.

Ladson-Billings, G. (1994). *The dreamkeepers: Successful teachers of African American children.* San Francisco: Jossey-Bass.

Loredo, E. (1996). *The jump rope book.* New York: Workman.

Martin, J. R. (2002). *Cultural miseducation: In search of a democratic solution.* New York: Teachers College Press.

Masten, A., Best, K., & Garmezy, N. (1990). Resilience and development: Contributions from the study of children who overcame adversity. *Development and Psychopathology, 2,* 425–444.

Mattox, C. (1989). *Shake it to the one that you love the best: Play songs and lullabies from black musical traditions.* El Sobrante, CA: Warren-Mattox Productions.

Morrison, T. (1990). The site of memory. In R. Ferguson, M. Gever, T. Minh-Ha, & C. West (Eds.), *Out there: Marginalization and contemporary cultures.* New York: New Museum of Contemporary Art and Massachusetts Institute of Technology.

Morrison, T. (1992a). *Playing in the dark: Whiteness and the literary imagination.* Cambridge, MA: Harvard University Press.

Morrison, T. (1992b). *Jazz.* New York: Alfred A. Knopf.

National Education Association. (2006). *NEA addresses top five teaching trends and outlines portrait of American teacher.* Retrieved September 9, 2006, from http://www.nea.org/newsreleases/2006/nr060502.html

Nettles, S., & Pleck, (1994). Risk, resilience, and development: The multiple ecologies of Black adolescents. *Center for Research on Effective Schooling for Disadvantaged Students,* Report 44.

Nettles, S. M., & Robinson, F. (1998). Exploring the dynamics of resilience in an elementary school. *Center for Research on the Education of Students Placed At Risk,* Report No. 26.

Nettles, S. (2001). *Crazy visitation: A chronicle of illness and recovery.* Athens, GA: University of Georgia Press.

Ong, W. (2002). *Orality and literacy.* New York: Routledge.

Perks, R., & Thomson, A. (1998). *The oral history reader*. New York: Routledge.

Reid, I (1954). Integration: Ideal, process, and situation: Next steps in racial desegregation in education. *The Journal of Negro Education, 23*(3), 348–354.

Ritchie, D. A. (2003). *Doing oral history: A practical guide*. New York: Oxford University.

Reynolds, W., & Webber, J. (Eds.). (2004). *Expanding curriculum theory: Dispositions and lines of flight*. Mahwah, NJ: Erlbaum.

Shor, I. (1992). *Empowering education: Critical teaching for social change*. Chicago: The University of Chicago Press.

Shor, I., & Pari, C. (1999). *Critical literacy in action: Writing words, changing worlds: A Tribute to the teachings of Paulo Freire*. Portsmouth, NH: Boynton/Cook.

Shujaa, M. (1996). *Beyond desegregation: The politics of quality in African American schooling*. Thousand Oaks, CA: Corwin.

Siddle-Walker, V. (1996). *Their highest potential: An African American school community in the segregated south*. Chapel Hill, NC: University of North Carolina Press.

Siddle-Walker, V., & Snarey, J. (Ed.). (2004). *Race-ing moral formation: African American perspectives on care and justice*. New York: Teachers College Press.

Tatum, B. (2007). *Can we talk about race? And other conversations in an era of school resegregation*. Boston: Beacon.

White, D. (1999). *Too heavy a load: Black women in defense of themselves, 1894-1994*. New York: W. W. Norton & Company.

Wink, J. (2002). *Critical pedagogy: Notes from the real world*. New York: Longman.

CHAPTER 6

USING MULTICULTURAL LITERATURE TO DEVELOP EMPATHY AND COMPASSION IN PRESERVICE TEACHERS

A First Step in Preparing Culturally Responsive Teachers

Lyndall Muschell

AUTOBIOGRAPHICAL ORIGINS OF THE STUDY

As a young girl, I could not understand why I could not drink from what I consid-ered to be the most beautiful glasses in my grandmother's kitchen. These glasses were kept in a cabinet separate from the others we used for every day and the ones we used on Sundays. Then, one day when I was about five or six years old, the realization hit me. It was quite a rude awakening for me. I didn't have the words to describe it, but I knew I didn't like what was happening. It was hay baling season. My father had hired several Black men to help in the fields. Papa drove the truck

Personal~Passionate~Participatory Inquiry Into Social Justice in Education, pp. 93–108
Copyright © 2008 by Information Age Publishing
All rights of reproduction in any form reserved.

for hauling the hay to the barn. Daddy drove the tractor until all the hay was on the ground; then he joined the Black men in the back-breaking work of loading, unloading, and stacking hay. The work was long, hard, and hot. During a break in the work, I saw my grandmother come out of the house and approach the Black men with a gallon jug of ice water and those beautiful glasses. At this point, I still did not realize the gravity of what was happening. It was not until the break ended, and the men went back to work that it all became clear. My grandmother collected the glasses, returned them to the kitchen, made a pan of steaming hot dish water, added bleach to the water, and proceeded to sterilize the glasses. Without a word spoken, I understood why the glasses were forbidden. I can remember beginning to question my grandmother but received only the admonition to go on outside to play.

I begin with this story because I truly believe this to have been one of my most meaningful life changing experiences. It was this experience that opened my eyes to difference. For years after this, I continued to notice obvious examples of prejudice. Many were related to race, but not all. I watched as some of my classmates were shunned or ridiculed because of their physical appearance or socioeconomic backgrounds. Those with disabilities were the brunt of jokes. I saw how gender determined expectations for education and other opportunities. Even as a child, these experiences disturbed me. I needed to find a way to reconcile them. For this reason, I took my stand early on in elementary school by making the decision to refuse to participate in such activities and to advocate for those being exploited.

I was in the fourth grade. A new girl, Chris, had recently moved into town and was in my class for the first time. She had an outgoing personality, and everyone seemed to like her immediately. Almost overnight she became one of the most popular girls in the class. On a warm autumn day, a small group of girls and I were enjoying some "girl talk" while sitting under a huge elm tree on the edge of the playground. After a few minutes, Chris joined our group. Immediately she began making hurtful comments about one of our classmates. This was a boy who walked with a very definite limp and spoke in a slow, slurred voice. Chris did not know or seem to care that this boy had made what all considered to be a remarkable recovery after being hit by a transfer truck. I can easily recall the anger that I felt. I spoke up, asking her to stop, trying to explain. At that instant, in order for her to save face in the group, I became the target of her ridicule. As a result, I was no longer accepted by many of my peers. My memory is of this group of girls along with Chris walking away leaving me alone, standing on the outside wondering how things could change so quickly. I became an outcast, one of the "others."

From this time forward, I always seemed to fall outside the group. I had different ideas, opinions, and goals. I chose, however, to remain on the outside looking in because I was determined not to compromise my own principles by playing the game where the rules were based upon exclusion, ridicule, and harassment. For years, I accepted this self imposed position rather quietly. I tried always to appear as if being excluded did not bother me. Most of the time, I successfully hid my feelings of hurt and rejection while inside the anger at the rudeness and disrespect of others' behavior festered.

As an educator for over 20 years, I now realize that these are the feelings that have influenced me in my study and have guided my practice both as a classroom teacher and teacher educator. This passion was the motivation in my own kindergarten classroom where groups of diverse children were encouraged to form supportive communities. This force was the motivation for seeking the strengths within all children rather than focusing endlessly on their weaknesses. I now remember many of these children, appreciating greatly the opportunities they offered me. I thank the child with prosthetic legs, who as an infant had both legs amputated just below the knees. One day, as he climbed on the monkey bars, his mother entered the playground area. She gasped, "I didn't know he could do that!" I quickly responded, "I didn't know he couldn't!" We both celebrated the moment. This child taught me to look for possibilities rather than limitations. I thank the child with Down syndrome who followed the same rules and completed the same activities as the rest of the class. She helped me to see her strengths and taught me not to set my goals too low, to expect the best from each child, and to find ways in which everyone could participate in meaningful ways. I thank the child from Korea who came to me with no knowledge of the English language. I am sure that I learned more from her than she did from me. My memories are long and full. These children and others were an inspiration reminding me of the importance of honoring and respecting difference.

The influences from my experiences continued to shape my practice as I moved from the kindergarten classroom to teacher education. Over the years, I have observed countless lessons conducted by both preservice and inservice teachers in which the culture, experiences, inquiries, and interests of the children were devalued or ignored. To some, many of these lessons such as the one described below might seem quite innocent.

I sat quietly to observe a lesson in a kindergarten classroom. Most children gathered anxiously on the carpet, sitting informally around the teacher. A couple of children had been separated from the rest of the group. These children were in chairs on opposite sides of the back of the classroom. The teacher was in a prominent position in front of the group, perched in a chair placing her on a higher plane than the children. The lesson began with the teacher showing a picture of a baby to the class. The picture was actually of the teacher when she was about a year old. Upon seeing the photograph, the children became very excited. It was obvious that they knew a great deal about being a baby and the changes that take place as "growing-up" occurs.

Impatient hands waved in the air. Some children who just could not wait to be recognized called out enthusiastic comments to the teacher. As the children, who were visibly excited to have a direct connection to the impending lesson, offered their ideas, experiences, and questions, they were firmly reminded by the teacher that it was time to listen and not to share. Eventually the children sat quietly, attentive to what the teacher was saying. Emphasis was placed over and over upon the fact that the picture and the events related to being a baby and growing up centered on the experiences of the teacher. The teacher told the children that there would be a time at the end of the lesson for sharing. This lesson was about how babies change over time. The children needed to listen to the teacher in order to learn what she had previously determined as important information. The time for sharing never came; other more important information needed to be covered in order to meet the objectives for the day.

What was wrong with this scenario? The children were interested and enthusiastic. The lesson was obviously connected to the prior knowledge of the children in the class. Children who had trouble being a part of the group had been removed so as not to cause distractions. The teacher was visibly in control of the lesson. So, what could possibly be inappropriate? This is a question that many may ask. I contend, however, that there is much to be found "wrong." Sadly too, this description represents what happens quite frequently in many early childhood classrooms today. The teacher is the dispenser of knowledge. The children are not seen as being knowledgeable, capable, or legitimate. They are the "blank slates" upon which the teacher must make her mark. The experiences, prior knowledge, and interests of the children are not valued or respected by the teacher. Those children, who for whatever reason are different, are excluded from the group and ultimately from the lesson itself. The contributions of these children, the ones excluded, are the least valued of all. The teacher encourages the children to conform rather than to think, to question, to challenge.

As I moved in and out of many schools within various systems observing lessons which were many times unresponsive to the children for whom they were planned, I realized that if I were to indeed respond to the dilemma which I faced, I needed to investigate the possibility of preparing a population of teachers who "see each student as a growing, dynamic, developing, stretching being—a fellow human creature—with specific needs and demands and hopes and desires and potentials" (Ayers, 1995, p. 2); teachers who establish classroom environments that challenge and nurture diverse groups of students; teachers who strive to create a classroom, a school, and a world for all children, a place characterized by peace and justice (Ayers, 1995).

PARTICIPATORY RESEARCH PROCESS

In response to the challenge to prepare teachers to become more culturally responsive in their practice, my goal was to design and implement a
study that would have implications for teacher education programs as
educators face the dilemma of preparing an overwhelmingly White
teacher population to teach for diversity in today's schools. To address
this dilemma I looked to the work of Geneva Gay (2000), Maxine Greene
(1978, 1995), and Martha Nussbaum (1997) as a foundation for study. I
developed questions to identify ways to increase sensitivity to and understanding of diversity as well as finding ways of inviting dialogue about
race, racism, and discrimination. What revisions could be made in the
current Early Childhood Education Program at my university that would
ultimately lead to the preparation of teachers who are more culturally
responsive in their practice? What experiences could be effective in
encouraging preservice teachers to explore their own cultural roots, to
question stereotypes, and to develop an appreciation for differences?
Could multicultural literature be used to encourage the development of
empathy and compassion for those who are different from oneself? Could
stories be helpful in opening up conversations that can challenge the
silence surrounding issues of race and racism?

To answer these questions, I made plans to work with a group of White,
middle class females who had entered the Early Childhood Education
Program in the fall of 2003. As one of the two mentor leaders who headed
the cohort of students who began at that time, I worked closely with each
participant, serving as an advisor, a field placement supervisor, and an
instructor. Because of the nature of the program, my relationship with the
students was unique. Unlike many professors, as a mentor leader for a
cohort of students, I was able to spend 2 years with the same group. At the
beginning of the program, I participated with the students in team building experiences, orientation activities, counseling sessions, and social
events. In addition, I taught part of the required course work each semester, arranged field placements, conducted field placement supervision,
and provided advisement. The design of the program lent itself to the
creation of an environment of trust and interdependence. The cohort
members became a cohesive group which provided a space where risks
could be taken.

At the time that the study began, I had worked closely with the participants for two semesters. They were seniors in the Early Childhood
Education Program. All participants had taken part in orientation events
and counseling sessions, had fulfilled the course work requirements for
the first two semesters of the program, and had completed four 7 week
placements in a range of classrooms within two school systems. In

addition, during the time that data were collected, each participant was enrolled in a course that I had specifically designed for the purpose of increasing awareness and understanding of the role of imagination in the development of culturally responsive pedagogy. As a part of the course, I arranged opportunities that allowed the participants to explore their own Whiteness, examine Maxine Greene's (1995) concepts of imagination, and engage in narrative imagination (Nussbaum, 1997) through multicultural literature.

The study was conducted using the cross-cultural narrative method of inquiry (He, 2003), which emphasizes and values lived experience along with the development of understanding, empathy, and compassion for those who are culturally different. Data collection methods included the school portraiture, participant profiles, autobiographies that explored the cultural roots of the participants, critical writings completed by participants, and participant interviews. Data were analyzed to determine existing stereotypes; to assess the participants' awareness of group dominance, stereotypes, racism, and/or oppression; and to ascertain whether or not the experiences of the study influenced change in the personal, cultural and/or racial attitudes and beliefs of participants who I hoped would become more culturally responsive in their teaching practices.

Having read and studied the writings of Nussbaum (1997), Greene (1978), Delpit (1995), Howard (1999), LeCompte and McCray (2002), McIntyre (1997), Landsman (2001), and Nieto (2000) which strongly support the self examination of one's identity and beliefs as a beginning step to the development of cultural responsiveness in teaching, I planned the first research activity as one which required the participants to engage in a critical exploration of their autobiographical roots. After searching for their cultural roots, reflecting upon their backgrounds, and examining their cultural values and beliefs, each participant composed an autobiographical paper. At this time, I truly believed that I understood the importance of exploring and sharing personal histories in the development of empathy and compassion for others and the role that this examination plays in encouraging teaching practices that are culturally responsive. I fully expected the confirmation of this claim, but I was not, however, prepared for the comprehensiveness and richness of the results.

I had shared my autobiography with the participants. I chose to do this for two reasons. The first was to help them to understand more fully the nature of the assignment. The second was to build a greater sense of trust between me and the participants. As I shared my story with the class, I noticed that what the faces of the students communicated was unexpected. I saw the concerns in their eyes and heard the resonance of my experiences in their comments. For this group of students, I felt that I had become more than a mentor leader, more than a field placement supervisor, more than the professor for the course. I had become "real." I was real in the sense that they could relate to my experiences. I was a person who had experienced hardships and triumphs. By sharing my story, I had become someone that this group of students could connect with and begin to understand.

When the time came for the participants to share their stories, I reminded them that they were not required to share anything that would make them uncomfortable. They could convey as much or as little information as they chose. As I expected, the sharing began slowly. However, after a short time, the monologue of sharing became a conversation. They listened and responded empathetically to one another. Their connections were evident. They began to comment openly about commonalities that even after a year together in the cohort they had never realized. I listened while acting primarily as facilitator to the discussion by asking clarifying or guiding questions. As I listened, I learned. I thought that I knew these students. I was wrong. It was only by listening to their stories that I began to understand these young women. Unconsciously and unintentionally, I had prejudged them. I had made assumptions about their experiences or the lack thereof. Having heard their personal stories, I could now see them in a different way. This experience was a demonstration of the type of connections that are needed in classrooms where a culturally responsive pedagogy could be developed. We had begun to develop empathy and compassion for one another.

As I became more connected with my participants, I realized that people "are more likely to ask their own questions and seek their own transcendence when they feel themselves to be grounded in their personal histories, their lived lives" (Greene, 1978, p. 2). As expected, the experience confirmed that critically examining one's autobiographical roots, reflecting upon one's background, and examining one's values and beliefs help develop empathy and compassion toward others who are different. As my participants began to understand more about each other, they began to see one another as individuals who could be understood, respected, and valued. This beginning process, however, was different for each one. For instance,

> I had been at the park, and I had heard people being loud, and I thought, "Oh, Black people are just so loud." It was like my mother's voice that I could hear in my head. I had just grown up with that. But, I don't believe that. So, it is just things like that that I learned about myself, things that I really didn't know that I had within me. (Warren, 2004, p. 191)

Realizing that these feelings of prejudice were a part of her life experiences gave Amy the opportunity to confront these and to continue in the development of empathy and compassion for others.

Exploring her personal, cultural, and racial beliefs was a challenging experience for Rebecca as well. Unlike Heather and Amy, this activity helped her to define herself as an individual, to separate her personal beliefs and values from those of her family.

> That paper really challenged my thinking about who I am as an individual, not who my mom is, or who my dad is, or how I was raised, but who I am today and what I believe is right and wrong when it deals with different cultures and races. (Warren, 2004, p. 205)

Confronting their beliefs about race, prejudice, and culture through the exploration of their cultural roots through autobiography was the first step for the participants as they moved toward culturally responsive teaching.

To determine the participants' awareness of group dominance, stereotypes, or social values that are communicated through media, they created and responded to a cultural collage. Their participation required them to address their own Whiteness in terms of White dominance. The cultural collage was assembled by the participants from pictures of people that were collected from popular magazines, sale papers, travel brochures, newspapers, and so forth. Afterwards, the participants closely examined the collage as a whole to reflect upon the messages conveyed by the visual representation.

As I read the participants' written responses to the collage, I began to see a primary theme that was common to all. The theme that emerged from the responses was the concept that the media presents the standard to which many people try to conform. I found that the acknowledgment of the representation of White dominance within the collage was almost completely absent. Where all the participants recognized the standard represented by the photographs, no one questioned how people of other races would respond to these. Only one participant, Heather, commented in her writing about the presence of White dominance, and even this comment was limited to recognition. "Most of the people are young, beautiful, skinny, White females or young, handsome, buff, White males. There are some African Americans thrown in there, but even the African Americans are young, beautiful, and skinny" (Warren, 2004, p. 129).

After composing their individual responses to the cultural collage, the participants engaged in a discussion related to their interpretations and reflections. Throughout discussions, I noticed that conversations always seemed to drift away from issues of race. I remember becoming inwardly frustrated that the participants continued to deny the monocultural nature of the collage. They were, however, sensitive to the absence of the elderly, the overweight, and the unattractive. These were all conditions that each one could directly relate to through personal experiences. When asked about the absence of other races, the group first argued that "they" were represented. I continued to question, to probe, playing the devil's advocate. As I continued to ask about the absence of different races or cultures, the atmosphere in the room became defensive in nature as if they knew that my pointing out the lack of representation was legitimate, but they could not voice the admission. Frustrated by my continuous probing, one student finally asked, "Why does everyone have to focus on color? Why can't all people just be treated the same?"

These reactions and comments, though disturbing, are consistent with current research on White identity development. "Whites are taught to think of their lives as morally neutral, normative, and average, and also ideal" (McIntosh, 1990). For this reason, it is difficult for those who have typically benefited from social position, race, or gender to examine the ways in which their own attitudes and practices are influenced by their backgrounds or their ignorance (Nieto, 2000). When considering differences such as race, religion, gender, and social position, people tend to be placed in the role of either the victimized or the victimizer. Once these issues are confronted openly by individuals, they become vulnerable; by opening themselves up to others, they open themselves up to a multitude of feelings and emotions including guilt, blame, denial, and responsibility. For this reason, this type of critical reflection upon personal realities is something that many avoid (Greene, 1978). Because of this tendency to avoid difficult issues, many preservice teachers have had very little practice confronting racial issues in meaningful and productive ways (Nieto, 2000). As they examine their own Whiteness, individuals often find themselves struggling to find something good about Whiteness, making excuses for the White race, or denying responsibility for participating in a system that perpetuates oppression and privilege based upon skin color (McIntyre, 2002). The participants' responses had demonstrated that acknowledging and confronting Whiteness, White privilege, and White dominance are complicated processes that involve risk taking and openness and also lead to vulnerability.

As I began to recognize the difficulty experienced by the confrontation of Whiteness, I began to search for a comfortable way for these explorations and discussions to occur. I knew, based on the work of Florio-Ruane (2001), that if in-depth discussions and conversations related to difficult issues such as equity, discrimination, prejudice, race, and racism were to occur, participants required the security of a safe space that was open and respectful. In addition, having studied the writings of Nussbaum (1997) and Greene (1978), I realized that because stories allow individuals to enter an imaginary world of awareness and permit the author to lead the reader on a journey, multicultural literature could provide this risk-free place where conversations could be initiated (Phillion & He, 2004). Through the story, the author has the power to shock readers, causing them to think, to notice, to question, to search for meaning, to realize possibilities (Nussbaum, 1997). Multicultural literature could engage the narrative imagination to help develop within readers the emotions of empathy and compassion for those who, for whatever reason, were different from themselves. For these reasons, I began to use multicultural literature as a vehicle for exploring the possibilities for cultivating narrative imagination—developing empathy and compassion towards others.

First, the participants read and discussed Vivian Gussin Paley's (1979/ 2002) book, *White Teacher*. This text provided a safe space to discuss the hard topics of race, prejudice, and discrimination. The book is a White teacher's personal account of how she dealt with the challenges of racial and cultural differences within her classroom. Paley's practices and beliefs challenged the participants. By discussing the prejudices, motivations, and actions of Paley, these topics became less personal, allowing the participants to feel less vulnerable and more willing to open up to honest and critical discussions. It was through the stories in *White Teacher* that the participants came to know the characters, sought understanding for their actions, connected to their emotions, and found commonalities in experiences. Through this reading, the reflections, and the discussions, I found that multicultural literature did indeed help to create a safe environment for these preservice teachers to generate difficult conversations related to racism, prejudice, and oppression.

Multicultural literature did indeed provide a risk free place where difficult issues related to difference could be addressed; therefore, I began to search for more channels through which my participants could confront these issues. I chose *Conrack,* a movie based on the book, *The Water is Wide,* by Pat Conroy (1972/2002). The text is based on a true story of a White, liberal teacher who is sent to substitute at a poor, all Black school on an island off the coast of South Carolina. the story describes how one teacher used whatever was available to educate illiterate, impoverished children.

Before the participants viewed the movie, *Conrack* (Ritt, 1974/1985), I encouraged them to concentrate on their understanding of narrative imagination as it related to the movie. As they watched *Conrack,* I asked them to focus on the importance of understanding and respecting the unique culture represented by a group of students in addition to addressing the individual needs of students; the motivation and actions of *Conrack,* administrators, and the students; and the relationships between the text and personal experience. As a result, four major themes emerged from the participants' written responses: the importance of respecting and valuing students, the significance of family and community support, the value of an experiential curriculum that is focused on the needs and abilities of the students, and the need to persevere in order to affect change. The existence of White power and privilege, however, was not acknowledged by the participants. This lack of recognition presents a concern, for throughout the movie are demonstrations of how the imposition of White power and privilege affects others as well as examples that were concealed within the motivations of characters. This absence of acknowledgment by the participants further confirmed that the confrontation of the issues surrounding Whiteness is a complicated and difficult process.

I realized, however, that through their reading of *White Teacher* (Paley, 1979/2002) and their viewing of *Conrack* (Ritt, 1974/1985), the participants were challenged to view issues and situations from the point of view of others. This provided an opportunity for the participants to engage in the process of developing the narrative imagination which allowed them to explore worlds that were quite different from their own. Being able to imagine one's self in the place of others allowed for the understanding of their condition, their motivations, and their actions. "Using your imagination can provide a window into someone else's life and encourage a sense of empathy in the person who is doing the imagining" (Warren, 2004, p. 139). It is through the narrative imagination that concern for the characters is inspired and empathy and compassion for others can develop (Nussbaum, 1997). Through narrative imagination, the reader is able to recognize that the other person is qualitatively different yet worthy of respect.

Throughout my inquiry, narrative imagination allowed the participants to think, to question, to search for meaning, to look beyond the habitual and the mundane, and to see possibilities (Greene, 1995; Nussbaum, 1997). Stories provided the participants with a safe environment where they could further their development of empathy and compassion by exploring the world from another's point of view, where they were better able to understand the context of the "other's" history and social world as well as the meanings behind actions.

As the participants continued to engage in critical examination and reflection upon their cultural values and beliefs; to acknowledge and to confront Whiteness, White privilege, and White dominance; to join in difficult conversations related to racism, prejudice, and oppression through multicultural literature; to question the habitual and mundane; and to search for possibilities for change, I began to realize that they were becoming more culturally responsive in their teaching practices. During my interview with Amy, she described to me how participating in the experiences of the study influenced her as she planned and implemented a family literacy project. The students in her class had been learning the format of a friendly letter. She took this opportunity to send a letter to the parents and the students asking that they, as a family, write a letter addressed to the class about a tradition they had as a family. Through this project she found a way to include families and to be respectful of their cultures and traditions. Like Amy, Allison used what she learned from participation in the experiences of the study to guide the development of a family literacy project. The project helped her not only to learn more about the children in her placement and their families but also to develop empathy and compassion for her students and their families.

As I interviewed Rebecca, I realized that she had used the knowledge and understanding that she gained from her experiences in a different way from Amy and Allison. During her placement in a kindergarten class, she was struggling to manage the classroom effectively. As she continued to develop empathy and compassion for the students in this classroom, she began to question classroom discipline practices.

> We only have one White child who will get her name on the board most days, but then we have three or four Black children that get their names up for something every single day. I have been trying to figure out why that is. It has made me think about the need to become more aware of differences in behaviors. (Warren, 2004, p. 213)

After fully analyzing the data gathered during the inquiry, it became clear to me that the participants' teaching practices were positively affected by participation in the study. The examples of their practices which were described are consistent with both Gay's (2000) definition of culturally responsive teaching and the essential characteristics of culturally responsive teachers. Cultivating empathy and compassion had fostered the development of culturally responsive pedagogy.

OUTCOMES OF THE INQUIRY

Preparing teachers to become culturally responsive in their practices is challenging and time consuming. It requires much dedication, energy, patience, and strategic planning. As I worked with the participants, I realized that each one came into this study with unique life experiences that had defined her personal, cultural, and racial beliefs. Each, depending upon these beliefs, was challenged differently by the experiences which were completed as a part of the study. The participants approached and engaged in the experiences at different levels of development in regard to empathy and compassion for others who are different from themselves. Therefore, they moved at their own rates toward culturally responsive pedagogy. At the end of the study, each participant had changed and progressed toward more cultural responsiveness in her practice; however, the change was unique to the individual.

These findings have affected change not only in program decisions but also professional practice. As a mentor, field supervisor, and instructor, I now see through a new lens. I find it more important than ever to get to know my students and to understand who they are. I make decisions based on individuals rather than strict requirements and guidelines. Equity has become more important than equality. As I observe students in their teaching, I find myself focusing specifically on culturally responsive practices, always guiding them to move in this direction. I encourage them to confront difference in a way that is respectful, to value the opportunities that diversity brings.

To assist students in their move toward culturally responsive pedagogy, decisions have been initiated programmatically to allow for more opportunities for students to develop an understanding of themselves and others. The examination of one's cultural roots is a critical experience that is now required of all students. Students are involved on many levels in the process of narrative imagination as a strategy for understanding differing perspectives. More experiences are now in place for students to examine the communities in which the children in their classrooms live, to develop relationships with both the children and their parents, to actively involve parents in the classroom in meaningful ways that honor their culture and beliefs, to be cautious of the personal bias that my occur in the assessment of children from different backgrounds, and to plan and implement lessons that are truly meaningful to the children whom they teach.

Where this would represent only the first step in an effort to move preservice teachers toward more culturally responsive teaching practices, my hope was that through the dialogue that was encouraged by the exploration of personal and cultural self-identity, narrative imagination, and multicultural literature these prospective teachers would become more comfortable and confident in talking frankly to each other about differences; would be less likely to be silent in the face of prejudice, racism, and discrimination; and would encourage their own students to speak out, to question, and to take risks. Ultimately, I hoped to build the understanding that listening to alternative points of view "takes a special kind of listening, listening that requires not only open eyes and ears, but open hearts and minds" (Delpit, 1995, p. 46). To do so, however, means that "we must be vulnerable enough to allow our world to turn upside down in order to allow the realities of others to edge themselves into our consciousness" (p. 47)

The findings of this study could be considered as challenges as well as possibilities. Each one has the potential to present a hurdle to be negotiated. The challenge lies in whether or not those of us in teacher education choose to realize the possibilities by tackling these or simply to maneuver around them thus perpetuating a system that is resistant to difference. Accepting the challenge of preparing teachers who are responsive to diversity is essential, for not only within the teacher preparation programs at my university but also throughout the nation, there exists a population of White teachers that should not be ignored or discounted. The preparation of teachers who are culturally responsive in their practices, however, does not represent a quick and easy answer to the problem of addressing growing diversity.

Culturally responsive pedagogy defies the conventions of traditional educational practices specifically as they relate to racial, cultural, and ethnic differences. It assumes that teaching is a contextual and situational process, therefore challenging the Eurocentrtic framework which currently shapes our schools. In many ways it requires teaching against the grain by challenging cultural neutrality and the syndrome of homogeneity in teaching and learning (Gay, 2000). As a challenge to traditional methods, culturally responsive teaching, with all its possibilities, is not without obstacles.

Education is "an arena of hope and struggle—hope for a better life, and struggle over how to understand and enact and achieve that better life" (Ayers, 1998, p. xvi). Therefore, educators should enter this arena by teaching consciously for social justice and social change. They should embrace "teaching that arouses students, engages them in a quest to identify obstacles to their full humanity, to their freedom, and then to drive, to move against those obstacles" (p. xvi). Many times, this type of teaching requires that educators challenge the status quo and seek possibilities rather than accept what exists. It demands that teachers see the students and the world in which they live, focusing not only on the students' identities, skills and abilities, and aspirations, but also on context, including significant historical events, cultural influences, and economic realities. When teachers teach in this way, they provide students with multiple entry points for learning and a wide range of pathways for success. Education becomes an avenue for opening doors, challenging minds, and offering possibilities. The Chinese ideogram for person summarizes the role of teachers.

> The Chinese ideogram for "person" depicts a figure grounded in the earth and stretching toward heaven. What is she reaching for? What dream is she pursing? Why so seemingly becalmed on one end, yet so relentlessly restless on the other? The character suggests the destiny of every human being: to be fated, but also to be free; to be both free and fated. Each of us is planted in the mud and the muck of daily existence, thrust into a world not of our choosing, and tethered then to hard-rock reality; each of us is endowed with a mind able to reflect on that reality, to choose who to be in light of the cold

facts and the merely given. We each have a spirit capable of joining that mind and soaring overhead, poised to transgress boundaries, destroy obstacles, and transform ourselves and our world. (Ayers, 2004, p. xiv)

The time has come for teacher educators to undertake the task of transforming teacher education by confronting the difficult issues of culture, race, racism, and oppression as well as accepting the challenge to become "awakened" to the world around them, seeing the possibilities of what can be rather than focusing on what is. It is time for teacher educators to critically analyze current teacher preparation programs and to initiate reforms that will better prepare teachers to more effectively deal with the issues of diversity that they will inevitably face as they enter public school classrooms. The challenge presented by the findings of this study is one of implementation. As a teacher educator, I must take this responsibility by working toward changes within the teacher education programs at my university; by preparing teachers, both graduate and undergraduate, to become comfortable and confident in acknowledging and confronting differences rather than to be silent in the face of racism, discrimination, social injustice; and by encouraging them to allow their students to speak out, to question, to take risks, and to reach their highest potential.

REFERENCES

Ayers, W. (1995). Introduction: Joining the ranks. In W. Ayers (Ed.), *To become a teacher: Making a difference in children's lives* (pp. 1–4). New York: Teachers College Press.

Ayers, W. (1998). Foreword: Popular education—teaching for social justice. In W. Ayers, J. A. Hunt, & T. Quinn (Eds.), *Teaching for social justice* (pp. xvi–xxv). New York: Teachers College Press.

Ayers, W. (2004). *Teaching toward freedom: Moral commitment and ethical action in the classroom.* Boston: Beacon.

Conroy, P. (2002). *The water is wide.* New York: Bantam Dell Publishing Group. (Original work published 1972)

Delpit, L. (1995). *Other people's children: Cultural conflict in the classroom.* New York: New Press.

Florio-Ruane, S. (2001). *Teacher education and cultural imagination: Autobiography, conversation, and narrative.* Mahwah, NJ: Erlbaum.

Gay, G. (2000). *Culturally responsive teaching: Theory, research, and practice.* New York: Teachers College Press.

Greene, M. (1978). *Landscapes of learning.* New York: Teachers College Press.

Greene, M. (1995). *Releasing the imagination.* San Francisco: Jossey-Bass.

He, M. F. (2003). *A river forever flowing: Cross cultural lives and identities in the multicultural Landscape.* Greenwich, CT: Information Age.

Howard, G. R. (1999). *We can't teacher what we don't know: White teachers, multiracial schools.* New York: Teachers College Press.

Landsman, J. (2001). *A white teacher talks about race.* Lanham, MD: The Scarecrow Press.

LeCompte, K. N., & McCray, A. D. (2002). Complex conversations with teacher candidates: Perspectives of whiteness and culturally responsive teaching. *Curriculum and Teaching Dialogue, 4*(1), 25–35.

McIntosh, P. (1990). White privilege: Unpacking the invisible knapsack. *Independent School, 90*(49), 31–36.

McIntyre, A. (2002). Exploring whiteness and multicultural education with prospective teachers. *Curriculum Inquiry, 32*(1), 31–49.

McIntyre, A. (1997). Constructing an image of a white teacher. *Teachers College Record, 98*(4), 653–681.

Nieto, S. (2000). *Affirming diversity: The sociopolitical context of multicultural education* (3rd ed.). New York: Addison Wesley Longman.

Nussbaum, M. C. (1997). *Cultivating Humanity: A classical defense of reform in liberal education.* Cambridge: Harvard University Press.

Paley, V. G. (2002). *White teacher.* Cambridge: Harvard University Press. (Original work published 1979)

Phillion, J., & He, M. F. (2004). Using life based literary narratives in multicultural teacher education. *Multicultural Perspectives: An Official Journal of the National Association for Multicultural Education, 6*(3), 3–9.

Ritt, M. & Frank, H. (Producers). & Ritt, M. (Director). (1985). *Conrack* [Motion Picture]. (Available from Playhouse Video, Industrial Park Drive, Farmington Hills, MI, 48024). (Original work published 1974)

Warren. L. (2004). *Using multicultural literature to develop empathy and compassion in preservice teachers: A first step in preparing culturally responsive teachers.* Unpublished doctoral dissertation, Georgia Southern University.

CHAPTER 7

A CURRICULUM OF IMAGINATION IN AN ERA OF STANDARDIZATION

Robert Lake

AUTOBIOGRAPHICAL ROOTS OF THIS INQUIRY

"Now Charley, you can put that ax down! I love your daughter and will take good care of her," my father said. "I won't let you take away my best worker," was my grandfather's reply. Eventually my dad talked Charley Gainey into putting down the ax, and he took my mother away from a North Carolina sharecropper's home to live in Tecumseh, Michigan. My mother came from a family of eleven brothers and sisters and started working in the cotton fields with all of them when she was five years old. My father had been stationed nearby at Fort Bragg, North Carolina during the Second World War. My mother finished the seventh grade, and my father finished the eighth grade. My paternal grandfather served as a migrant laborer in logging camps that stretched from Northern Michigan to Saskatchewan, Canada, and would leave home for months at a time. After World War II, my father found work in a refrigeration compressor

Personal~Passionate~Participatory Inquiry Into Social Justice in Education, pp. 109–125
Copyright © 2008 by Information Age Publishing
All rights of reproduction in any form reserved.

factory where he worked for thirty years. While I was growing up, my mother was a waitress in small restaurants, serving locals and truckers. We were considered "the working poor." The cultural roots of my family and repressive and suppressive experience my family has encountered invigorate my passion for responsive and imaginative teaching and researching for social justice.

I received three "Ds" in kindergarten and was placed in "group two" in first-grade reading. Like many students today, I remember always having a hard time sitting still for too long. This was further complicated by the onset of puberty during which time I laughed and caused frequent disturbances in class. Sometimes I would be sent out in the hallway or to the principal's office. More than once, I was placed in the back of the classroom underneath the science lab sink with tape on my mouth. This experience has become a very personal metaphor for the "taping shut" of individual student voices, interests and abilities through standardized practices that have increasingly dominated the culture of schools to the present time.

Because I received such poor grades and scored so poorly on standardized tests, I was never considered "college material." In high school, I remember being placed in social studies for slow readers, general math, general science and industrial arts. *The tragic part of this is that I was convinced that I belonged there.* One day a caring teacher came as a substitute to "slow reader's" social studies. He told me that I did not belong there and placed me in his World History class. I still continued to do poorly in school, but I will never forget that teacher. I have sought to model his example in looking past the test scores with my own students.

At the same time that I was having such a struggle as a high school student, outside of school, I began to flourish as a musician. One defining moment took place in my second year of high school, just after my parents' divorce. I remember hearing a song by the Lovin' Spoonful (1965) featuring a harmonica solo by John Sebastian called *Night Owl Blues*. I was so drawn in by the emotional tone and skill expressed in that song that I said to myself, "I will learn to play just like that!" A few months later, I could play most of it! Not long after that, I was asked to play in a band. My self-esteem soared! Through the creative power of music the "tape" came off my mouth, and I began to find my voice.

Eventually, I broke through the class barrier through music by "marrying up" into the world of my wife's upper middle class family. She once confessed that she married me "because I was nice and played the guitar." On several occasions we lived with her parents. Her father was a lawyer, her mother was an art teacher, and their home was rich with academic language and books. With my auditory style of learning, I found myself speaking, reading, and writing in a much more sophisticated manner. My musician friends told me I sounded like a different person. It was also through music that I began my teaching career by teaching language through songs to English as Second Language students.

These experiences as a student and a teacher/researcher have provided me with a firsthand perspective on the negative effects of standardized testing and the resulting tracking and marginalization of students. These encounters have fueled my passion against dehumanization of every kind and, at the same time, implored me to move beyond the predictable and the given for my own life as well as the lives of those whom I teach. For more than 12 years, I have worked as a teacher of English for immigrant children and adults and high school dropouts preparing for the GED as well as "developmental" reading students at a technical college. My work with these groups drove my passion for relevant teaching even further as I looked for ways to help them move beyond both academic and social obstacles through discovery of personal voice, personal interests and abilities. Now as a teacher of preservice education students, I share my story of release from class barriers and the effects of tracking as I help them make sense of their own personal history by encouraging them to weave the positive and negative features of their lives into a garment of caring and imaginative teaching in this present climate of highly scripted methods and standardized practices in schools.

THE FOCUS OF MY INQUIRY

Reflections on the causes of marginalization and disenfranchisement of students and the power of imagination in cultivating multiple discourses of literacy, both in and out of schools, led me to ask these questions in this personal, passionate and participatory research. By reflecting on my own experience, I came to understand the power that imagination played in my release from the walls of negative self-expectation and standardized thinking. These deeply personal musings helped me come to a focused purpose of my inquiry in the following question. How does imagination, which permeates every aspect of our life experience, help develop personal and political awareness by enabling us to look beyond what is taken for granted, to question the normal, and to develop various ways of knowing, seeing, feeling, and acting upon positive social and educational changes in this current climate of accountability? I sought to understand what role imagination plays in helping us develop awareness of personal perspective and identity in an era of standardization. And further I inquired: How can we develop ways of imagining that will cultivate the opening of personal spaces of thought and expression beyond the status quo? How can the imagination be used to enhance both personal and communal ways of knowing, seeing, and being in the world? As I sought to answer these questions, I came to recognize the value of reflective/reflexive autobiographical inquiry in helping me understand.

WRITING AS INQUIRY

As I looked for a way to express my passion for a curriculum of imagination that would make personal sense to me and my readers, I was thrilled to discover the work of Laurel Richardson (2003). She sees the act of writing as a "method of inquiry, a way of finding out about yourself and your topic" (p. 499). Writing is a form of thinking and an extension of the reading process. And yet the field of educational inquiry is still influenced by nineteenth century forms of static methodology in which writers are expected to "silence their own voices and to view themselves as contaminants" (p. 501). The more I read Richardson's notion of writing to find personal connection and voice, the more I resonate her position. She concludes that positivistic methodology's quest for "pure" objectivity tends to "validate a mechanistic model of writing, shutting down the creativity and sensibilities of the individual writer/researcher" (p. 502). Conversely, it is through imaginative engagement of personal sensibilities, where the divide between the objective and subjective aspects is transcended, that learning is most likely to occur. I began to see possibilities in the act of writing as a means of creating personal metaphoric connections with a wide range of forms of discourse (Moffett, 1968). By intertwining theory and personal story, I found a continual unity in using imagination and metaphor in a multilayered, nonlinear process that explored the contrast between imaginative ways of being with the cultural effects of standardization.

I found that autobiographical writing makes "the personal the political, the personal is the grounding for theory" (Richardson, 2003, p. 506). I also found that dialogue provides one way to make the connections between the personal and the political, the theoretical and the practical, the reality and imagination, and the author and the audience. In dialogue with others, private musings become more alive and relevant.

IMAGINATIVE DIALOGUE

This experience compelled me to look for historical connections between dialogue and imagination. I traced the traditions of classic intellectual conversations in Socratic dialogues. Plato's (380 B.C.) *Meno* is a good example of one of the clearer and more focused uses of this variety because it involves a shared definition and discussion of the question:

"What is virtue?" I was also introduced to *A Rap on Race*, the work of Margaret Mead and James Baldwin (1971), which

> juxtaposes Baldwin's apocalyptic despair, based on his profound emotional response to his life in America as a black lost among whites, to Margaret Mead's enduring faith in redemption from racial doom, based on her own experience as a white among nonwhites, and articulated with relentless fiery logic. (Mead & Baldwin, 1971, backcover)

They used a dialogue format to discuss race issues. During their discussion, they also draw from a wide range of sources as varied as Peter Ustinov (p. 127), and Allen Ginsberg (p. 249) to support their points of view.

Building on these examples of dialogue as well as those that I mention below, I created an imaginary intellectual dialogue between Maxine Greene and Paulo Freire. The works of Greene and Freire epitomize two aspects of imagination: artistic and critical, that are crucial to understanding what exactly is meant by this term when it is applied to the context of education. Together they express a holistic view of creative and critical applications of imagination. In addition Freire and Greene's works contain a number of examples of dialogue in the form of intellectual conversations.

In the introduction to *The Landscape of Qualitative Research*, Denzin and Lincoln (2003), two notable voices in qualitative research, share the metaphor of the qualitative researcher "as *bricoleur* or maker of quilts (that) uses aesthetic and material tools of his or her craft" (p. 6). This metaphor extends beyond the pragmatic to the "aesthetics of representation" into the concept of montage. This term is used in cinematography to describe the process of creating an aesthetic fusing together to form a newly created composite from footage shot in real time. The fusing together of film is often done in juxtaposition in ways that create greater depth and width to the representation of images. In a similar way, I created a montage of quotes from Greene and Freire, in writing, that provided a way to internalize a discursive interaction between the creative and critical aspects of imagination by the blending of their written voices with my own inner voice of personal musing. The conversations were arranged in a way that helped me understand the role of imagination in developing my own personal agency in removing barriers to social justice, first within me, and then in the lives of those whom I teach. For example, I have used the following section of the dialogue between Greene and Freire to teach the concept of imagination. It adds a humanizing dimension and makes it come alive in clear and understandable terms.

> Paulo: You refer to imagination quite often in your writing, and that is a very broad term. What is your personal understanding of its meaning?

Maxine: I'm glad you emphasized the word "personal" because that is the modus operandi of imagination. Indeed, "out of all our cognitive capacities, imagination is the one that … allows us to break with the taken for granted, to set aside familiar distinctions and definitions" (Greene, 1995, p. 3) and break with what is supposedly fixed and finished (p. 19). This must be why Dewey (1934) described this capacity as a gateway through which meanings derived from past experiences find their way into the present in what he calls the "the conscious adjustment of the new and the old." He goes on to say that imagination more than any other capacity "breaks through the inertia of habit" (p. 272) while it allows us to "glimpse what might be and what is not yet" (Greene, 1995, p. 19).

Paulo: I see imagination as a humanizing capacity that enables us to act upon and transform our world through the first-hand discovery and naming of our own worlds of meaning. This is what my friend Richard Shaull had in mind when he said that: [this] *world* to which he relates is not a static and closed order, a *given* reality which man must accept and to which he must adjust; rather, it is a problem to be worked on and solved. It is the material used by man to create history, a task which he performs as he overcomes that which is dehumanizing at any particular time and place and dares to create qualitatively new (Shaull, 2003, p. 32).

By means of dialogical discourse, I am able to more fully grasp the emphasis in both these statements on the personal meaning-making capacity of imagination as well as the emphasis on action. It reminds me of Dewey's notion that "mind is a verb" and, therefore, involves the whole being. Imagination integrates the cognitive, the emotional, and the physical by connecting concepts or images with our experience in comprehension and personal meaning-making. This process involves more than the ability to "reflect" and recapture images. Imagination enables us to perceive, uniquely interpret, and express in a new way.

NEW VISTAS IN FOUR COMMONPLACES

As I reflect upon what I have learned from this inquiry, I turn to Schwab's (1969) notion of four commonplaces to envision a curriculum of imagination in the making. Schwab had much to say about the need to open the field to democratic dialogue and forms of inquiry that focused less on "proof" while opening spaces for "discovery and invention" (through) pluralities of knowledge (Westbury & Wilkof, 1978, p. 336). I am intrigued by some of the terminology that Schwab brought to the field of education from his background in biology because a curriculum of imagination is rich with metaphors of life and nature. I remember that it was Schwab (1969) who referred to the field of curriculum as "moribund" (p. 1). Another potent word he brought from biology is "coalescence" (Westbury & Wilkof, 1978, p. 365) which literally means to grow together in forming new living organisms.

Coalescence is an important aspect to understanding Schwab's (1969) notion of four commonplaces because they continually grow together in organic oneness and like every living organism, they overlap in function. They are delineated for the sake of inquiry and discussion. The four commonplaces (milieus, teacher, learner, and subject matter) are integral parts of curriculum. Drawing from my observations and evolving notions, I use these four commonplaces to reflect upon the findings that emerged from my inquiry and to imagine what these four commonplaces would look like in a curriculum of imagination in the making.

IMAGINATIVE MILIEUS

Westbury and Wilkof (1978) used the term "milieus" (p. 366) to describe the context of learning that included school and classroom environment, community and family, class and ethnicity, as well as values and attitudes that in the learner's environment comprise the "cultural climate" (p. 367). The current curriculum milieus that characterize a standardized curriculum are dehumanizing, abstract, and impersonal with a focus on individual achievement, singular interpretation, predefined answers, and a downward configuration of authority.

To counter static curriculum milieus, imaginative milieus are comprised of a number of elements that work together to create the environment of problem posing, personal discovery, and shared understanding that are central to a curriculum of imagination. The most vital elements in this commonplace are the milieu of hope; a milieu of shared interests; the milieu of fluid language, incubation, and dialogue across differences; and a sense of belonging and care. I will briefly examine each of these in connection with what I have already written, as I envision a curriculum in the making.

The one constant feature that I have discovered which is always present in the curriculum of imagination is the milieu of hope. This is so much more than the "eternal sunshine" of optimism. Hope is allowed to exist by choice. In an educative and personal dimension, I have learned that hope exists because we refuse static representation and given knowledge, while reaching out toward that which is not yet expressed or experienced or created.

One of the places where hope needs to be generated the most is in the teacher academy. Teacher preparation is so overloaded with methodology and mandated practices that there is little content that can lift our students out of the predefined and two-dimensional at a time when teachers are in short supply. During this past year of teaching, I found myself continually drawing from the energy, enthusiasm and hope that my preservice education students carry. In spite of all the nightmarish problems that face educators today, these young people are courageously stepping forward to guide the lives of the next generation. I continually tell them that I believe in them. They certainly need all the encouragement they can get. Instead of increased methodology, teachers in the making need to see and hear from those whose hope remained strong in the face of seemingly insurmountable obstacles. Honest and personal stories of persistence by inventors, social reformers, writers, artists, musicians, and athletes and first hand accounts of the triumph of the marginalized need to be brought continually into the vision of both teachers and students.

Another milieu is described by He, Phillion, Chan, and Xu (2008) as a "curriculum of shared interests" (p. 231). This is described in very positive and hopeful language.

> We envision this curriculum of shared interests as one where all members of the school community and policy making milieu have shared common interests. Families connect their concerns about the education of their children with those of the larger society. Schools share their interests in educating immigrant students with families and communities. Individuals have equal opportunities to "take and receive from others" and to have "free interchange of varying modes of life experience" (Dewey, 1916, p. 84), and are willing to adjust their interests to the interests of others in a larger society. In a curriculum of shared interests, teachers cultivate cultural competence to recognize contributions of ethnically and linguistically diverse students. They develop pedagogical competence to enrich the curriculum for immigrant and minority students. Students are encouraged to value their cultural and linguistic heritages, respect and accept difference, critically examine their position in society, and perceive themselves as agents of positive curriculum change. Policy makers and administrators learn the nuances of immigrant students' experience of curriculum. They value the knowledge held by teachers, students, parents, and other curriculum stakeholders and incorporate this knowledge into policy making. Families and communities share responsibility with schools and government organizations to create a school environment that is equitable, safe, and caring. This environment is the ideal milieu for developing a curriculum of shared inter-

ests that commits to a high level of achievement, not only for immigrant and minority students, but for all students. (pp. 231–232)

This passage describes an "ideal" environment for a curriculum of imagination in the making. While I am aware this is far from what actually takes place in the present, it is very important to continually cultivate our dreamscape in hope. Think what inspiring effects Dr. Martin Luther King's speeches had on the listeners, for example. Speaking and cultivating one's vision is a very powerful aspect of milieu. The language of imaginative milieu is characterized by fluidity and flexibility that resists predefinition, dead metaphor, and second hand meaning in every domain of knowledge. Instead, the prevailing language is created out of personal connection through metaphoric and experiential blending of background knowledge and present experiences.

Almost every assignment I give my preservice teachers is designed to draw out this kind of language. I encourage them to write in their own words and tell their own stories about why they are considering the field of education. These stories are then shared in a number of ways throughout the semester. I also give them much freedom to personally reflect in their school observation journals. I tell them I am more concerned about reading their personal reflections about what they encounter than just getting the what, who, where, when, questions straight. Also, I try to see to it that my students read examples of creative personal writing in a wide range of discourse. The milieu of future classrooms is being determined now, in schools of education! Teachers who write in a static way produce the same kind of students.

Another discovery I made about the commonplace of imaginative milieu is that it operates on organic time, not mass production time. Personal meaning and discovery necessitate a milieu of incubation. In this inquiry, I have learned that this is one of the greatest features of a curriculum of imagination. Through sensing gaps in the given and the status quo, personal questions are formed which have the power to implore the learner into the environment of incubation out of which the learner discovers space to creatively and critically think things through. Teachers and parents need to carefully respect the organic and personal processes that are required for each one to peck their own way out of the shell. This can take many forms. I have had many fruitful episodes of rumination while mowing the lawn or riding a bicycle as well as times that were so quiet that I was aware of my heart pumping blood all the way to my feet. Of course, this is not always possible in school, but I feel very strongly about making room for silent reading and writing and some form of incubation "time." This aspect of milieu is tragically lacking in an age of instant information, drive-though dining, and performance standards that specify exactly what content should be covered and how long that should take.

The milieu of a curriculum of imagination should inspire people more about how to inquire rather than provide answers in isolated and decontextualized ways to questions that students are not asking. When I look at all these features together as part of a commonplace of a curriculum of imagination, the milieu is one of hope and possibility that encourages growth beyond the confines of controlled meaning and orthodox interpretation.

Dialogue across differences is another key element in imaginative milieu. This should be welcomed in every role of relationships. Parents, policymakers, teachers, learners, community members, and all stakeholders in education need to be brought under the influence of the power of dialogue and the auditory aspect of curriculum as conversation.

In my foundations of education classes, I encourage the students to raise their voices to discuss controversial issues with one another. In fact, I seek to engage them in dialogue and, at times, debate on a wide range of issues without providing them with my own patent answers. I tell them that one of the greatest needs in our culture is the ability to listen. This capacity requires imagination because, by its influence, we are able to hear multiple meanings presented in polyphonic expressions that require inner attunement not just the narrow sounds of cliché or the kind of inward thoughts that cause knee-jerk reactions to what we hear. The prejudiced person is only in tune with themselves.

The last element of this commonplace that I discovered includes all the others. It is the sense of belonging and personal care that is present when all the other aspects of imaginative milieu are contributing to the environment. When every voice is welcomed and personal meaning is treasured, when organic time to incubate is honored and the art of imaginative listening is continually cultivated and difference is seen as strength, not weakness, the sense of belonging and personal care will flourish. In this milieu, critical consciousness and questioning will become more effective because learners will be less likely to be cynical in an environment of hope. By the same token, hope can become more substantial when myth and cliché, stereotype and insincerity are brought to the light by critical questioning.

IMAGINATIVE TEACHER

My understanding of the commonplace of the teacher in a curriculum of imagination has been shaped very strongly by Freire's (1971) concept of critical pedagogy. In this perspective, the teacher is also a learner. In the milieu of dialogue, the teacher and the learner discover together. Knowledge is enhanced in both directions and is always new because no two interlocutors are ever the same in outlook or personal history.

Looking back on these experiences through the lens of this present inquiry, I have come to understand the teacher as an improvisational artist (Bateson, 1990) who has the flexibility to work spontaneously and yet deliberately toward the opening of creative vision and expression in learners. This notion reminds me of something that my wife Elizabeth's art teacher told her when she began oil painting classes, "I can't teach you to paint, but I can teach you to see" (personal communication, 2003). That statement says so much about the teacher as an improvisational artist. In this role, the teacher helps to give birth to personalized meaning and self-expression and, at the same time, challenges the learner to greater quality through appropriate criticism. Individual care and concern and an awareness of the process of organic time in the learner is of primary concern. By this, I am not referring to generalized categories of life span developmental psychology. This knowledge is more intuitive than information derived from a collection of pathologies that are applied in an objective way. What I have come to understand instead is that a curriculum of imagination is a relationship between the teacher and the learner wherein both teacher and learner exercise reflective, critical, and generative imagination to discover, express, and evaluate desired learning.

The conjoining of creative and critical aspects brings me to another dimension of the teacher in a curriculum of imagination that should be included. This is the notion of the teacher as a connoisseur (Eisner, 1998). This role is important "in any realm in which the character, import, or value of objects, situations, and performances is distributed and variable, including educational practice" (p. 63). The critic is the public side of the same role. "Connoisseurs simply need to appreciate what they encounter. Critics, however, must render these qualities vivid, by the artful use of critical disclosure" (Eisner, 1985, pp. 92–93). By presenting connoisseurship and criticism as two aspects of the same concept, Eisner supports a creative/critical aspect of imagination that helps to recognize and distinguish the finely nuanced aspects in every domain of inquiry. The critical aspect is the public expression of connoisseurship that involves the communication of detailed distinctions in such a way that they are recognized and understood by others.

In a curriculum of imagination in the making, the teacher is a learner, improvisational artist, and a model of what is taught. As a learner, he or she discovers meaning in a shared ontology. Education is dialogical, and all participants have something added to their understanding. As an improvisational artist, the teacher helps create personalized meaning and self-expression in the learner through personal concern and care along with an intuitive sense of timing and understanding of learner potential. This requires both the creative and critical aspects of imagination in every encounter with the student. You cannot give what you do not have yourself. A teacher of curriculum of imagination must be a living model by refusing static meaning and dead metaphors and by actively engaging in a passionate pursuit of understanding, while at the same time being willing to admit that he or she is still learning. This is what this inquiry has taught me about the commonplace of the teacher.

IMAGINATIVE SUBJECT MATTER

I first discovered the nature of the commonplace of subject matter in a curriculum of imagination by contrasting it with standardized and static knowledge. I saw, for example, the lack of engagement that is present when the subject matter is presented in isolated and decontextualized units as a product of the canon of "official knowledge" (Apple, 1993). This is often enforced on passive recipients that have learned to play the game in order to get a good grade or, by the same token, to those who despair because their strengths are not measured by tests of standardized subject matter. This condition has been further exacerbated by accountability requirements from both federal and state legislation in the form of benchmarks. This curriculum is mostly prescriptive and confining rather than descriptive and narrative of lived experience.

Also, the subject matter of a standardized curriculum is comprised of objective facts and skills that are often detached from real life contexts by rote and mechanistic imitation. Often this is accomplished through means of verbal learning alone. I love how Lisa Delpit (1995) described the way this approach might be used to teach African Americans to dance. This would involve a workbook with "200 hundred mastery units" (p. 39) for each dance, and as a result, at the end of the year, there would be many African American students in remedial dance classes. No! We learn to dance by dancing.

In a curriculum of imagination in the making, the commonplace of the subject matter is boundless and multidimensional, yet holistic and personal. It is not contained in any one discipline rather it shuns fragmentation. It welcomes multiple meanings and newly created metaphoric connections. The only limitations on its scope are the present circumscribed horizons of the imaginer. The subject matter can be anything from the microcosm or subatomic dimension to the macrocosm so many light years away that even the most powerful telescope on earth cannot detect its presence because any light that may be present is so distant that it is out of the range of measurement.

There are also an infinite number of ways that the subject matter can be represented in a curriculum of imagination even when students are given the same assignments. I have found that my preservice education students are remarkably creative when they are encouraged to release their imaginations on required writing tasks. Recently, one of my students created a book review in the form of a hanging mobile. It was creative and covered all the requirements. Another student wrote and performed a song as a review of Kozol's (1991) book, *Savage Inequalities*. Last year, some of my reading education students created their own children's books that connected reading theory and their personal accounts of literacy experiences.

I have also discovered that in a curriculum of imagination, the dichotomy between objective and subjective understanding disappears. The subject matter is comprised of the metaphoric blending of the old with the new, lived experience with the inexperienced, and the emotions along with mental faculties. It is through these connections that subject matter becomes personal as well as social. This takes place through the language of metaphor, an important component of the commonplace of subject matter in a curriculum of imagination. I have learned that it is almost impossible to exercise imagination about any subject matter without metaphor. This was easy for me to understand in grasping personal meaning because metaphor is simply seeing one new concept through one that is already part of personal schema.

One completely new part of this for me was the use of metaphor when the subject matter is the "other." How thrilled I was to read Ozick (1991) on this matter! She says, "Metaphor is the reciprocal agent, the universalizing force: it makes possible the power to envision the stranger's heart" (p. 279). Through metaphor, we are able to see our lives in the lives of others. This has very important social and political implications for reaching out across barriers in so much more than a superficial, patronizing way. Metaphor has the power to create empathy by revealing human connections that transcend race, class, gender, and ethnicity.

I have also learned that subject matter of this kind is holistically explored across multiple content areas. For example, my son, William, wrote a paper for a math class about the use of algebraic computation in the computer programming language that is needed to create video games. He also is learning music composition through the sound track of video games. In the subject matter of a curriculum of imagination, the whole universe and all that is in it can be a text.

IMAGINATIVE LEARNER

This inquiry into a curriculum of imagination grew out of my desire to understand who I am as a learner in a way that would help me understand all learners. As I recall my own personal history of discovery, I recognize points in my life when imagination was conspicuous by its absence as well as its presence. The obstacles to learning in my early personal history were largely the result of a standardized system that was running at full strength during my years in school. When imagination has been present in my life, I recognize it as what I would call a spirit of exploration that embraces the unknown and imagines against the grain. When faced with contradiction and obstacles of every kind, the imaginative learner refuses stasis and the line of least resistance and challenges orthodox thinking. It is very clear to me now that I am at my best as a learner and a teacher when this spirit of exploration is cultivated. Here is a closer look at imaginative learners in the making.

The learner is first an inquirer, seeking personal understanding out of his or her own desires, interests, aptitudes, and questions. This is likely to bring the learner into an internship with given forms of knowledge and experiences with others, either directly or indirectly. Through sensing gaps in the predefined body of knowledge and questioning the status quo in every given domain, the learner enters into the dimension of generative imagination as a creator. This can be anything from personal voice expressed in poetry, to an act of resistance (i.e., Rosa Parks), to the invention of the airplane. The last example bears further mentioning at this point.

One of my favorite books as a child was the biography of the Wright Brothers written by Quentin Reynolds (1950). It is easy to recognize the role that passionate inquiry played in their identity as learners. Out of their own desire to know, they diligently read and applied all the previous body of knowledge about flight and all else that could be known about the principles of aerodynamics. I now understand this as a curriculum of reflective imagination in the making. Here, the two brothers are marked as interns to the given body of knowledge and to each other as they experimented with flight. These experiences brought them to the dimension of learners as creators through many painful episodes of imagining against the social, scientific and even political grain in their day. Many people thought that their experiments were on the lunatic fringe, including the federal government, but as they continued to imagine against the grain, they eventually changed the culture of the entire world!

CURRICULUM OF IMAGINATION IN THE MAKING

Through these four commonplaces, I am able to envision an imaginative curriculum that is both theoretical and practical. At the same time, I acknowledge that a curriculum of imagination can never be turned into a method. It cannot be mass produced with singular specifications but is constantly created through engaging and participatory discovery. There are aspects that are learned with others, of course, but as every human is unique, life itself is never static in its creative dynamic. No two trees are exactly alike, but when they stop growing, they are dead. Every living thing is dependent on others within the same and other species in order to perpetuate life. Even a stalk of corn must interact with others in order to produce nutrition; otherwise, it is just a weed. Imagination expresses these features of the power of life in vibrant and creative milieus, teachers, learners, and subject matter. The sphere of life is never static; through forces of self-preservation it is constantly changing and being changed by the environment of social and political and natural movement Education is an important aspect of the sphere of life in which the power of biological, sociological, and cultural sustainability is either directly or indirectly passed on to succeeding generations. Education needs to continually renew itself through continual creative reflection and action, and a curriculum of imagination is always in the making.

As I reflect on the content of this inquiry, I recognize an element that unites the four commonplaces in holistic oneness. It is the principle of life itself, active and dynamically present within each commonplace that creates a condition out of which personal meaning is continually created *from within* the participants. This notion reminds me of the living connections between true democracy and a curriculum in *the making*. They both involve the whole being through imaginative connections, in naming and transforming from within. In this perspective, a curriculum of imagination and democracy in the making are fashioned from the same life dynamic.

I view democracy in the making as a metaphor for a curriculum of imagination in the making. For example, the problem with an external adaptation of "democracy" is that it results in what Freire (1971) called adaptation. In countries like Iraq, their recent history is one of adaptation. People live with what they will tolerate. If the people of Iraq chose to tolerate an unjust and inhumane dictatorship for so long, what external forms of power are they merely passively accepting now? Change must come from within, but it cannot stop with theory. A curriculum of imagination begins within but requires corresponding outward action in order to bring change. I find a powerful catalyst to this kind of action in this stunning excerpt from Ayers (2006) essay, "Trudge Toward Freedom."

> If a fairer, more sane and just social order is both desirable and possible, if some of us can join one another to imagine and build a participatory movement for justice, a public space for the enactment of democratic dreams, our field opens slightly. There would still be much to be done, for nothing would be entirely settled. We would still need to find ways to stir ourselves and our students from passivity, cynicism, and despair, to reach beyond the superficial barriers that wall us off from one another, to resist the flattening social evils like institutionalized racism, to shake off the anesthetizing impact of the authoritative, official voices that dominate so much of our space, releasing our imaginations and act on behalf of what the known demands, linking our conduct firmly to our consciousness. (p. 96)

In the beginning of the history of the United States, transformation came from an awakened citizenry that named their walls and put their own lives on the line to move beyond the control of the political and religious empire of Colonialism. At present, special interest groups silence the voices of true democratic conversation. This condition is endemic in our schools because all too often, they are dominated by business practices that close the door on imaginative and democratic milieus. Neither education nor democracy is a product that can be governed by the rules of commerce. Democracy and schools are made up of people with culturally specific needs and experiences that must be newly addressed in each generation. As Dewey (1916) said, "Democracy must be born anew in every generation, and education is its midwife" (p. 139). There can be no finalized and completed form of democracy or a curriculum of imagination. This is why sensing gaps, raising questions, challenging the given and the static are such important concepts. In the environment of ongoing inquiry, constant innovation and critical appraisal, there is life, and where there is life, there is a curriculum of imagination in the making, connecting the known with the newly discovered until the "old" is made new again through very personal connections. I am reminded of T. S. Eliot's (1943) lines from *Four Quartets*.

> *We shall not cease from exploration*
> *and the end of all our exploring*
> *will be to arrive where we started and know the place for the first time.* (p. 59)

REFERENCES

Apple, M. (1993). *Official knowledge: Democratic education in a conservative age.* New York: Rutledge.

Ayers, W. (2006). Trudging toward freedom. In G. J. Ladson-Billings & W. Tate (Eds.), *Education research in the public interest: Social justice, action, and policy* (pp. 81–97). New York: Teachers College Press.

Bateson, M. C. (1990). *Composing a life*. New York: Plume.

Delpit, L. (1995). I just want to be myself: Discovering what students bring to school "in their blood." In W. Ayers (Ed.), *To become a teacher: Making a difference in children's lives*. New York: Teachers College Press.

Denzin, N., & Lincoln, Y. (2003). *The landscape of qualitative research*. Thousand Oaks, CA: SAGE.

Dewey, J. (1916). *Democracy and education*. New York: Free Press.

Dewey, J. (1934). *Art as experience*. New York: Perigee Books.

Eisner, E. W. (1985). *The art of educational evaluation: a personal view*. London: Falmer.

Eisner, E. W. (1998). *The enlightened eye: Qualitative inquiry and the enhancement of educational practice*. Upper Saddle River, NJ: Merrill.

Eliot, T. S. (1943). *Four quartets*. New York: Harcourt Brace.

Freire, P. (1971). *Pedagogy of the oppressed*. New York: Seabury.

Greene, M. (1995). *Releasing the imagination*. San Francisco: Jossey-Bass.

He, M. F., Phillion, J., Chan, E., & Xu, S. J. (2008). Immigrant students' experience of curriculum. In F. M. Connelly, M. F. He, & J. Phillion (Eds.), *Handbook of curriculum and instruction* (pp. 219–239). Thousand Oaks, CA: SAGE.

Kozol, J. (1991). *Savage inequalities*. New York: Crown Publishers.

Lovin' Spoonful. (1965). Night owl blues. On *Do you believe in magic* [CD]. New York: Kama Sutra Records.

Mead, M., & Baldwin, J. (1971). *A rap on race*. Philadelphia: Lippencott.

Moffett, J. (1968). *Teaching the universe of discourse*. Boston: Houghton Mifflin.

Ozick, C. (1991). *Metaphor and memory*. New York: Knopf.

Plato. (380 B.C.). *Meno*. Retrieved June 1, 2006, from http://classics.mit.edu/Plato/meno.html

Reynolds, Q. (1950). *The Wright brothers: Pioneers of American aviation*. New York: Random House.

Richardson, L. (2003). Writing: A method of inquiry. In N. Denzin & Y. Lincoln, (Eds.), *Collecting and interpreting qualitative materials* (2nd ed., pp. 499–454). Thousand Oaks, CA: SAGE.

Shaull, R. (2003). *Foreward*. In P. Freire (Ed.), *Pegagogy of the oppressed*. (pp. 28–34). New York: Continuum.

Schwab, J. (1969). The practical: A language for curriculum. *School Review, 78,* 1–23.

Westbury, I., & Wilkof, N. J. (Eds.). (1978). *Science, curriculum, and liberal education: selected essays: Joseph J. Schwab*. Chicago: University of Chicago Press.

CHAPTER 8

A QUIET AWAKENING

Spinning Yarns From Granny's Table in the New Rural South

Angela Haynes

This is an inquiry into generational stories from my Granny's table. It is an exploration of my lived experience as a first generation doctoral student who negates the truths of a rural Southern upbringing steeped in issues of race, class and gender. Building upon the work of Falk (2004), Freire (2002), He (2003), He and Phillion (2008), Weis (2006) and Weis and Fine (1998, 2003), I explored the arenas of place, class, and race, particularly the intermingling of multiple realities and contested in-between space and Southern female identities.

Family members who raised and nurtured me are the main characters in the stories. Using oral history, I documented the place and people that live as a single family entity and collected stories and memories to create a representation of an identity meshed within a place and time. Oral history allowed me to capture the stories in order to better understand the complex lives that allow subjugation of and by these people who cling to family, land, and their way of life. Each story became my own. I fictionalized

Personal~Passionate~Participatory Inquiry Into Social Justice in Education, pp. 127–143
Copyright © 2008 by Information Age Publishing

the accounts by telling the story through one primary lens. The character lived the events that I had experienced and witnessed in my life and the lives of my family as stories that I had experienced vicariously through the oral tradition of family stories became text. I seek to explore possibilities for a new order through the flow of these words.

Much of the current literature on the South deals solely with race, sex, or class. Few texts explore life in the South from the vantage point of a lower-class, White female caught between reality of the place and the promise of education. Yarns spun from my Granny's table revealed a contested way of life stifled in an ever-changing new rural South. Those stories raise questions about Southern legacy and heritage, one of the most complex, controversial, and significant issues lived by teachers, administrators, parents, and students in the South. Education becomes the key to doors long locked, allowing my personal awakening. Many people in the rural communities need to awake from their slumber and demand change. Possibilities for the future—my children, their children, a lost generation—destined to be locked in the stilted mind-set of this place need to be realized.

TRACING THE ROOTS—
FINDING THE STARTING POINT FOR THE UNRAVELING

My grandmother's house, a whitewashed square fashioned from cement blocks, centers my world. Our farmland surrounds the domicile allowing my granny a bird's eye view of the comings and goings of the members of her flock. The fields have long lay bare; farming fell by the wayside as bankruptcies sucked the will out of the men who had for so long worked the ground for their meager subsistence. The land is all that is left. Nestled within these fallow fields are foot-trails winding through wooded acres where deer and children roam. Nowhere in this world have I ever felt as free as I did when I was a child trekking throughout this mundane wildness. Protected from the dangers of the outside world by the enveloping sanctuary of family, my siblings, cousins, and I were left free to roam the woods and fields as we pleased. The biggest threat we ever happened upon was the occasional water moccasin or rattlesnake. We learned to navigate these dangers from earliest childhood; it was and often still is the dangers of the civilized outside that perplexes and confounds our human sensibilities. Nowhere in the world nurtured and trapped me as steadily as the place that I love as home.

Family traditions run long and uncontested in my rural community, and the tradition of the quiet, subservient female rests at the crux of the family tree. Looming large in the foreground resides my grandmother's kitchen table—a symbol of family togetherness and female subservience. While the men sit in the living room, the women prepare the meal and watch the children—a dance as old as my granny herself. My steps in this choreography have evolved over the years. As a child, the lessons conveyed subversively were inherently more than the "Eat everything on your plate" admonishments. All grown up, I sit at the table that centers my universe; my hands unconsciously tap out a rhythm as syncopated as the daily beat of our lives. The unraveling of my reality, as complex as the staccato beat bursting forth from unconscious fingers, started with a desire ingrained in the community—I wanted to make more money. Graduate school loomed as the means to an end; however, each new class in the curriculum studies program developed ideas that caused a stutter-step in the day-to-day cadence of my life. The rhythm no longer contributed harmoniously to the steady beat of family life; instead its fragmented notes provided discordant cacophony to the otherwise melodic rhythm of life in this backwoods community. I exist in-between the slow waltz-like pulse of my childhood memories and home-life and the frenetic samba-esque tempo that education infused into my consciousness. As important as money had always been to me, there entered an unceasing emptiness within me that I continuously sought to fill. I finally begin to recognize a sense of self that made the superficial view of success fall by the wayside.

The concordant disharmony that became my world developed into my inquiry. One night, I would sit in a college class and discuss Falk's (2004) recognition of the limiting aspects of place, the next night I would watch my mother fix my father's plate and carry it to him in his recliner because that is what wives do where we live. On another day I might sway in the old wicker porch swing reading Freire's (2002) call for *conscientization* while my daughters learn subjugation and fear-mongering at the knees of their grandmother's and great-grandmother's effortless religious dia-tribes and ingrained actions. Behaviors that peppered my lived experi-ence from my earliest memories began to unravel as the literature I experienced in my academic life opened my eyes to ingrained prejudices and oppression.

At first, flashes of clarity would occur in rapid bursts of irritation, brief rays of light streaking through the clouds of subversion that obscured my vision. So many occurrences seemed to start at family gatherings, usually centered around my paternal grandmother's kitchen table where we gath-ered once a week for lunch on Saturday. Little actions or comments at these meals made me stop and take note of things I had always taken for granted, like the incessant griping of family members about the sorry state of the world outside of the community boundaries—where morals and values were falling into rapid disrepair. I entered into a mental alter-cation with each comment: Do I question why they need to denigrate every person and thing that differs from them—socially, racially, economically? Why does one half of every relationship have to kow-tow to the other to keep harmonious relations? It is hard to vocalize dissent in conversation with those people who raised you to be seen and not heard. When I was younger, I knew without any doubt that my comments were to be curtailed in the midst of adult conversation. Lying beneath the skin resides the dark-eyed waif who feared the repercussions of treading into adult conversation. Flashes of irritation morph to episodes of brooding with each semester that illuminate what McLaren (2005) states, "[t]o be colorless is to be white, and white—in particular, white males—currently function as the colorless, normative standpoints of humanity" (p. 99). In addition, Greene (2001) states:

> Convention, taken-for-grantedness, routines: all these encase the perceiver. The informed awareness I have been speaking of involved a breaking through, a free play. Dewey was not only asking for a rejection of the routine and the automatic; he was asking that the same attention be paid to the arts as to reading and writing and arithmetic ... he was objecting to the traditional dualistic separations—between feeling and perception, imagination and thought. (pp. 58–59)

Instead of retreating into silence, I venture comments and critiques of behaviors long ingrained, but I found myself continuously at odds with those who raised me, nurtured me, created me.

This feeling of being out-of-place and completely antagonized at home mirrored a similar feeling of unease that occurred when I went to the same college classes that had started the eye-opening process. In those quiet and hallowed halls I ventured only hesitantly, certain that at any moment someone would recognize me for the intellectual imposter that truly did not belong to the setting. Insecurity became my modus operandi. Reflecting upon my childhood leads me to believe that there was no possibility I could have ended up any other way than insecure. As an adult, my insecurity flavors every decision I make or fail to make. As McLaren (2005) notes, "[a] class involves, therefore, the alienated quality of the social life of individuals who function in a certain way within the system. The salient features of class—alienated social relation, place/function, and group—are all mutually dependent" (p. 127). I functioned precisely as I had been programmed to function as a lower-class female in the rural South. For the majority of my education, I occupied a space in college classrooms where I failed to contribute to conversation because of an innate fear of appearing out of place. To find education through texts and dialogue with classroom teachers allowed me to understand various components that shaped my world and helped me to begin the research process as I grappled with questions posited by Provenzo (2005),

Why have certain groups historically had privileges over others? How has this worked out in terms of race, gender, and ethnicity? How has this contributed to structural inequality in our culture? What problems are evident in our culture as a result of inequality? How can inequality best be addressed? (p. 63)

I struggled with these questions and feelings of not belonging, and from this struggle flowed my motivation.

MY MOTIVATION

Place has been a recurring theme in many of the texts I have read and stories I have heard and lived. While these sources often flirted tangentially with the ideas of being poor, White, and rural Southern, most did so only fleeting while focusing on either race or place or socioeconomic class or a melding of the three that did not represent the situation that has been my experience and the experience of my family and neighbors for decades. There is a mind-set, a way of believing and living that is created by the location, the level of wealth (or lack of), and the identity of race (being poor and White and in this area) that creates an extremely limited concept of reality—a reality I believe even more limited for females in this world. This actuality, narrow and constricting, propels girls into early marriage (at age 16, 17, 18) for fear of becoming an old maid (being unmarried at age 21, 22, 23); this reality (thanks to a strong, patriarchal fundamentalist religion) promotes a male-dominated household that entraps females into lives of subservience (to their husbands and their children) that they never question; this reality limits, even renders unimaginable, ambitions of a life in any other form. The entrapment is subtle, yet stratifying, and usually of one's own design, leaving one unaware of the oppression even as it suffocates you.

For generations, my family has lived within a 10-mile area that has colored and molded our behavior, our beliefs, our thoughts, our identities, and our futures. This area and our way of life effectively trapped us without our noticing the snares that effectively gripped us, preventing our expansion. Our minds, entrenched in a reality that stifled variation, were kept as narrow and rigid as predecessors before us; meanwhile, we remained oblivious. Entrenched in our poverty as well as our place, we perpetuated a mindset that was rapidly being outpaced in other areas of the country. Anti-intellectualism and sexism were inherent parts of this mindset. Education—the only panacea—was bitter medicine. Ironically, the beliefs we held so dear kept us from evolving—now, I understand that it is intentionally so. Statistically, I should not have experienced graduate studies or earned any advanced degrees, learning ideas that negate the truths that have been instilled in my life since birth. There were countless times when I thought, "I don't belong here."

Paradoxically, I have felt this idea in my own community and in the learning community; I am a stranger with no world. As described in Giroux's (1992) *Border-Crossings* and He's (2003) *River Forever Flowing*, I find myself at odds in the familiar situations that I have experienced all of my life and in the world of academe where I have sought refuge. I have witnessed the dismantling of ideas that I held to be as necessary to life as the oxygen that infuses my lungs. I observe the intermingling of three generations—my grandmother's, my mother's, and my own. The females of each generation exhibit certain levels of submissive behavior in regards to their husbands and children. There is also a general trend towards a changing society, one that mirrors the females in Weis' (2004) *Class Reunion*. While these females' roles in society are gradually changing as they become key players in the work world, their roles in our community and in their homes remain the same. The passage of time is barely noticeable once you leave the paved road and enter the dirt road community that we call home.

There is a darkness that seeps into the soul of the place. The beauty of our woods and our world marred with the poisonous traits of bigotry and sexism. My pretty little girls, dark curls and laughing eyes, play out the roles of the submissive. My Maggie, precocious at age 4, bats her eyes and believes that girls should be petite and perfect. At age 8, Grace's quiet intuition internalizes grandmothers who serve. Their brother, fair-haired and determined, dominates; he is the boy, and he will be heard. These children are pitied by their relatives. They have a mother who refuses to take them to church and instill in them proper values. Family members try to intervene; it's not the children's fault. I only wish to avoid the fearmongering that marred my own religious experiences, but every point I make is met with a counterpoint. Leaving is never an option. We are family. So, I continue, and I research, and I learn, and I teach and un-teach my own.

PARTICIPATORY RESEARCH PROCESS

My granny's table is the central axis of my world. One Sunday, while we were eating breakfast with her, my uncle asked me why I was still in school. His recent divorce had landed him back at home with his mother, my granny. My father's younger brother—he had always been something of a rounder—continuously in trouble from gambling. When Granny warned me about having kids, I always felt like it was him that hurt her heart more than anyone. It was hard for me to try to explain to him why I felt the need to continue my education. Certainly, the opportunity for more money was a strong motivator, but there was so much more to it than just the financial reward. As I tried to explain my love of learning to him, he quickly lost interest. His closing comments on the situation were that I needed to be more like his long-term girlfriend—Candie. The two of them had been seeing one another on the sly for over 10 years. His divorce was only several weeks old at this point. Candie was a convenience store clerk who had recently quit her job so that she could ride with him in his big truck hauling logs. I had to ask; I couldn't resist, "Why should I be more like her?"

I had no idea where this conversation would go. Why would I, a college graduate working on an EdD while maintaining a household and a full-time job as a teacher want to be more like a former convenience store clerk who never completed high school? His answer was steeped in certainty.

> Well, she loves a man like he ought to be loved. She puts me first, even when I was with Dana. She quit her job to spend time with me. She doesn't question me, and when I want to do something, I just do it. No questions asked. That's how a woman ought to love a man.

Somewhere along the way, we (women, me, my mom, my granny, etc.) are supposed to lose ourselves. Who am I, if not someone's wife or mother? That's why I fell short of Candie's perfection, at least to my uncle. His point of view prevails. That is why my parents feel sorry for me because I have to work instead of getting to stay at home with my kids like my sister does. That I choose to work does not really occur to them. When I leave for a conference or other work related trip, they note the neglect that I heap on my family. I have my own guilt issues to work through.

What can one person do? What can my story contribute that might be worth hearing? What is it about being female, poor, and Southern that demands an audience? These questions play around the corners of my mind as I grapple with anecdotes and incidents that permeate my experience. Assuredly, there are fantastic scripts noting the particularity of being Southern. Southern poverty frames many narratives from Faulkner (1932/ 1959) to Morrison (1987). Certainly, when one reads of the South there are themes that stand out. A Southern identity is built around nuances such as Southern gentility laced with the iron-casings of a fundamental religion. The South as place is pivotal, but yet it is only one component of my narrative. Admittedly, "class matters" (hooks, 2000), but there are already stories guided by the delineation of class, so why go there? What about gender? Entire portions of libraries are filled with verse about the role of male/female interplay in modern society, so how important can one more story be? As valid as the various existing stories are, they can not speak for me.

Throughout my reading adventures in graduate school, I realized that MY place, MY class, MY gender intertwined in a unique weave that created a tapestry unlike any other. Why my story and the stories of my family? Because of all the things I have learned from the graduate school experience, the one that affects me the most is the knowledge that each person has a story worth telling. Each person is shaped and molded by her or his environment in a manner so subtle, yet so efficient, that the subsequent generation is often a mirror image of the one before. This pattern seamlessly transcends from one generation to the next. Only a major incident can provide the key to unlocking new possibilities. My travels through the Curriculum Studies program opened doors that were not only previously closed, but hidden. Through the writings of Pinar (1994, 2004), Greene (1995), hooks (2000), Freire (2002) and many other curriculum scholars, I realized that education and the educational system as I had experienced it limited my perception of the world. This narrowing of reality was perpetrated in conjunction with the desires of society-at-large. Uncovering the "hidden curriculum" (Jackson as cited in Pinar, Reynolds, Slattery, & Taubman, 1996) generated an epiphany in my educational career; the result was the upending of my beliefs and truths in search for a new manner of existing in my world.

The inquiry process became the bridge that helped me navigate between two distinctly separate worlds. As I listened to the stories and chronicled events from the lives of my loved ones, I began to see patterns emerge that echoed themes in society. I lived the stories, the injustices—no longer were these ideas only theoretical words marching across paper. There were real faces and emotions to color every injustice. If nothing else, the realization of problems such as racism, sexism, and classism struck home after narratives provided faces for the problems.

Every family gathering became fodder for the next chronicle of our lives. Family members became wary when my mother warned them that they were the subjects of scrutiny, but the self-certainty that their personal beliefs and life-style constitute the only "correct" way of life left them assured that I would find nothing negative to report. I have never tried to influence the reader in terms of seeing anyone's actions in a negative or positive light; I simply want the reader to see the unflagging conviction with which lives are lived, prejudices expounded, hate perpetuated. The subjects in my inquiry are real to me, precious to me, and I do not set out to make anyone seem like a monster. There are horrific stories to tell, but each word is wrought with love for the subject and characters. I want to ensure that everyone could find positive aspects in every character, no matter how steeped in societal evils he or she might be. My love for my family and their inherent and unflagging love for me and each other had to show through my writing. Each word appears on the page after I feel assured that it captures the entire essence of our lives—not just the good or just the bad.

I exist under the banner of an uneasy truce between the way things are and the way I envision that they could (or should) be. Many days I wish that I remained couched in the comfort of ignorance as I experience an acute awareness of the two distinct worlds in which I operate and my inability to reconcile myself to the inadequacies of each world. I search through the myriad of my memories to determine how I arrived at this point in an effort to justify the path I forge away from my background. From family experience to educational experience, every aspect of my upbringing should have prohibited me from finding these between-spaces that allow for "lines of flight" (Reynolds & Webber, 2004). In revisiting my educational experience, I become intensely discomfited. Through this exploration, I recognize the funneling process that I experienced as my education, closely akin to what Darling-Hammond (2006) describes as occurring in urban, low-income schools, "many low-income and minority students receive a steady diet of low-level material coupled with unstimulating, rote-oriented teaching" (p. 223). This recognition leads me to present my story as indisputable evidence of its existence because one can not fight what one does not recognize or understand to be inherently wrong. To present my story as a "counternarrative" (Peters & Lankshear, 1996, p. 2) eases my guilt about existing in worlds that do not respect/accept/recognize me. I owe my dichotomous existence in multiple realities, the every-wary maneuvering between them, and a new-found thirst for social justice to graduate studies that made me stop and think about current practices in education, religion, and politics. I learned to ask myself questions about the status quo or the current scheme of things, like why standardized testing is the one thing that could detect a student's achievement.

The "participatory" part of the inquiry—telling the harsh truths about the South—pained me, yet the repercussions are cathartic. With each story, my understanding of my place and people groaned against my new understanding of the world. With each theme uncovered—issues of racism, classism, sexism—the stories of my family and my life lead me back to the texts that liberated me. Each word that captured the essence of my indoctrination liberated me to write the next one. For each story that I included, I turned my back on three of equal importance. To staunch the flow of blood through letters, I had to find the right balance of angst and ecstasy. The life I know is steeped in trial, but tempered with love; to capture this dichotomous truth my stories had to speak for me. Because I live this world of which I write, I wrote many of the stories from a personal point of view even though the events may not have actually happened to me. I want to be able to go home again; to air dirty laundry reeks of treason to the family. I can only hope that allowing the stories of our lives to become the story of my life provides each individual charged in the matter the understanding of my pride in them and love for them. My inquiry allowed me the opportunity to merge reality with theory. I found support from the likes of Freire (2002), He (2003), and Ayers (2004) to counterbalance the lived experience depicted in my narratives.

SEEKING SOCIAL JUSTICE—SOCIETAL IMPACTS OF THE STUDY

This exploration could not occur at a more opportune moment situated in the current turmoil that is the American educational system. Miller (2005) recognizes the current strain on a system "pressured to present predetermined, sequential, skills-oriented and measurable versions of 'English' to … students" (p. 46). How accurately her observations translate not only to English classes but also across a prepackaged, static curriculum. Education has been reduced to coaching students to mindlessly regurgitate random facts and information. Higher order thinking skills are left by the wayside as teachers worry about test scores. "Teachers are reduced to technicians, 'managing' student productivity. The school is no longer a school, but a business" (Pinar, 2004, p. 27). Ten years in a rural high school classroom helped me envision how the lived experience of many of my students mirrored my own upbringing. The school I worked in, a carbon-copy of the one that I attended as a student, upheld many of the traditions taught by my family as die-hard truths. Again, I recognized that school for me and these students that came to my classroom every day existed only as a means to an end; education fell by the wayside in the quest for marketability. Counts (as cited in Kliebard, 2004, p. 158) surmised that

> the feverish and uncritical fashioning of tests in terms of the existing curriculum and in the name of efficiency has undoubtedly served to fasten upon the schools an archaic program of instruction and a false theory of the nature of learning.

How well I recognize the strident belief that time-tested worksheets and rote memorization generated educated individuals.

It took my personal awakening during my own educational experience to help me envision the disservice currently perpetrated on America's youth in the name of education. I was no longer content to just occupy time and space, but for me as a teacher to push the idea of time, space and reality. As Greene (1995) states,

> [w]e who are teachers would have to accommodate ourselves to lives as clerks or functionaries if we did not have in mind a quest for a better state of things for those we teach and for the world we all share. (p. 1)

The precepts of social justice and critical theory enabled me to verbalize the intrinsic discomfort that had tweaked my conscience during skill-and-drill moments in the classroom and find a language for the critique of the current injustice perpetrated by the modern educational system. Through studying the nature of female entrenchment in the rural South, I can offer my Deleuzean "AND" (as cited in Reynolds & Webber, 2004, p. 3) that allows me to navigate between the parallel worlds of academia and my home community that can not be reconciled one with the other. Like Anzaldua's (2004) "dual identity" (p. 497), I have to find an in-between space that allows me to find peace in both worlds. When I enter a classroom as teacher or student, I need to be able to find merit in the simplistic comforts that I call home—watching children bronzed by the sun running on a riverbank in search of a new adventure, perching on a tailgate with a beer in one hand and a fishing pole in the other, or watching bull-riding and cheering for the bulls. I need to be able to maintain the value of the simplistic pleasures that I adore because I grew up the child of have-not and wife instead of the affluents.

Conversely, I must overcome the desire to fade behind a silent façade to keep the peace on the home front. For many males in my South, there is a simple hierarchy that exists. The man is the head of the household answerable to no power but themselves. My South does not encompass all of the males in the South, in Georgia, or even in the county in which I live, but my South is a mind-set that is not particular to just one area and no where else. There are traces of the single-minded domination that marked my childhood throughout realms of society. Daly (2004) articulates the problem, "[i]f God in 'his' heaven is a father ruling 'his' people, then it is in the 'nature' of things and according to divine plan and the order of the universe that society be male-dominated" (p. 544). Patriarchal religion provides the foundation for the perceived image of the perfect family. From this understanding, I watch as my mother subjugates herself because God decreed men to be the head of the family. The skewed identity I have found for myself rails against the woman she is yet respects her for all she has done. There is strength in a woman that works eight hour days, comes home and assumes her role as caregiver to children and husband, yet still defers to the decrees meted out from the husband in his rocker/throne.

The importance of one story, one situation, one particular situation is, as Pitt (2001) states, when one, "grapples with what it means to read and write autobiographically from a place marked by traumatic experience—in this case, the traumatic experience of being a woman living in a patriarchal culture" (p. 91). Pinar (1994) says, "I take myself and my existential experience as a data source" (p. 20). I am marked by what I experienced as a child. I share those stories with my mother who remembers the same episode, but her story is completely different from mine. I can still remember when I was a little girl not yet in school; my mother stayed at home with me and my two siblings—both in diapers. My father worked swing shift during the week. Saturday mornings were my favorite time. I would wake up to and climb in bed with my mom. Dad would come in with a candy bar that he had purchased from the store, and he and I would watch cartoons while my mom cleaned the house and took care of the babies. These lazy mornings are marked in my memory as perfection. Later conversations with my mother revealed glaring distortions in the story that resulted from our differing vantage points. While I remember these mornings as lazy Saturdays in which I basked in my father's love, my mom remembers hectic mornings when she would juggle household chores, children, and an entirely indifferent husband who would watch TV or sleep, rousing only enough to quiet us down if we became too noticeable. For my father, these memories slant again, as he remembers working hard to support his family and returning to a house where he was nagged until he found somewhere else to go. In catching these multiple truths, one realizes the subjectivity and frailty of reality.

Through my inquiry, I found my voice and the desire to question my world. Using my work as an educator, I am able to bring the ability to question to students who are much too often taught to be silent vessels filled with aging rhetoric. By starting the dialogue, my contribution continues with each new question that springs to the mind of my students. Encouraging the seed of thought becomes motivation and reward.

FINDING MY PLACE IN THE WORLD

As pivotal as my experience with gender is to my story, it could not have occurred as it did if it were not for the place and time it occurred. The South is an entity full of beliefs—both valid and backward—that are native to its borders as inherently as is grits and sweet tea. In discussing a Southern-situated curriculum, Pinar (2004) notes,

> Such a curriculum not only represents a place, it also becomes place, a curricular embodiment and contradiction of peculiarly southern experience,

taught in ways appropriate to the reconstruction of that experience, toward the end of demystifying southern history and culture. (p. 94)

Place, especially thinking of the South as place, goes beyond recounting anecdotal material in an effort to delve into the unconscious to look past the actions and uncover where the seeds of motivation were planted. Robison (1997) describes the importance of regional writing explaining,

> writing "our side" is a hegemonic project that can tell us a great deal about how cultural difference was perceived ... local color literature can be understood as having a cultural function that goes beyond the offered by traditional literary history. (p. 55)

In this place, poverty flows like the deadly undercurrent that allows you to barely keep your head above water gasping for breath, carrying you to the point of almost giving in until suddenly you break through the surface gasp, and go under again. Lines from *Weighted With Lack*, a poem by Nardi (Schubert & Nardi, 2006), catch the hopeless void of poverty, "My mind said giddy-up all day/But only time moved/Only time went away/ The dray/ Horse of my nothingness/Stayed" (p. 63). When one lives in the throes of poverty, all to be had is the hope for a better life. However, the endless monotony of day-after-day entrenchment in the debilitating effects of drudgery without the fruition of hopes and dreams leaves one bitter and angry.

From this interplay of place, gender, and class, I draw my identity and throw it into the arena for criticism and critique. He (2003) mentions, "[a]s participant and researcher in my inquiry, I lived through and observed the flows of both traditions from the inside out and the outside in" (p. 111). I am fortunate enough to find a new vantage point from which a new perception flows. A new awareness allows me to see how the fusion of different elements creates perception. Just living in the South creates a reality to this particular place and time. Doll (2000) states, "[i]t is in the South that Whites have developed a fantasy about aristocracy and landed privilege. The fantasy is based on false histories, yet it persists in codes of privilege that are given respectability and visibility" (p. 7). The mindset of this place clings to outdated ideals of White supremacy and warps/twists those who live the experience. Lived experience—autobiography—deconstructs a subjective reality and allows us to learn from and through our worlds. Miller (2005) cites this learning,

> recent autobiographical work, particularly from feminist poststructural perspectives, encourages individuals to review those relationships within larger contexts of predominant discourses that, in part, construct "selves" as well

as accompanying relations of power and authority that frame every teaching practice and curricular creation or choice. (p. 151)

Reflective practice must be encouraged in education and our schools. Determining how the various pieces of our society weave within one another to create our everyday reality helps us realize the influence that our world has on us, and conversely, the influence we can have on our world.

Critical theory provides the cornerstone for the foundation that helps me reconcile my two conflicting identities. Oakes and Rogers (2006) recognize that our schools must provide education in which students are "learning about power in American society and about where and with whom the power over their education and futures resides" (p. 3) so that they might "produce knowledge and use it to effect change" (p. 3). I had to see the marked shaping through the mandates and commands that propelled everyone into proper behavior—the dual education system that tracked students into their designated futures (Kozol, 2005). One does not wake up one day and realize that the truths they hold to be valid and just are inherently flawed. Higher education helps me to adjust some values, create new truths and understandings, and open my eyes to possibilities. It is an unflagging hope and desire for understanding that compel me to tell stories, "[p]edagogy is a referent for understanding the conditions for critical learning and the often hidden dynamics of social and cultural reproduction" (Giroux & Giroux, 2004, p. 97). Educators are the key components to unraveling the current system. "Teachers can become witnesses to the notion that intelligence and learning can lead to other worlds, not just the successful exploitation of this one" (Pinar, 2004, p. 31). Each day, students walk into classrooms full of preconceived notions/truths about place, class, gender and identity. The classroom must espouse a dialogue for tolerance and move beyond literal levels of thought to push students to consider what constitutes their realities versus the constructs that shape those realities.

Our system is stymied in the current mode of operation, yet the quest for social justice can be as painful as the lack of it. Smith (2000) recognizes,

> when education is for the practice of freedom both teacher and students are at risk. We are at risk for pain, unwanted dangerous memories, and a form of nakedness that seems uncoverable. However, there is a dialectical relationship at work whereby we stand to gain justice, freedom, and healthy, nurturing relationships and communities. (p. 196)

We need the critical lens, but it is not an easy thing to deal with it. Ayers (2004) speaks of a search for social justice through education in which students are recognized and valued for their roles as members of the human race. This realization values the narrative that situates a place, time and person in the tapestry of society and demands a curriculum for social justice.

HERE WE GO ROUND AGAIN

As my research approached completion, I felt contradicting senses of joy and loss. To finish such a daunting project filled me with a vast sense of satisfaction, but the void created by the marked absence of being on a mission left me wanting. I realized that I had to unpack all that I had wrapped into my research process and build it into my life. Instead of playing around the edges, the refrains that characterized my research waft through the daily interludes. "Education does not substitute for political action, but it is indispensable to it because of the role it plays in the development of critical consciousness" (Freire & Macedo, 1987, p. xv). I find myself rather pleased by the conspicuous lack of complacency; the stories that I heard, lived and captured should not be cast aside at the completion of my degree because as Weis and Fine (2003) note, "in a sea of parallel lives stratified by geography, class, color, friends, language, dress, music, and structures of tracking around them, the moments of working together, not always friendly or easy but engaged across, are worth comment" (p. 120). I have been surrounded with people willing to talk, listen, learn, and teach. My inquiry made me a better person and my world a better place. I found a voice inside me that I did not realize existed and a passion that suddenly needed an outlet. Writing my life ripped apart my identity while steadfastly forging a new sense of myself in this world. Words on paper translated into the self-confidence that eluded me. Finding the ability to articulate this new concept of the world and my experience in it made me feel alive. Experiencing and participating in academic conferences created within me a sense of possibility for what I might accomplish in this world. My inquiry creates a sense of possibility— of what I might now be capable of through writing and speaking—academic, or personal, or the inescapable entwining of the two.

REFERENCES

Anzaldua, G. (2004). How to tame a wild tongue. In G. E. Kessler (Ed.), *Voices of wisdom: A multicultural philosophy reader* (pp. 496–502). Belmont, CA: Wadsworth.

Ayers, W. (2004). *Teaching toward freedom: Moral commitment and ethical action in the classroom*. Boston: Beacon.

Daly, M. (2004). Beyond God the father. In G. E. Kessler (Ed.), *Voices of wisdom: A multicultural philosophy reader* (pp. 544–548). Belmont, CA: Wadsworth.

Darling-Hammond, L. (2006). *Powerful teacher education*. San Francisco: Jossey-Bass.

Doll, M. A. (2000). *Like letters in running water: A mythopoetics of curriculum*. Mahwah, NJ: Erlbaum.

Falk, W. W. (2004). *Rooted in place: Family and belonging in a Southern Black community*. New Brunswick, NJ: Rutgers University Press.

Faulkner, W. (1959). *Light in August*. New York: Vintage. (Original work published 1932)

Freire, P. (2002). *Pedagogy of the oppressed*. New York: Continuum.

Freire, P., & Macedo, M. (1987). *Literacy: Reading the word and reading the world*. Westport, CN: Bergin & Garvey.

Giroux, H. A. (1992). *Border crossing: Cultural workers and the politics of education*. New York: Routledge.

Giroux, H. A., & Giroux, S. S. (2004). *Take back higher education: Race, youth, and the crisis of democracy in the post-civil rights era*. New York: Palgrave.

Greene, M. (1995). *Releasing the imagination: Essays on education, the arts, and social change*. San Francisco: Jossey-Bass.

Greene, M. (2001). *Variations on a blue guitar: The Lincoln Center Institute lectures on aesthetic education*. New York: Teachers College Press.

He, M. F., & Phillion, J. (Eds.). (2008). *Research for social justice: Personal~passionate~participatory inquiry*. Greenwich, CT: Information Age.

He, M. F. (2003). *A river forever flowing: Cross-cultural lives and identities in the multicultural landscape*. Greenwich, CT: Information Age.

hooks, b. (2000). *Where we stand: Class matters*. New York: Routledge.

Kliebard, H. M. (2004). *The struggle for the American curriculum: 1893–1958* (3rd ed.). New York: RoutledgeFalmer.

Kozol, J. (2005). *The shame of the nation: The restoration of apartheid schooling in America*. New York: Crown.

McLaren, P. (2005). *Capitalists and conquerors: A critical pedagogy against empire*. Lanham, MD: Rowman & Littlefield.

Miller, J. (2005). *Sounds of silence breaking: Women, autobiography, curriculum*. New York: Peter Lang.

Morrison, T. (1987). *Beloved*. New York: Penguin.

Oakes, J., & Rogers, J. (2006). *Learning power: Organizing for education and justice*. New York: Teachers College.

Peters, M., & Lankshear, C. (1996). Postmodern counternarratives. In H. A. Giroux, C. Lankshear, P. McLaren, & M. Peters (Eds.), *Counternarratives: Cultural studies and critical pedagogies in postmodern spaces* (pp. 1–39). New York: Routledge.

Pinar, W. (1994). *Autobiography, politics and sexuality: Essays in curriculum theory 1972–1992*. New York: Peter Lang.

Pinar, W. (2004). *What is curriculum theory?* Mahwah, NJ: Erlbaum.

Pinar, W., Reynolds, W., Slattery, P., & Taubman, P. M. (1996). *Understanding curriculum: An introduction to the study of historical and contemporary curriculum discourses.* New York: Peter Lang.

Pitt, A. (2001). The dreamwork of autobiography: Felman, Freud, and Lacan. In K. Weiler (Ed.), *Feminist engagements: Reading, resisting, and revisioning male theorists in education and cultural studies.* New York: Routledge.

Provenzo, E. F. (2005). *Critical literacy: What every American ought to know.* Boulder, CO: Paradigm.

Reynolds, W. M., & Webber, J. A. (2004). *Expanding curriculum theory: Dis/positions and lines of flight.* Mahwah: NJ: Erlbaum.

Robison, L. (1997). Why, why do we not write our side? In S. A. Inness & D. Royer (Eds.), *Breaking boundaries: New perspectives on women's regional writing* (pp. 54–71). Iowa City, IA: University of Iowa Press.

Schubert, D., & Nardi, M. (2006). Special handling. In G. Lenhart (Ed.), *The stamp of class: Reflections on poetry and social class.* Ann Arbor, MI: University of Michigan Press.

Smith, D. (2000). Outlaw women writers, (un)popular popular culture, and critical pedagogy. In T. Daspit & J. Weaver (Eds.), *Popular culture and critical pedagogy: Reading, constructing, connecting* (pp. 183–199). New York: Garland.

Weis, L. (2004). *Class reunion: The remaking of the American white working class.* New York: Routledge.

Weis, L., & Fine, M. (2003). Extraordinary conversations in public schools. In G. Dimitriadis & D. Carlson (Eds.), *Promises to keep: Cultural studies, democratic education, and public life* (pp. 95–123). New York: RoutledgeFalmer.

CHAPTER 9

AFRICAN AMERICAN STUDENTS WITH READING DISABILITIES

A Critical Race Inquiry

Margie Wiggins Sweatman

Obstacles to learning are prevalent in today's educational system (Bennett de Marrais, & Le Compte, 1999). These obstacles interfere with adequate learning conditions for students with disabilities. Many of these obstacles are instructional related and hinder students from reading well enough to function in society. African American students with learning disabilities and their families may face additional problems caused by a lack of social and political capital, dearth of necessary, and knowledge of the dynamics of the educational system (Rothstein, 2004). Educational policy often follows the world view of the dominant culture. African American students are thought to benefit by association with little regard for their individual or cultural needs (Gay, 2000; McLaren, 1991). Low achieving African American students frequently have difficulty grasping curriculum standards identified as the norm. This difficulty is manifested in high stakes

Personal~Passionate~Participatory Inquiry Into Social Justice in Education, pp. 145–159
Copyright © 2008 by Information Age Publishing

testing which reinforces the concept of low achievement. As argued by McClaren, new interpretations regarding the way race, gender, and class interact to affect the role of public schooling in equalizing opportunities for all students must be developed.

My study explored the current instructional trend of using grade level textbooks as the primary source in teaching reading to students with reading disabilities. The investigation took place in an urban metro Atlanta middle school that serves a majority African American student population. A critical race inquiry method (Bell, 1995) was used to capture the perceptions of teachers, students, and parents towards reading and reading instruction. Thoughts, feelings, and understandings, from the perspective of these participants, are important in associating influences that may have impelled or allowed the use of grade level textbooks in teaching reading to students with disabilities.

AUTOBIOGRAPHICAL THOUGHTS OF LITERACY

When thinking of literacy, the ability to adequately read, write, and communicate comes to mind. This inquiry has deepened my understanding of literacy. Being literate gives one power and control over life the way nothing else can. I often think about literacy and my own family background. At a young age, I felt saddled with the responsibility of helping everyone in the house with reading. Reading was always a fun past time for me, but not for my two brothers who struggled in school; and not for my grandparents whose access to the opportunity to read was replaced by the necessity to work. It is strange how access to literacy can be granted or denied.

I remember my grandparents buying a set of encyclopedias from a traveling saleswoman. I was excited because the encyclopedias were accompanied by a set of readers designed for children. I can remember sitting in the living room with my grandmother as she negotiated monthly payments with the saleswoman, who coincidentally was one of my elementary school teachers. Reflecting on those encyclopedias and more importantly, my grandmother's negotiation for literacy, I understood this as a way she invited language into our house. The saleswoman was White as all my teachers were. She had a place in my mind as being seriously concerned about her students' achievement and about me. I felt honored that Mrs. Chisholm would come to my house with books for me to read.

As an elementary and middle school special education teacher, I have noticed that educational trends tend to come and go. One of the most recent trends with special education students is inclusion and immersion in the general education curriculum (Lipskey, 1997). While it is a popular practice, this has challenged many special education students to the point of frustration. When contesting this curriculum, *the bureaucracy of the way things were* was always a constant force. The fact that curriculum for these students would not be changed, even if students were not achieving, sparked an interest in why this is the case in my research site—a predominantly African American school and community.

Attempts to address a need for more varied literacy opportunities for students with reading disabilities in minority schools bring me back to my childhood of being the *reader* in the house. I think of my grandparents who were non-readers themselves, yet given the responsibility to educate and raise three grandchildren with the assistance of the public school system.

Adding fuel to my desire to investigate this phenomenon was my experience with and knowledge of students with disabilities in the public school system. Through these experiences, I have gained valuable knowledge about the conditions under which students benefit the most. Every year, each class of students I have taught contains students whose reading levels range from pre-primer to 1 year below their respective grades. My mission as a teacher has been to ensure that each student receives appropriate instruction to be successful in their challenge of learning to read. Over the years my students have shared many of their learning experience with me. I have often heard the voices of middle school students with reading disabilities as they express a strong desire to be able to read like their general education peers. Many students progressed to the point of becoming readers. Some, however, never did.

DEVELOPING A LANDSCAPE OF INQUIRY

As an educator, I choose to take a critical stance on literacy for students with disabilities. Even though federal laws serve to protect the rights of these students, there are reading education programs that fail to address their individual needs. This evokes the question of what kind of instructional practices are better for teaching of reading; and, for whom are these best fitted? Critical inquiry of the structure of education for students with disabilities helps stir the embers of a fire that must not be extinguished. A critical stance not only enables researchers to recognize the social, cultural, and political beliefs that influence pedagogy such as the use of grade level textbooks to this population of students, but also allows for the critiquing of these practices. The purpose of special education is to reposition students to a point of ableness by utilizing instructional tools. Educational policymakers must be careful not to develop policies which are ability neutral as they relate to the needs of students.

As contended by Nussbaum (1997), differences of race, gender, class, and religion interfere with understanding others. These differences "shape not only the practical choices of people but also their 'insides,' their desires, thoughts, and ways of looking at the world" (p. 85). This also applies in the case of differences related to disabilities. Most educators who are charged with delivering instruction to students with disabilities do not have a disability themselves. Therefore, they have limited knowledge of students' internal feelings about the teaching strategies used. The question of how students can reposition themselves as able and literate in classrooms with grade level texts must be considered. Suggested methods of instructional modifications include recording stories or using books on tapes, oral reading by the teacher or a more capable student, and oral reading of the book at home by a family member or some other capable person (Price, Mayfield, McFadden, & Marsh, 2001). These recommended modifications still lead to further questions. Are these modifications effective and do they consistently take place? Is it more important for students to have an instructional strategy that teaches them to read themselves or to listen to someone read for them?

Nussbaum (1997) suggests that narrative imagination may assist in developing a sympathetic consciousness of how students feel about reading instruction. As stated by Nussbaum, narrative imagination develops empathy, elicits a "sympathetic responsiveness to another's needs, and understands the way and circumstances that shape those needs" (p. 90). This compassion enables us to consider with a more accurate awareness what type of instruction students with disabilities need. Awareness that stems from the students' revelations provides a clearer picture of their struggles. Through narrative imagination we are able to see into the minds and hearts of students with reading disabilities and to understand and support their parents and teachers.

THEORETICAL FOUNDATION FOR THE STUDY

My initial inquiry into "why," specifically why the needs of students with disabilities were not being met, came without a knowledge of critical race theory or other theories for social justice to help me determine what was going on in this particular school as opposed to other schools in which I had worked. I wanted to know what other teachers as well as parents thought about the way things were for their students and children. I soon learned of an avenue which would help me to constructively address issues of schooling for African American students. I began to count on critical race theory to guide me in my quest for answers. Although at first I was confused by all that was happening, the structure of schooling made it seem impossible for one teacher to make a difference. I wanted to provide a venue for my fellow teachers, my students, and their parents to begin to move away from what I felt were the power restraints that suppressed them in hidden ways.

Teaching in a special education program at the middle school level helped the progress of my research. I had transferred from an elementary school to a middle school which was a new experience for me. It took the first year to grasp the mindset behind the curricular concepts for special education students and which strategies and structures would allow my students to be successful based on the curriculum at hand. Yet, year after year, I felt the resources available were not sufficient for my students. I began to question whether other teachers felt the same way as I did. I began to question what my students and their parents thought of the type of education being offered. As I journeyed through this research, I have concluded that one of the best way to address these concerns is to listen. By listening to others over the years, I have heard much, and I hope to hear more to inform and guide my practice.

In describing possible influences that may lead to the implementation of certain instructional practices, it was important to use methods of inquiry that allowed me to examine what went on in the school setting with students and teachers. The voices of students' with reading disabilities, their feelings and experiences needed to be heard. Teachers' experiences of teaching students with reading disabilities, their instructional practices, and influences that determined practices needed to be examined and described. Listening to the voices of parents of students with reading disabilities contributed an understanding of the experience of being located on the margins as related to their children's reading ability and achievement. This was an opportunity to explore parents' sense of empowerment, knowledge of parents' rights, and types of instructional practices used with their children.

I started my inquiry with the intent to open up more literacy opportunities for students who learned differently. This required deconstructing beliefs which had been taken for granted about schooling for minority students and the outcomes that resulted from those beliefs. My preservice teacher training had enabled me to identify and utilize a variety of methods for teaching students to read. When beliefs held within the school system conflicted with my knowledge of what was suitable for my students, I was forced to deconstruct my own personal perceptions of teaching and to determine how to best serve the needs of my students with the resources at hand.

For many years, I had known that the reality that I was experiencing did not make sense in a democratic society where resources and opportunities were said to be boundless. When I looked to postmodern and poststructural understandings of the ideas and questions that engrossed me, I began to see new ways of thinking about democracy, agency, and power. The new ways of thinking allowed me to change my perspective of the situation from a local to a more expansive context.

When I interviewed students, their parents, and their teachers in the middle school in which I taught, I learned that parents, though interested in their children's achievement, in many ways lacked knowledge of the inner workings of the school system. They felt that the school and teachers were the experts and that these experts knew and practiced the best strategies for their students. These parents trusted the schools to provide an appropriate education for their children. Listening to the parents resonated with my own experience. Over 25 years ago, I knew my grandparents never questioned school administrators or teachers about why my older brother experienced problems with reading or the decision to send my younger brother to a school for students with mental retardation. Feelings of unworthiness to question those who were in authority came with a huge price—illiteracy. Likewise, the students in my study talked about personal feelings of embarrassment and their struggles in their quest to learn to read. It was difficult, yet heartwarming, to hear them vocalize their feelings. In addition, my colleagues and fellow teachers at the school spoke of how their voices were often inhibited by power structures that govern the school system.

Contributing an important foundation for shaping this study, critical theory enables me to look beyond the individual or the situation to an underlying cause or source. This, along with four other factors, solidified my choice of inquiries. It was important to me to be able to understand a phenomenon and to link "the problem to some greater wrong operating at some grander scale" (Wolcott, 1999, p. 181). Second, because critical theory raises awareness, change may be affected. For issues related to ethnic background, critical theory brings forth "important questions about the control and production of knowledge—particularly knowledge about people and communities of color" (Denzin & Lincoln, 2003, p. 423). Third, critical theory can be used to uncover potential negative effects and hidden meanings behind established power structures and traditions. Lastly, critical theory is appropriate for the researcher to be "cast in the role of instigator and facilitator" (Schram, 2003, p. 35) to understand beforehand that changes are necessary in a situation. In addition, Denzin and Lincoln (2003) offer that critical race theory "asks critical qualitative researchers to operate in self-revelatory mode, to acknowledge the double (or multiple) consciousness in which she or he is operating" (p. 423). According to Schram,

[t]he values of the researcher inevitably influence the inquiry as he or she foregrounds the judgment call that an injustice is holding back someone from something better. This places the particular demand upon researchers to make explicit how their own class, status, ethnic or gender orientation, and power relationships relative to research participants affect what is investigated and how data is interpreted. (p. 35)

Critical race theory first emerged as a legal concept, but has since grown rapidly to include other disciplines such as education (Valdes, Culp, & Harris, 2002). Ladson-Billings and Tate (1995) apply this concept to education to show how the school curriculum is designed specifically based on dominant ideologies. Dehyle (2005) explains how this may happen:

As institutions, schools respond to and reflect the larger society. It is therefore not surprising that racism finds its way into schools in much the same way that it finds its way into other institutions, such as housing, employment, and the criminal justice system. (p. 136)

Thus, the goal of critical race theory is to develop pedagogy that takes into account the role of race and racism in education and to recognize forms of subordination that have occurred as a result. As I reflected on my school community and my participants, I felt comfortable in knowing this method of inquiry would be the best mechanism for exploring this aspect of their lives. For me, critical race theory illuminated the meaning my participants made of their experiences.

CRITICAL NARRATIVE INQUIRY

To help communicate the experiences of this school community, the methodological grounding for this study is based on storytelling and narratives. Closely connected to storytelling, narrative inquiry (Clandinin & Connelly, 2000) is often used as a conduit into the personal experiences of individuals. Clandinin and Connelly describe the concept of individual life experiences as being significant to the field of education. In doing this, they reflect on Dewey's (1916) conception of effective education as being directly linked to the ongoing life experiences of children. As suggested in Dewey's theory, the life experiences of all people play a crucial role in how they react and interact within their daily lives. Narratives hold great potential in capturing these stories and the meanings behind them. Not knowing exactly what types of stories would emerge as a result of my inquiry, I constructed the reality as it was offered and described by the participants.

Phillion, He, and Connelly (2005) agree that the increasingly diverse and complex nature of experiences warrant the use of narratives in reflecting the lives of others. These scholars highlight several aspects of narrative inquiry that support its suitableness for this practice. One aspect is that narrative inquiry is the "inquirer's recognition of sociopolitical and cultural contexts in shaping experience" (p. 10). This feature is important because it encourages an understanding that society is shaped by the experiences of different people, thereby legitimizing these experiences. Another aspect is that narrative inquiries give the possibility of "effecting social change beginning with the individual and expanding into the greater community" (p. 10). This helps to fill an appeal to view individuals' lives and epistemologies from a more forthright perspective while involving a broader audience.

Narrative inquiry can be used to implement critical race theory. Creating a critical race consciousness, it serves to "see the world from the point of view of oppressed persons of color" (Denzin & Lincoln, 2003, p. 479). Additionally, it confronts underlying assumptions about existing systems and social structures. Claims to truth are challenged based on criteria of personal and cultural knowledge. According to Sirotnik (1991) critical narrative inquiry is a "knowledge building process where what is presumably known is continually re-known through questioning, arguing, counter arguing, reflecting, challenging, contradicting, reconciling, modifying, revising, and so forth" (p. 247). This particular inquiry raises the questions regarding academic achievement of African American students and whether or not their best interests are being served. What meaning is applied to the type of instruction rendered to students? Do parents, teachers and students perceive the use of grade level text as beneficial? Why or why not? The worldview of teachers should reveal how they come to utilize a particular practice. Special education teachers are generally aware of the type of instruction that is best for meeting the individual needs of their students. Considering this brings an additional concern to the forefront. In coming to this process, do they acknowledge or address subconscious knowing of what is best? In seeking and collecting responses to these questions, participant-observer researchers must learn to live "in-between" (He, 2003) their own cultures and those of their participants. Like He, a Chinese immigrant woman and scholar who explored the variations in cultures as she moved back and forth between different countries, the researcher must learn to live in-between the culture of the participants and that of their own. Doing so will help the researcher avoid the appearance of being an outsider looking in (Phillion, He, & Connelly, 2005).

Marshall and Rossman (1999) describe how narratives can take several forms. One is to focus on individuals' meaning of their experiences. The individuals in this case would be "those who are socially marginalized or oppressed, as they construct stories (narratives) about their lives. Marshall and Rossman add that "storytelling is integral to understanding lives and that all people engage in the construction of narratives" (p. 5). Using critical narrative inquiry helped reflect the lived experiences of my participants and their perceptions of the use of grade level textbooks at the middle school. The stories collected from teachers and students helped me to understand how a school's culture and environment contributed to the use of practices that may not be in the best interest of the students.

REFLECTING ON MEANING: EDUCATIONAL AND SOCIAL CHANGE RESULTING FROM THE INQUIRY

The meaning behind this inquiry compels me personally and professionally to listen carefully to the voices of local school communities. As the participants began to share their experiences about reading instruction in this school, the importance of hearing their views was apparent. Society can derive more meaning and understanding about what benefits students academically if it considers the views of local groups.

Voices of teachers in this particular school revealed that different power influences such as state mandated curricula affect the manner in which instruction and resources are delivered to their students. These influences restrained their abilities to administer reading programs as they desired. These teachers defined their roles based on dominant constraints which gave them little authority to construct knowledge for themselves. Apple (1995), Bennett, de Marrais, and LeCompte (1999) defined this emerging trend over 10 years ago as one of deskilling the teacher to the point that much of decision making about curriculum, instructional delivery, and resources is no longer in their hands. Taking away decision making by teachers regarding the type of resources used and instruction rendered leaves a feeling of powerlessness, not to mention a disregard of the actual needs of students. Dr. Harvey, a teacher participant offered his reasoning.

> I think schools use textbooks because they match the objectives of the general curriculum that is handed down by the state.... However, being that we are exceptional education teachers, I don't think they cater to what we actually need or what we actually want or what we feel is best for our students. (Sweatman, 2005, p. 95)

Mrs. Wade, a teacher participant, confirmed this when she stated,

> the trend has changed because we now are required to test them (students) on grade level. So, in preparation for the CRCT, it's like we've had no other

choice but to blend in with regular education teachers and what they are teaching from the same textbook. (p. 97)

Teachers' hands are tied, as their students' performance on high-stakes testing affects their yearly performance evaluations. Mrs. Wade points out, "It's on our annual evaluation. They (administrators) say your evaluation is contingent upon the results of the CRCT. So, we don't have a choice in the matter. We are in a position where we have to teach the curriculum" (p. 112).

Even though teacher participants felt that students did not benefit from grade level textbooks, a general sense of powerlessness to change the system was voiced. As suggested by Spring (1998), "Teachers are at the bottom of the chain of command and the objects of power from above" (p. 74). This idea supports teachers' feelings of helplessness regarding their abilities to change the manner in which instruction and resources are delivered to their students. Decisions about their students and schooling were made at a higher level than the classroom teacher or even the school administrators. Without connecting this concern to race, they felt that special education teachers are ignored as to the wants and needs of their students. Teachers are pressured to use whatever resources are provided to them. They expressed the feeling that special education teachers do not have enough influence or power to affect change in their pedagogical practices.

In addition to a lack of power, teacher participants felt there was nowhere to turn for alternatives. They expressed the need for student and teacher advocates who could support and voice their concerns to those in authority. As these teachers shared their experiences, I began to realize what was happening. Through this type of control, the dominant culture is able to sustain the ideologies that promote their lifestyle and the type of education they desire for their children to experience. Even though the teacher who participated in the inquiry voiced feelings of powerlessness to change the system, I believe they felt valued in sharing their thoughts and saw this as a means of gaining the authority to speak about their lack of power. Corroborating this, Delgado and Stefancic (2001) suggest that storytelling provides a powerful means for minorities to bring their experiences to the attention of the public. In addition, Phillion, He, and Connelly (2005) agree that we must recognize "sociopolitical and cultural contexts in shaping experience" (p. 10). Society as a whole needs to pay closer attention to concerns such as these and seek out ways to help local schools address the need for developing pedagogy sensitive to cultures as well as student abilities.

As I reflected further on the comments of these teachers, I felt there was a confused nature of responsibility at work within this school. The teachers who participated perceived their given role as delivering instruction with the resources handed down to them; while parents and students expected teachers to be the experts and deliver resources and instruction appropriate for student needs. Additionally, teachers shared an expectation of a role of ownership and partnership with the students and their parents. Students were expected to take ownership and seek materials which they could read, while parents were expected to be partners in helping their children with not only reading but also other school objectives. This is supported by Mrs. Wade, a teacher participant, who feels that "parents play a really big role because they're there to encourage and support the child" (Sweatman, 2005, p. 107). However, both students and parents often lacked the knowledge, resources, or assistance required to solidify this ownership.

Poverty as well as race has a great impact on the quality of education received by minority students. Describing the impact of socioeconomics on student learning, Knapp and Woolverton (2004) indicate the quality of education available in schools is primarily shaped by policymakers of the community. These policymakers are generally from the middle class populations whose children are not likely to be members of minority or lower income schools. In addition, the research literature highlights how society is organized along racial lines and hierarchies (Delgado & Stefancic, 2001). Therefore, it is important to realize that these degrees of separation exist in order to change injustices. The participants in the study continually cited examples of how situations differed in their school cultures as compared to others. For example, most parent participants felt that this middle school received fewer resources than other schools. One parent, Ms. Brown, claimed "services, they're not the same which shows up in the scores" (Sweatman, 2005, p. 188). Some parent participants thought that teachers and parents exhibited the same characteristics in minority schools as other schools. However, Ms. Brown a college educated parent, acknowledged that "where there is one parent in the home, parent involvement in the school is going to be much lower" (p. 188). This is due to the many responsibilities of single parents that may interfere with time set aside for assisting their children with schoolwork.

Researchers and educators may not be able to remove factors that contribute to poverty, but we can learn to understand and value the unique characteristics of students and families who are affected. We can help them to realize that the obstacles they may encounter in pursuing an appropriate education can be overcome, as well as provide guidance in how to accomplish this. A critical race theory perspective offers a critique of discourse as it relates to location in situated experiences. Race and socioeconomic status represent two spaces within which experiences are based. Therefore, as described by Rogers (2002), success depends on whether the less powerful learn the discourse of power. The connection between socioeconomics and race presents an important implication that should be addressed on a larger scale. Siddle-Walker and Snarey (2004) suggest that more color consciousness is needed to recognize how race influences the educational outcomes of African American and other minority students. There are patterns of thought, hidden rules, cognitive strategies, and social interaction patterns that are particular to different groups (Daspit & Weaver, 2000; Payne, 2001; Rothstein, 2004). These factors must be considered when developing a culturally applicable curriculum.

The stories of student and parent participants teach us that reading and education are important to them. Students saw themselves as deficient in their abilities to read and sought help at school and home. This is confirmed in comments by Ingrid, a student participant, who values reading because "it feels good when you can read something" (Sweatman, 2005, p. 166). As indicated by Cook-Sather (2003), the views of students and how "they reinforce, contradict, or complicate the perspective offered" (p. 25) in public education are important to making curriculum more relevant to their lives. The student perspectives in this study serve both to contradict and complicate factors related to the effectiveness of their reading instruction. All student participants verbalized their difficulty in reading grade level textbooks. They indicated their perceptions of inferiority and being teased by others because of their reading abilities. Kelly, a student participant, stated, "My challenge is that kids from outside of class say 'yeh, yeh, yeh, you're special ed. You don't know how to read right.' " (Sweatman, 2005, p. 164). Students sought help at home in reading because they realized they needed assistance. This substantiates students' attempt to be involved in their own learning. Two students reported receiving assistance at home in reading and in completing schoolwork. Melanie, however, stated that she did not receive help at home. Where as Jonell, who reported receiving little assistance at home from a parent, sought help from her sisters. She continues by sharing that "at home my mom don't have time for me. At school the teachers have more time" (p. 171). Through this narrative inquiry, it was evident that students were interested in their own achievement in school. These experiences demonstrate students' efforts to help themselves in ways they knew how. Generally, reading acquisition skills for struggling readers require training from someone knowledgeable of these procedures. Students' attempts to assist themselves and seek help from home often led to frustration and a general feeling of helplessness about reading. Students express their desire of wanting to learn to read, but not being able to, due to lack of knowledge of effective strategies. Students' stories tell us that there is a need for development of opportunities and experiences through which students can be successful, instead of assuming that they are not interested in reading.

Most parents who participated in the study evidenced some knowledge of how children learn to read, but none compared this knowledge to actual instruction being administered in their children's reading programs in school. Additionally, parent comments exhibited their faith in the school system to provide an appropriate education to their children. As stated by Ms. Ross, "The school is doing pretty good" (Sweatman, 2005, p. 196). Yet, in order to ensure their children's success in school, parents should have knowledge of how to effectively participate and enhance performance. This would require an understanding and knowledge of whether or not classroom reading programs are appropriate for their children. Hill and Craft (2003), however, found that "African American parents might define involvement in school as carefully monitoring but not intervening because they may feel limited in their ability or knowledge to intervene" (para. 9).

Critical race theory assists in the effort to listen to and accept the voices of local communities. It identifies and brings awareness to areas of injustice faced by those within these communities. As promoted by Delgado and Stefancic (2001), this "may begin a process of adjustment in our system of beliefs and categories by calling attention to neglected evidence and reminding readers of our common humanity" (p. 43). In schools, we should be looking for equality in educational outcomes. To attain this equality, a range of resources and instructional methods must be utilized. Determining the appropriate tools requires knowledge of what actually transpires in the classroom and, more importantly, the reasoning behind why instruction is rendered in the manner which it is.

Since the completion of this study, I have continued to encourage my fellow teachers, parents, and pre-service teachers to maintain dialogues that promote school community authorship which acknowledges the needs of diverse groups in education. As poverty and race continue to have a great impact on the quality of education received by African American students, I work with fellow teachers and teacher candidates enrolled in teacher education classes to understand new perceptions and interpretations of equality as it relates to race and ability to enable them to effectively address the needs of marginalized groups in their school communities. As I have moved from the middle school classroom to university as a mentor and advisor to preservice and in-service teachers, I now have the opportunities to instill the idea of empowerment of self and respect for the knowledge and responsibility of parents and students. I can work with teachers and administrators to stimulate change.

I continue to advocate for culturally relevant teaching for all students in an effort to achieve equality of education. The idea of curriculum based upon the needs of local communities may be contested by society in general. However, if the type of curriculum local teachers and parents desire for their students is seriously considered, we might be able to develop a culturally responsive curriculum which includes culturally responsive teachers, students, subject matters, and learning environment. With such a culturally responsive curriculum, which moves beyond mandates and incorporates beliefs and needs of teachers, parents, and students within a community, all students might have equal opportunities to learn and to thrive.

REFERENCES

Apple, M. W. (1995). *Educatin and power.* (2nd ed.). New York: Routledge.

Bell, D. (1995). Serving two masters: Integration ideals and client interests in school desegregation litigation. In R. Delgado (Ed.), *Critical race theory: The cutting edge* (pp. 228–240). Philadelphia: Temple University Press.

Bennett de Marrais, K. B., & LeCompte, M. D. (1999). *The way schools work: A sociological analysis of education.* New York: Addison Wesley Longman.

Clandinin, D. J., & Connelly, F. M. (2000). *Narrative inquiry: Experience and story in qualitative research.* San Francisco: Jossey-Bass.

Cook-Sather, A. (2003). Listening to students about learning differences. *Teaching exceptional children, 35(4),* 22–26.

Daspit, T., & Weaver, J. A. (Eds.). (2000). *Popular culture and critical pedagogy: Reading, constructing, connecting.* New York: Garland.

Dehyle, D. (2005). Journey toward social justice: Curriculum change and educational equity in a Navajo community. In J. Phillion, M. F. He, & F. M. Connelly (Eds.), *Narrative & experience in multicultural education* (pp. 116–140). Thousand Oaks, CA: SAGE.

Delgado, R., & Stefancic, J. (2001). *Critical race theory.* New York: University Press.

Denzin, N. K., & Lincoln, Y. S. (2003). The discipline and practice of qualitative research. In *The landscape of qualitative research: Theories and issues* (2nd ed., pp. 1–45). Thousand Oaks, CA: SAGE.

Dewey, J. (1916). *Democracy and education.* New York: Macmillan.

Gay, G. (2000). *Culturally responsive teaching: theory research, and practice.* New York: Teachers College Press.

He, M. F. (2003). *A river forever flowing: Cross-cultural lives and identities in the multicultural landscape.* Greenwhich, CT: Information Age.

Hill, N. E., & Craft, S. A. (2003). Parent-school involvement and school performance: Mediated pathways among socioeconomically comparable African-American and Euro-American families. *Journal of Educational Psychology, 95*(1), 74–83.

Knapp, M. S., & Woolverton, S. (2004). Social Class and Schooling. In J. A. Banks & C. A. McGee Banks (Eds.), *Handbook of research on multicultural education* (2nd ed., pp. 656–681). San Francisco: Jossey-Bass.

Ladson-Billings, G., & Tate, W. (1995). Toward a critical race theory of education. *Teachers College Record, 97*, 47–68.

Lipsky, D. K. (1994). National survey gives insight into inclusion movement remaking of American society. *Harvard Educational Review, 66*(4), 769–796.

Marshall, C., & Rossman, G. G. (1999). *Designing qualitative research* (3rd ed.). Thousand Oaks, CA: SAGE.

McLaren, P. (1991). Critical pedagogy: Constructing an arch of social dreaming and a doorway to hope. *Journal of Education, 173*(1), 9–34.

Nussbaum, M. (1997). *Cultivating humanity: A classical defense of reform in liberal education.* Cambridge, MA: Harvard University Press.

Payne, R. K. (2001). *A framework for understanding poverty.* Highlands, TX: Aha! Process.

Phillion, J., He, M. F., & Connelly, F. M. (2005). The potential of narrative and experiential approaches in multicultural inquiries. In *Narrative & experience in multicultural education* (pp. 1–14). Thousand Oaks, CA: SAGE.

Price, B. J., Mayfield, C., McFadden, A. C., & Marsh, G. E. (2001). *Special education for inclusive classrooms.* Retrieved April 27, 2005, from http://www .parrotpublishing.com/Inclusion_Chapter_2.htm

Rogers, R. (2002). Between contexts: A critical discourse analysis of family literacy, discursive practices, and literate subjectivities. *Reading Research Quarterly, 37*(3), 248–277.

Rothstein, R. (2004). *Class and schools: Using social, economic, and educational reform to close the black-white achievement gap.* Washington, DC: Economic Policy Institute.

Schram, T. H. (2003). *Conceptualizing qualitative inquiry: Mindwork for fieldwork in education and the social sciences.* Upper Saddle River, NJ: Pearson Education.

Siddle-Walker, V., & Snarey, J. R. (2004). *Race-ing moral formation: African American perspectives on care and justice.* New York: Teachers College Press.

Sirotnik, K. A. (1991). Critical inquiry: A paradigm for praxis. In E. C. Short (Ed.), *Forms of curriculum inquiry* (pp. 243–258) New York: State University of New York Press.

Spring, J. (1998). *Conflict of interests: The politics of American education* (3rd ed.). New York: McGraw Hill.

Sweatman, M. W. (2005). *A critical race inquiry into the use of grade level textbooks for students with reading disabilities: The perspectives of teachers, students, and parents.* Statesboro, GA: Georgia Southern University Press.

Valdes, F., Culp, M., & Harris, A. (2002). *Crossroads, directions, and a new critical race theory.* Philadelphia: Temple University Press.

Wolcott, H. F. (1995). *The art of fieldwork.* Walnut Creek, CA: AltaMira.

CHAPTER 10

LANGUAGE, CULTURE, AND IDENTITY

Immigrant Female Students in U.S. High Schools

Joanna Stoughton Cavan

AUTOBIOGRAPHICAL ROOTS

I grew up in a small southern town in the mid-1960s. My parents were both school teachers and struggled to support five children. Although we had little in a material sense, I later realized that I was one of the privileged (McIntosh, 1998) simply because of the color of my skin. Growing up in this small town, I felt that something was wrong with a system that allowed discrimination against others. These others were the Blacks who went to separate poor schools in neighborhoods overrun with poverty. When I was old enough to drive, I used to go these neighborhoods to pick up our maid. Yes, as poor as we were, there were those willing to work for practically nothing. I recall the empty feeling I had when I saw this very sweet and gentle woman who would always be standing on her rickety porch waiting patiently for me. Against her many protests, I always

Personal~Passionate~Participatory Inquiry Into Social Justice in Education, pp. 161–175
Copyright © 2008 by Information Age Publishing

insisted that she sit up front with me, not in the back, as we chatted on the way to the house. As I grew older, I began to examine my own privileged life in comparison to those not so fortunate. In doing so, I realized that I owed much to my ancestors who fled other countries in pursuit of a future that held hope for a better existence. My paternal grandfather's family left Ireland during the potato famine. They were also Protestant and sought more religious freedom. Some of the family emigrated to Canada while others sought work in the West Indies on sugar plantations. In Canada, my grandfather and his brothers became wheat farmers while some of my great uncles lost their lives working the plantations. Again seeking a better life, my grandfather emigrated to Georgia to find a more substantial living. He was never able to reach his potential.

My maternal great grandparents came to this country from Alsace-Lorraine in northeastern France. They were of German decent and left the country because of political and religious reasons. My paternal grandfather was accepted more easily here because he spoke English. My maternal ancestors had more of a challenge because they spoke German and were German. My mother often told me that she never heard her grandparents speak German. They were too embarrassed to do so, and they forbade their children to speak the language. Furthermore, they changed the spelling of their last name so that it did not resemble German. My mother and I often discussed the shame they must have felt simply because of their culture and language. I also realize now that my family lost much of its heritage because my grandparents came here during a time when Germans were not in the privileged center of American life.

Although I grew up in the South, I never considered myself a South-erner. I spent my summers in Canada with family. and it was there that my love for diversity of language and culture began to soar. The blood of my ancestors runs through me bringing with it a love and a passion for diversity. I was 22 the first time my feet were on French soil, and I knew that I was home. Like Feuerverger (2005), the "texture" (p. 175) of my life began to "take shape" (p. 175). That texture has much expanded since those younger days. Having taught the French language over twenty years, the texture of my life has increased beyond a simple passion for one language and culture to many languages and cultures.

PARTICIPATORY RESEARCH PROCESS

As a French teacher, I have had the pleasure of teaching many Hispanic students, African students, and Asian students. I have become a mentor to these students because they know my passion for diversity of language and culture. As such, I began to listen to their stories of hurtful and painful bias that they had experienced in the school setting. During my doctoral studies, I was encouraged to become an advocate for my students and get together some of my students after school or during the weekend where the students could tell their stories without fear of recrimination. It is from these gatherings that my research process began and from which I chose three immigrant females for the research process. They were Marcela (Mexican), Sara (Pakistani), and Tayo (Nigerian).

My research was grounded in John Dewey's (1938) theory of experience and education and narrative theory (Carger, 2005; Clandinin & Connelly, 2000; He, 2003). Clandinin and Connelly state that narrative "begin[s] with experience expressed in lived and told stories" (p. 40). John Dewey espoused the importance of experience which became the cornerstone for narrative theory. He argued, "I assume that amid all uncertainties there is one permanent frame of reference: namely the organic connection between education and personal experience" (Dewey, p. 24). This vital connection between education and personal experience became the foundation for the questions I sought to answer in my research.

The theoretical framework of narrative inquiry extended into a cross-cultural narrative inquiry which Carger (2005) calls the fourth dimension of narrative inquiry. She states that a cross-cultural narrative is "a comprehensible unfolding and humanizing of cross-cultural situations that elude the fixed, scientifically based terminology" (p. 239). Like Carger, my research process could not remain an academic exercise in which I would remain objective. I would "not evade the emotion in my inquiry, but embrace it, and describe it richly" (p. 240). I began to understand that the participants in this study had suffered discrimination due solely to their diversity. I also came to realize that although our school proclaimed to embrace diversity, it did not. I, like Ayers, (2004) realized that "[e]ducation systems ... have not adapted successfully to such diversity" (p. 7).

Other studies by Carger (1996), He (2003), Soto (1997), and Valenzuela (1999) encouraged me to question how learning a new language and new culture while maintaining the heritage languages and cultures impact immigrant students' school success. I also questioned how identity development in cross-cultural environments impacts immigrant students' experience of schooling. In this cross-cultural narrative inquiry, I, the researcher, worked with the participants to "explore and portray the shifting, often paradoxical, nature of our [their] cross-cultural lives" (He, 2003, p. 5). Like He, my participants were pushed and pulled between languages and cultures. They faced frustration, tension, and anxiety not only in their school experiences but in the process of revealing these experiences. On several occasions, my participants could not hold back tears of sadness or tears of joy when someone finally heard and listened to their stories.

My field texts included a school portraiture, participant profiles, participant conversations, and three audio recorded interviews with each participant, each lasting approximately 45 minutes. Some of the interviews were conducted on the school site while others took place in the participants' homes. Participants chose their pseudonyms. I also encouraged participants to keep a reflective journal in which they could write about experiences they had in school and reflections on our interviews. I also kept a researcher journal to reflect upon the interviews as well as what I observed in the school setting. Field texts were coded and interpreted for particular themes involving language, culture, and identity development.

INQUIRY OUTCOMES

Silencing Language

Participants revealed that they had been silenced in the school system because of their language difficulties. Tayo was often ridiculed when she spoke because she had a heavy accent from her heritage language, Yoruba. As a consequence, she became silent in class and gave up her hopes to become a lawyer because she would have to speak in front of people. She also refused to ask for help in the classroom when she knew she did not understand the lesson. She also stated that the teachers never asked her if she understood, and she began to internalize feelings of unworthiness. She stated, "They never talk to me anyway so I guess I do not matter" (Cavan, 2006, p. 146). She was also given an American name in some classes because the teachers could not pronounce her African name. She told me this made her sad because she was not an American; she was African. Not learning her name meant to her that teachers and students did not care enough about her to try to pronounce it.

In spite of the fact that Tayo could have benefited from English to Speakers of Other Languages (ESOL), she chose to withdraw because she felt that other students made fun of ESOL classes. In her interview she told me that she was called a SPED (Special Education Student) because she was taking ESOL. Because of her fear of speaking and asking for help, Tayo failed two language arts classes and ultimately changed from the college prep degree to the vocational degree.

Sara had some of the same experiences in school as Tayo. There were occasions when she tried to explain class instructions in her heritage language to her cousin who had recently arrived from Pakistan. She was told not to speak this language but to speak English in class. Her teacher stated, "He will learn faster if you speak English to him" (Cavan, 2006, p. 159). Sara told me that some people at the school were racist. She felt they looked down on her because she was different. When she spoke her heritage language, Urdu, she said others laughed and stared at her as if she were weird. She, too, began to internalize feelings that she was not good enough or smart enough to succeed. She ultimately decided she did not want to become a doctor because she did not believe she was capable. At the end of the year, she had chosen to be a cosmetologist.

Marcela's experience was tragic. She dropped out of ESOL classes because the teacher disallowed Spanish in the classroom. Although she stated that the other students and she understood much better when they helped each other in Spanish, this was not allowed. Her teacher told her, "This is English class. This is America" (Cavan, 2006, p. 167). Like the other two participants, she never asked questions in class, nor did teachers inquire about her understanding of the subject. She stated that everyone looked at her when she spoke in class. She felt that those around her did not want her to do well and that people thought of her as stupid. She said her teachers ignored her and she began to blame herself for her failing grades. She, too, changed from the college prep degree. She told me a counselor advised her that a vocational degree would suit her better. She knew the counselor meant that she was not capable of pursuing an academic path.

Marcela experienced discrimination from other students especially when she was speaking Spanish with other Hispanic students. She recounted, "This place is just discrimination. Just walking down the halls. Stuff people say like, 'Oh, I hate these Mexicans.' I feel their breath on my neck when they say it. My mind just goes blank" (Cavan, 2006, p. 170).

Cummins (1989) says our nation sees bilingualism as a handicap rather than a resource. Instead of viewing the participants' heritage languages as a powerful tool for school success, the participants were treated as if they were deficient and their heritage language was viewed as inferior to English. Soto (1997) says that schools are a part of a "systematic repressive system" (p. 27) which denies language opportunity. In contrast, research supports the idea that bilingualism is "key for the survival and success of language-minority students" (Beykont, 2000, p. 3). Tayo, Sara, and Marcela were not allowed to stay connected to their languages in the school system. As a consequence, they lacked a healthy self-image and suffered "the psychological scar of disconnection from their heritage language" (Anzaldua, 1987, p. 108). These participants had experienced the "Yanking out of the tongue" (p. 108). Their heritage languages could have been a tool for empowerment and success (Jankie, 2004), but the contrary was the case. Each participant experienced failure in several classes and ultimately gave up hopes and dreams of careers which they had envisioned as possible in this country.

Cultural Marginalization

Being on the margins, being left out, was a consistent theme throughout the interviews. Tayo was proud of her Nigerian heritage. She would have valued an opportunity to share her heritage culture. However, she felt stressed about the fact that no one knew about her or cared to know. For Tayo, this meant that no one respected her heritage or her. She stated,

> Teacher never ask about my country. It would be good to tell people about my country but nobody [is] interested. Maybe people [would] understand me better, get to know me, not judge me. I feel this way. I feel not so good as other people here ... like we do not exist. We have our ways. They are just different. (Cavan, 2006, p. 149)

Tayo went on to explain that she was often ridiculed about her clothing. She was called "booty scratcher" (Cavan, 2006, p. 149) by other students. Students refused to sit by her in class or on the bus because they said she smelled and had diseases from Africa. Telling me this story, she began to cry. There was a time when she wanted to wear her African clothes to school, but she had since dismissed this idea for fear of ridicule. At lunch other students made fun of her food and her music. As a result she stopped bringing her food to school and ate when she returned home.

Practicing cultural traditions also became a burden for her. She stated,

> When I first come here I practice respect with teachers. Like I cannot give something to older person with left hand. I give with right hand. This is respect for them. I try to explain and teachers say, 'This is the way we do it in America. You [are] not in Africa.' I just try to be quiet because I know it do no good. (p. 151)

In a sad voice Tayo told me,

> "High school is terrible. I am a visitor here. I feel I do not belong. I am on the outside where people make fun of me.... It hurts to be on the outside.... I do not run track anymore because people make fun of the way I run.... People do not accept me cause I am different. (Cavan, 2006, pp. 151–152)

Sara's tales were similar to those of Tayo. People called her smelly and stinky and refused to sit by her in class. One of her teachers even sent her to the school social worker to address the issue. Sara said she was humiliated because she did not stink. The teacher moved Sara away from the complaining students when she returned to class.

Students made insensitive jokes about her and called her Osama Bin Laden's daughter. Although she is Muslim, she said she could not practice her religious customs at school. When she tried to wear her traditional head cover, she was told not to do so. On one occasion, a student snatched it off her head. The head cover policy has changed since then, but she still chose to reject her head cover for fear of ridicule.

Sara also experienced exclusion. She told me, "People like us are not popular at school. Teachers just ignore people like me. Everybody wants to be close to the sports players and the cheerleaders. Teachers help them to pass. They have power from teacher" (Cavan, 2006, p. 162). Like Tayo, Sara did not belong to clubs or other activities at school. She exclaimed, "I do not belong here. I have never belonged here.... I left everything behind. I am so sad at times.... It is hard to adopt a new culture which is totally different from yours" (p. 163).

Marcela told the same stories. At times my heart would break listening to her pain. She was often called a wetback and told she would never do anything but yard work. She was accused of stealing something in a physical education class. When she did not confess, other students bullied her by saying they would call immigration. She was insulted by this. She said,

> It made me feel like I don't deserve to be here. That this is their territory and the only way that we, being Mexicans, Latins, whatever, the only way we can earn the right to be here is by crossing the river.... They think that this is theirs and we don't need to be here. (Cavan, 2006, pp. 168–69)

She went on to say that the teacher also accused her of stealing and then reprimanded her for speaking Spanish in the class.

Marcela never held back in her stories. Her view on the school was that "The whole place is discrimination.... It seems everybody hates us here ... it is all favoritism. A person can get away with anything if he knows the right people ... not us" (Cavan, 2006, pp. 170–171). Like Sara, she believed that some had the power like the students active in sports and the cheerleaders. She also expressed that these students had power from the teachers. She stated, "I do not want to be left out. But you can't do it ... it's impossible to get in and impossible to get treated like others. Teachers and students just don't want us around" (p. 171).

She once tried out for the dance team and the flag team. She did not make either. When she questioned the judges, she was told that either she was too fat or too tall. She told me, "I know I did not make it because I was the minority ... I love to dance. But it wasn't going to happen" (Cavan, 2006, p. 172). Marcela wept when she told me she was used to being left out. She continued to say that, at first, she tried to conform, but that made little difference in how people treated her. She said it would make little difference to anyone what she did. She was still Mexican and excluded for that reason.

Acceptance of diverse cultures is often met with opposition that relentlessly seeks to place other cultures in submission. Suppression of culture maintains the privilege and power of the dominant group (Apple, 1995, 2001; Spring, 2001). Gay (2000) states, "Culture is at the heart of everything we do in the name of education" (p. 8). Tayo, Sara, and Marcela were all testaments to this belief. They were denied their own cultural existence which could have been a "fundamental anchor" (p. 9) for other behaviors like thinking, relating, and speaking. Their heritage cultures could have been a strong resource for success in the classroom (Gay, 2000; Nieto, 1996, McLaren, 1995). Weaver (2004) also shows us that when pedagogy has relevance and connects to one's life experiences, the student is more likely to be participatory and engaged in the learning process. Devine (1995) states, "Educative figures should strive in ... engaging the whole student-not just the disembodied mind" (p. 66). When the student is alienated from her own culture through "bicultural ambivalence" (Cummins, 1993, p. 105), inferior status, and discrimination, academic failure often ensues. These students cannot become whole students whom Ayers (2004) describes as "three-dimensional with hopes, dreams, aspirations, skills, and capabilities; a body and a heart and a spirit; experience, a history, a past, several pathways, a future" (p. 3). The interviews with these participants revealed they were all denied becoming a whole student.

Identity Struggles

All three of the participants were eager to tell me about how they struggled with identity issues. Tayo talked about how different life was here than what she had imagined. She said her life was very confusing because at times she found herself wanting to be American. This became a conflict for her because people did not accept her as an American. Furthermore, when she reverted to her Nigerian identity, she was still not accepted. Later she told me that she was no longer bothered by her non acceptance. She told me she would always be Nigerian and wanted to be buried in her country. Yet, there were occasions when I knew she struggled with who she really was. There were many things about the American culture that she liked such as being able to go out with boys. She knew that this was impossible because it was not allowed in her culture. She told me it made her feel badly that she wanted to do these things like other girls she knew.

Tayo's identity also revolved around her heritage culture. She wanted respect for whom she was but found that there was no respect for her or her heritage. Realizing this, Tayo began to doubt who she was and questioned why no one took the time to discover who she was. She was embarrassed to tell me during the interviews that at times she was ashamed of her culture and who she was. In the end, she came full circle to tell me that she had grown up and that the rejection of who she was no longer bothered her. She stated, "I no longer cry. I just let it go. I am ok to be different" (Cavan, 2006, p. 154). Tayo began to accept herself for other reasons which included finding a support group with Sara and other immigrants. She found a safe place at school where she could be herself without having to hide the person she was and who she was becoming.

Sara recounted stories of feeling lost. She said she felt half-Pakistani and half-American. She often struggled with having to be American at school and Pakistani at home. She stated, "I have to remind myself to be one way or this way. Then I forget sometime. Then I am like stuck. Like I am not really this and not really that. Sometime I don't know what to do. It is confusing … I just want people to respect me" (Cavan, 2006, pp. 164–65). She continued to tell me that she was not one culture; she was both. The fact that she realized she was both caused her anguish because she was not accepted by either. Her identity was challenged as that of Tayo, but she found a support group where she could be herself. It is also in this group that she, like others, found acceptance of self.

Marcela perhaps had a greater identity struggle than Tayo and Sara because she participated in the large Hispanic population in the community and at school. She recounted that many of her Mexican friends, as well as her father, accused her of trying to be American. Some told her she was not a Mexican. She admitted that she did like some things that were American but that her own cultural identity was important to her. She explained, "I do not want to lose it … I always am Mexican. One time I didn't know who I was" (Cavan, 2006, p. 178). Marcela was also lost not knowing whether to speak Spanish or not, try to be accepted or not, or try to practice her own culture or not. She confessed that she sometimes felt like a hypocrite because she wanted to do things that were not acceptable in her culture. "I feel like I am bad, like I am not true to my culture" (p. 178). She was also saddened to tell me that there were occasions when she wanted to just deny her identity and become American. Her reasoning for this was that then perhaps people would not look down on her. Her identity as a Mexican was described as this, "We are the lowest. Everybody treat us like the lowest. Teachers, everybody. We just don't count" (Cavan, 2006, p. 178). Like the other two participants, by the end of the interviews, she was telling me that it did not bother her any more. She wanted to have the freedom to be who she would become.

Apple (1995) addresses identity issues in schooling which promotes a reproducible individual for corporate needs. Such a curriculum is lacking in self-awareness, experience, and self-growth. Aronowitz (1989) emphasizes this: "[A] major purpose of schooling is the denial of identity "(p. 200). Wear (1997) believes that our school system is entrenched in dualisms where some students are valued and others are not. Promoting a monoculture leads to mono identities deprived of self-worth and value (Aronowitz & Giroux, 1985). Each of the participants revealed a negated identity development through rejections of language, culture, and self.

Identity is a process and is ever changing (Green, 1995). Green emphasizes that there must be space and safe haven for identity development. There must also be time for identity development to take place. All the participants told me that they did not have time to assimilate; they were rushed to conform and be like everyone else. All of them became confused and lost at times, not knowing which pathway to follow. He (2003) felt "tensions and challenges" (p. 75) in this abyss which I know Tayo, Sara, and Marcela also experienced. However, He describes a continuum that allowed her to flow freely from one culture and identity to the other. It is from this flowing that she was able to construct a new identity which included the past, present, and the future. The participants in this research were never given the same opportunity to experience a free flowing from one identity to the other. They were denied the "free spaces" (Raley, 2004, p. 151) needed to explore who they were and who they would become. The participants lacked these spaces in the classroom where they were ignored and rejected. A healthy identity development is critical for immigrant students to imagine what they might become instead of what is. Denying spaces for identity development to occur is described by Soto (2005) as "suffocating … forbidding our perspectives, our creativity, and our wisdom" (p. ix). Each of the participants began to internalize that she was not smart or capable of succeeding academically or attaining her dreams. This became a self-fulfilling prophesy for each of them.

EDUCATIONAL AND SOCIAL CHANGES RESULTING FROM THE INQUIRY

I would like to say that much has changed at my school since my research was completed. Unfortunately, that is not the case. The overall objective continues to be high stakes testing and making the marks for graduation.

To acerbate this madness for testing, the school did not make the annual yearly progress goal for the school year 2006–07. Consequently, more and more efforts are focused upon prepping students for the upcoming tests. I realize that there is little I can do to change the testing mode of the school or the powers that demand such an absurd practice.

As I look around the school on a typical day, I see the minority groups, Hispanics, Africans, and Asians, together in the halls, classrooms, library, and cafeteria. These groups are also subdivided into their own races. Likewise, there are the popular students in their groups. What I see also in my own classroom is a small microcosm of what takes place in the whole school. Although I try to place students into diverse groups for cooperative work, there is constant grumbling and moaning from all students who wish to be with their own races. In my heart, I would love to see otherwise; so I continue to try. My classroom is diverse, and that is a good thing. Culture is a large part of my curriculum so I am constantly asking students to share their cultural mores with the class. I also use role playing which includes students assuming new and uncertain lives which are very different from their own. These activities encourage empathy for others of different languages and cultures and those who experience unknown and often unwelcomed situations.

I am chairperson of the World Languages Department, and I am proud that I finally was able to institute Spanish for Native Speakers into the curriculum. This class is for students who speak Spanish, but whose writing and reading skills need improvement. Kwong (2000) writes that classes such as this offer an emotional support for immigrant students while they are learning English. They are together with their peers and a cultural role model who speaks the same language and understands cultural nuances. There are also those who contend that in these classes, students are engaged and motivated and that overall academic performance is increased (Ballenger, 2000; Ladson-Billings, 2001). As our Asian population increases, I foresee such a class for our Chinese students. We already have an ESOL teacher from China who is certified in teaching Chinese.

In the past, there has been little communication between the ESOL teacher and the core curriculum teachers. Although she has been available, teachers have not taken the time to discuss individual student needs or accommodations with her. At the time of my research, she told me that no one had ever approached her about one of her students. This supports Bartolome's (2000) view that monolingual teachers use little modified instruction for our ESOL students. However, this seems to be changing as a by-product of our testing procedures. As immigrant student numbers increase at my school, they will be considered as a subgroup and held accountable for passing mandated tests. As a result, more attention will be given to meeting the academic needs of these students. Although I oppose the high stakes testing which schools are required to administer, I am encouraged that more attention will be focused on our immigrant population for school success.

There are other glimmers of hope for change that are happening throughout my department. One of the Spanish teachers wrote a grant to start a girl's club at the school. Many of our immigrant population have shown a desire to join and become a part of this group. The focus of the club is to bring females together and to discuss critical social issues which include managing money, respecting one's body, applying for college, seeking aid for college, and many more topics to which these females do not have access or guidance. The grant includes workshops conducted at the school site by various companies and organizations. I praise this teacher for her efforts and vision in this project. I am certain many of our female students will benefit from this club, especially our female immigrant students.

I have come to realize that there are things that I can accomplish in my own classroom and my own department to fight against the injustice I see around me. They may be small steps, but then again, it is an effort to bring about change. It is my hope that other teachers in the school will begin to see the progress we are making in the department to end prejudice and bias toward our immigrant population. It is my hope that they will choose to follow us.

Everyday I am challenged personally and professionally to bring about change in our schools so that ultimately education will bring about social change. However, from my research, I am convinced, like Olneck (1995), that schooling continues to "inculcate dominate modes of social participation and belonging, and to periodically establish the 'once imagined neat fit between language, culture, and nation' " (p. 381). As a nation, we must implement an education that stresses the continuity of the immigrant student's language, culture, and identity. This requires a culturally responsive pedagogy. In doing this, we can promote learning, build self-esteem, and create opportunities for economic and social progress. If the opposite is pursued, we will continue to generate unskilled and uneducated students (Suárez-Orozco, Suárez-Orozco, & Doucet, 1999).

"Cultural continuity" (Sleeter & Grant, 1999, p. 47) in education develops academic skills in part because it is less confusing and frightening for immigrant students. Cultural continuity allows and accepts different learning styles, languages, and cultures. Furthermore it builds upon past experience which can enrich learning opportunities and develop literacy (Moll et al., 1992).

A culturally responsive pedagogy must include immigrant families (Moll, Amanti, Neff, & Gonzalez, 1992). We have made some headway in my school because the administration meet immigrant parents in the beginning of the year and inform them about issues concerning their children's education. However, more of these meetings need to be held. Involving the parents in the education process can enrich the process through the "funds of knowledge" (Moll et al., 1992, p. 133) these families hold. These funds of knowledge also extend to the children in the families. My research revealed that Tayo ran the household including financing and meals, Sara worked at her father's store keeping the accounts, and Marcela was in charge of housekeeping and cleaning. These are resources that could have been used to strengthen their education experience and success.

"Examining this intersection of factors contributing to these immigrant students' school success is of paramount importance, given the fact that significant numbers of immigrant students leave without a diploma" (He, Phillion, Chan, & Xu, 2007, p. 224). The oppression that immigrant students undergo in school ultimately excludes them from fully reaping economic, social, or political benefits in this country. A culturally responsive education must recognize that our nation is diverse and work toward implementing ideals for change. As Connell (1993) states, "Social justice requires … reconstructing the mainstream" (p. 44). Jelloun (1996) states that pedagogy must address the learned ignorance of and racist attitude of one group toward another. I am dedicated to teaching students not to fear diversity due to linguistic and cultural differences. I am also dedicated to teaching students to value sociocultural differences, to recognize that one is not more valid than the other, and to respect the "human dignity" (p. 39) of all others. When I do this, I am teaching for social justice and equality.

REFERENCES

Anzaldua, G. (1987). *Borderlands: La frontera*. San Francisco: Aunt Lute Books.

Apple, M. W. (1995). *Education and power* (2nd ed.). New York: Routledge.

Apple, M. W. (2001). *Educating the "right" way: Markets, standards, God, and inequalities*. New York: Routledge.

Aronowitz, S. (1989). Working-class identity and celluloid fantasy. In H. Giroux & R. Simon (Eds.), *Popular culture: Schooling and everyday life* (pp. 197–218). Granby, MA: Bergin & Garvey.

Aronowitz, S., & Giroux, H. (1985). *Education under siege*. South Hadley, MA: Bergin & Garvey.

Ayers, W. (2004). *Teaching the personal and the political: Essays on hope and justice*. New York: Teachers College Press.

Ballenger, C. (2000). Bilingual in two senses. In Z. Beykont (Ed.), *Lifting every voice: Pedagogy and politics of bilingualism* (pp. 95–112). Cambridge, MA: Harvard University Press.

Bartolome, L. (2000). Democratizing bilingualism: The role of critical teacher education. In Z. Beykont (Ed.), *Lifting every voice: Pedagogy and politics of bilingualism* (pp. 167–186). Cambridge, MA: Harvard University Press.

Beykont, Z. (Ed.). (2000). *Lifting every voice: Pedagogy and politics of bilingualism.* Cambridge, MA: Harvard University Press.

Carger, C. (1996). *Of borders and dreams: A Mexican-American experience of urban education.* New York: Teachers College Press.

Carger, C. (2005). The art of narrative inquiry: Embracing emotion and seeing transformation. In J. Phillion, M. F. He, & F. M. Connelly (Eds.), *Narrative and experience in multicultural education* (pp. 231–246). Thousand Oaks, CA: SAGE.

Cavan, J. (2006). *A cross-cultural narrative inquiry into language, culture, and identity development of three high school female immigrant students and the mainstream schooling experience in an Atlanta suburb.* Statesboro, GA: Georgia Southern University Press.

Clandinin, D., & Connelly, F. M. (2000). *Narrative inquiry: Experience and story in qualitative research.* San Francisco: Jossey-Bass.

Connell, R. W. (1993). Disruptions: Improper masculinities and schooling. In L. Weiss & F. Fine (Eds.), *Beyond silenced voices: Class, race, and gender in United States schools* (pp. 191–208). Albany, NY: State University of New York Press.

Cummins, J. (1989). *Empowering minority students.* Sacramento, CA: California Association for Bilingual Education.

Cummins, J. (1993). Empowering minority students: A framework for intervention. In L. Weiss & M. Fine (Eds.), *Beyond silenced voices: Class, race and gender in United States schools* (pp. 101–118). Albany, NY: State University of New York Press.

Devine, J. (1995). *Maximum security: The culture of violence in the inner-city schools.* Chicago: University of Chicago Press.

Dewey, J. (1938). *Experience and education.* New York: Touchstone.

Feuerverger, G. (2005). Multicultural perspectives in teacher development. In J. Phillion, M. F. He, & F. M. Connelly (Eds.), *Narrative and experience in multicultural education* (pp. 175–199). Thousand Oaks, CA: SAGE.

Gay, G. (2000). *Culturally responsive teaching: Theory, research and practice.* New York: Teachers College Press.

Greene, M. (1995). *Releasing the imagination: Essays on education, the arts, and social change.* San Francisco: Jossey-Bass.

He, M. F. (2003). *A river forever flowing: Cross-cultural lives and identities in the multicultural landscape.* Greenwich, CN: Information Age.

He, M. F., Phillion, J., Chan, E., & Xu, S. J. (2007). Immigrant students' experience of curriculum. In F. M. Connelly, M. F. He, & J. Phillion (Eds.), *Handbook of curriculum and instruction* (pp. 1–32). Thousand Oaks, CA: SAGE.

Jankie, D. (2004). "Tell me who you are": Problematizing the construction and positionalites of "insider"/ "outsider" of a "native" ethnographer in a postcolonial context. In K. Mutua & B. Swadener (Eds.), *Decolonizing research in cross-*

cultural contexts: Critical personal narratives (pp. 87–105). Albany, NY: State University of New York Press.

Jelloun, T. (1996). *Racism explained to my daughter.* New York: The New Press.

Kwong, K. (2000). Bilingualism equals access: The case of Chinese high school students. In Z. Beykont (Ed.), *Lifting every voice: Pedagogy and politics of bilingualism* (pp. 43–52). Cambridge, MA: Harvard University Press.

Ladson-Billings, G. (2001). *Crossing over to Canaan: The journey of new teachers in diverse classrooms.* San Francisco, CA: Jossey-Bass.

McIntosh, P. (1998). *White privilege: Unpacking the invisible knapsack.* Wellesley, MA: Wellesley College Press.

McLaren, P. (1995). *Critical pedagogy and predatory culture: Oppositional politics in a postmodern era.* New York: Routledge.

Moll, L., Amanti, C., Neff, D., & Gonzalez, J. (1992, Spring). Funds of knowledge for teaching: Using a qualitative approach to connect homes and classrooms. *Theory Into Practice, XXXI,* 132–141.

Nieto, S. (1996). *Affirming diversity: The sociopolitical context of multicultural education.* New York: Longman.

Olneck, M. (1995). Immigrants and education in the United States. In J. Banks and C. Banks (Eds.), *Handbook of research on multicultural education* (pp. 382–403). San Francisco, CA: Jossey-Bass.

Raley, J. (2004). "Like family, you know?": School and the achievement of peer relations. In M. Gibson, P. Gandara, & J. Koyama (Eds.), *School connections: U.S. Mexican youth, peers, and school achievement* (pp. 150–172). New York: Teachers College Press.

Sleeter, C., & Grant, C. (1999). *Making choices for multicultural education: Five approaches to race, class, and gender.* New York: Wiley.

Soto, L. D. (1997). *Language, culture, and power: Bilingual families and the struggle for quality education.* New York: State University of New York Press.

Soto, L. D. (2005). Teachers as transformative healers: Struggles with the complexities of the democratic sphere. In J. Phillion, M. F. He, & F. M. Connelly (Eds.), *Narrative and experience in multicultural education* (pp. 143–156). Thousand Oaks, CA: SAGE.

Spring, J. (2001). *Deculturalization and the struggle for equality: A brief history of the education of dominated cultures in the United States.* New York: State University of New York.

Suárez-Orozco, C., Suárez-Orozco, M., & Doucet, F. (1999). The academic engagement and achievement of Latino youth. In J. Banks & C. McGhee (Eds.), *Handbook of research on multicultural education* (pp. 420–490). San Francisco, CA: Jossey-Bass.

Valenzuela, A. (1999). *Subtractive schooling: U.S.-Mexican youth an the politics of caring.* New York: State University of New York Press.

Wear, D. (1997). *Privilege in the medical academy: A feminist examines gender, race, & power.* New York: Teachers College Press.

Weaver, J. (2004). Curriculum theorists as spawns from Hell. In J. Weaver, K. Anijar, & T. Daspit (Eds.), *Science fiction curriculum, cyborg teachers, & youth culture(s)* (pp. 21–37). New York: Peter Lang.

CHAPTER 11

READING THROUGH
BROWN EYES

Toward Developing a Culturally
Congruent Reading Curriculum

Clara Taylor

Six African American males, Que, Jermaine, Rico, Kobe, Tay, and Trae, participated in this research study, with two from each grade level of sixth grade, seventh grade, and eighth grade. Using critical race theory (CRT) as a theoretical framework and critical narrative inquiry as a methodology, I examined the reading motivations of these six African American middle grade males and investigate why some of them are more successful academically in reading than others. I also explored racial and ethnic identity as it relates to cultural backgrounds, popular cultures, learning styles as motivational factors for engaging African American males in reading and learning processes.

Personal~Passionate~Participatory Inquiry Into Social Justice in Education, pp. 177–198
Copyright © 2008 by Information Age Publishing
All rights of reproduction in any form reserved.

CONTEXT OF STUDY

A strong workforce is dependent on literacy as an important ingredient for a country's economic opportunities and growth. Yet, a large segment of youth labeled as "at-risk" academically in the United States experience reading problems, which in turn may affect their ability to participate in and contribute to society and their own economic security. These students are often labeled "at-risk" because of their race, ethnicity, gender, and socioeconomics status. Not only are reading skills required for success in education, they are just as important for successful economic and social interactions in a global society. Although, the United States of America is considered a world leader based on its wealth and technological advancements, a large portion of minority, immigrant, and poor children experience minimum success in reading literacy and academic achievement.

The growing population of minority students in public schools further exacerbates the problem. Carbo (1995) estimated that one out of every three students in American schools would come from a minority group before the year 2000. As early as 1955, Flesch expressed concerns about illiteracy and made the following predictions:

> Some 27 million American adults are functionally illiterate, and 45 million more are marginally literate. The number of adult problem readers is increasing by 2.3 million each year. At this rate, we'll soon join the ranks of such undereducated Third World countries as Bangladesh, Haiti, and Uganda. (p. viii)

Flesch (1955) and Carbo (1995), along with many educators, researchers and society at large validate my concerns about a large percentage of "at-risk" students with reading problems. African American males are particularly at risk. The racial gap has fluctuated more in reading than in any other subject. In 1971 Black students at ages 9, 13, and 17 were appallingly far behind whites, ranking in the 14th, 13th, and 11th percentiles, respectively (Chubb & Loveless, 2002). Chubb and Loveless also indicated that in 1988 Black 9-year-olds ranked in the 23rd percentile, 13-year-olds in the 30th percentile, and 17-year-olds in the 29th percentile. In 1999 the two older groups scored about the same as they had 15 years before, and 9-year-olds were performing at the low level they had achieved 24 years earlier.

It is well documented that many African American male students are reading substantially below grade level (Donahue, Daane, & Grigg, 2003; Kunjufu, 1995). Most of the data report the achievement gap based on ethnicity and gender in subgroups, but fail to provide specific data about African American males in the area of reading. The Achievement Gap Analysis of the State of Georgia reports that 28% of eighth-grade Black students do not meet the reading achievement standard as compared to 12% of eighth-grade White students as measured on the 2003 Georgia Criterion Referenced Competency Tests (CRCT) (Georgia School Council Institute [GSCI], 2004). The GSCI report also indicates a large percentage of students failing to meet the standard for reading fall into the following subgroups: economically disadvantaged (29%), special education (57%), and male (23%).

Comparatively, Kunjufu's (1995) analysis reports African American children comprise 17% of public school children in this nation; 41% of African American children are placed in special education, and 85% of those African American children are male. This validates the high percentage of African American males in the special education category. Equally important, reading scores for Black students nationally increased over the years from an average score of 237 in 1992 to an average score of 244 in 2003 (Donahue, Daane, & Grigg, 2003). The average reading score for male eighth-graders declined 2 points between 2002 and 2003; the average score in 2003 (258) was higher than in 1992 (254) (Donahue et al., 2003, p. 43).

The significance of the plight of an individual's position in the labor market and their socioeconomic status, specifically African American males, is linked to literacy achievement (Sowell, 2000). A brief literacy survey by Smith (1996) shows a correlation between basic skills and literacy skills with occupational skills (as cited in Sowell, 2000, p. 97). The study concludes that a correlation exists between literacy and occupational skills and suggests that the workplace demands an increased level of basic skills, and the amount of education and skill that workers have affects their occupation, performance, and pay.

Based on my professional experience as a reading teacher, I propose that this reading problem among African American males is not primarily a lack of student ability or even skill, but is fundamentally a lack of culturally compatible educational conditions that foster student motivation. Many African American males have become socially alienated by the current curriculums and methods of schooling, which are incongruent with their cultural identities, and, as a result, these young males have motivationally disengaged with school reading and learning in general (Gause, 2000; Gordon, 1990, 1993; Harrison & Harrison, 2002; Hilliard, 2003; Hilliard, Payton-Stewart, & Williams, 1995; Kunjufu, 1990, 1995). Having taught reading for 6 years in the public school system, I have first-hand experience and knowledge of the critical needs of "at-risk" African American male students in the area of reading instruction A major question to consider is: What makes some African American males succeed in reading when so many others experience a high level of failure from similar economic backgrounds? I propose that critically important for investigation

are the cultural factors that may facilitate or diminish the personal reading motivations of African American males.

AUTOBIOGRAPHICAL ROOTS OF MY INQUIRY

My family has often referred to me as a rebel. I have always had a voice
for the "underdog" and a desire to make life better for those often victimized by society, such as myself and many people of color. At the age of
fourteen, I was almost arrested for interfering with the duties of an
officer. I was visiting my girlfriend when one of our male friends dashed
in the door running from the police. As the police came to the door, I
insisted that they show a search warrant before entering the house. In my
heart I believed my friend was being unfairly targeted. Things are not
much different today for African Americans and especially African American males than they were then. Currently, two stories confirm the current
victimization and the continued injustices experienced by African
American males. Genarlow Wilson, a teen serving a 10 year prison term
for having consensual sex with a 15-year-old female when he was 17
(Lewis, 2006). The Jena Six, a group of Black students who are being
charged with attempted murder for beating up a White student who was
taunting them with racial slurs in a school that continued to support other
White students who hung three nooses from the high school's "White
tree" which sits in the front yard (Stewart, 2007).

As an African American female, mother, grandmother, daughter, wife,
sister, and community activist, I am deeply concerned about the plight of
African American males in a variety of roles in the United States and have
a vested interest in their success. This year, my daughter blessed me with
a beautiful grandson. Prior to his arrival, many questions haunted my
thoughts and pulled at my heart strings. How do I make life better for my
Black blood brothers and those related to me by our ancestry? Now, I
must consider how do I make life better for my grandson and those
around him? What bridges do I have to cross to make sure that he
receives the same opportunities (if not, greater) as every other child? I am
passionate and committed to making life better for all African American
males in our education system and others with similar experiences.

As an African American educator, it is important for me to provide
additional views to the notions of the dominant power group that feels
privileged to speak for all groups. I want to be included in the dialogue
about educating students that look like me, and I want my voice heard.
This is not easy in our current society. Often, the voices of people that
look like me, even in academe, do not receive the same level of respect
and acknowledgement as others. Why is that? Ladson-Billings (2003)

believed that CRT helps raise some important questions about the control and production of knowledge—particularly knowledge about people and communities of color.

As a middle school reading teacher for 6 years, it was a major challenge for me to get my students actively involved in the reading process. I was often frustrated trying to follow the county mandated reading curriculum with my eighth grade students. During those 6 years of teaching reading, many of my students, especially African American males, experienced a high failure rate academically. On many occasions my students would verbalize their dislike for reading and state that it was boring. I could not understand this because I have always been an avid reader. Despite the many tactics I used, I could not get most of my minority students to adopt the concept of becoming independent readers.

As an administrator and counselor, I have witnessed the frustration of many teachers assigned to teach reading to predominantly African American students. It appears that many of these teachers, despite their subject content certification area, loathed teaching reading to a group of students who appeared apathetic and detached from the subject. I am concerned about the survival of African Americans as viable and contributing citizens in this global society if this mind-set continues.

CRITICAL NARRATIVE INQUIRY

Critical narrative inquiry represents the marriage of two forms of inquiry, critical inquiry and narrative inquiry. The term critical, within a theory of research, has been used to connote the action of social critique (Moss, 2001). Kincheloe and McLaren (2003) suggests that critical inquiry is concerned in particular with issues of power and justice and the ways that the economy, matters of race, class, and gender, ideologies, discourses, education, religion and other social institutions, and cultural dynamics interact to construct a social system. Sirotnik (1991) considers critical inquiry as a paradigm for praxis and describes it as empirical, explanatory, interpretive, deliberative, reflective, instrumental, and action-oriented. Critical inquiry must also challenge directly underlying human interests and ideologies based upon a commitment to social justice. Critical inquiry is thereby explicitly normative and focuses on underlying values, beliefs, interests, intentions, and so forth (Sirotnik, 1991). Critical inquiry suggests that the paradigm offers realistic guidelines for more authentic communication, decision making, action taking, and evaluation by people who are genuinely and actively seeking a more democratic vision of schooling. The use of critical in this study is used as an adjective to describe the disposition of the narrative research method, the narrative stories of the African American males, the use of CRT, and my role as a researcher (Sirotnik, 1991).

Clandinin and Connelly (2000) also emphasized the dynamic and dia-logical nature of narrative research in their definition.

> Narrative inquiry is a way of understanding experience. It is collaboration between researcher and participants, over time, in a place or series of places, and in social interaction with milieus. An inquirer enters this matrix in the midst and progresses in this same spirit, concluding the inquiry still in the midst of living and telling, reliving and retelling, the stories of the experience that make up people's lives, both individual and social. Simply stated … narrative inquiry is stories lived and told. (p. 20)

I view my inquiry into African American males' reading motivation as leading to radical changes and emancipation from oppressive social structures. This will happen through collaboration with this oppressed group of participants, African American middle grade males, revealed through their storytelling in this research. My use of CRT as my lens of focus in this narrative process creates a critical narrative approach. This is critical narrative because using race as a factor makes this more than just a narrative by presenting a counter story from a racial viewpoint. The art of storytelling is part of the African legacy and a component of critical race theorists. Therefore, CRT will direct and guide me during this research process in research and framing the questions for the interview process. Critical narrative is the process of presenting the experiences of what was shared and learned during the research process.

One component proposed by critical race theorists is that the individual life experiences of people of color should be recognized and made public as a unique voice of color. This should be accomplished using language, narrative, speech, and words (Crenshaw, Gotanda, Peller, & Thomas, 1995; Delgado & Stefancic, 2001; Ladson-Billings, 2003; Olmsted, 1998). My goal was to use critical narrative inquiry to provide a loud and pronounced voice on behalf of several African American males and their stories, which are often silenced and marginalized in many hegemonic discourses. Some traditional social science research has silenced many marginalized and oppressed groups by making them the passive object of inquiry (Marshall & Rossman, 1999). Casey (1995/1996) highlighted the importance of the last 20 years that have witnessed an enormous burgeoning of oral history/narrative research projects explicitly connected to progressive political projects. An especially appealing attribute of oral history/storytellling is the way in which it can display the assets of those ordinarily considered to have none such as African Americans in general and African American males in particular. A lack of academic learning does not preclude expertise in narrative knowing or skill in narrative expression.

Ladson-Billings (2003) expressed the importance of narrative as the need to know and to be known as powerful aspects of the human condition. She stands critical of knowledge by and about people of color as being repressed, distorted, and denied by a Euro-American cultural logic that represents an "aggressive seizure of intellectual space" (p. 417). She continued to express that the value of storytelling in qualitative research is that it can be used to demonstrate how the same phenomenon can be told in different and multiple ways depending on the storytellers.

Critical race theorists have created a legacy experimenting with poetry, parables, personal anecdotes, chronicles, fiction, revisionist histories, counter-stories, music, aesthetics, nature, and short stories, all with the goal of illustrating and sharing how minority persons suffer from existing laws and the system of American justice (Crenshaw, Gotanda, Peller, & Thomas, 1995; Delgado & Stefancic, 2001; Ladson-Billings, 2003; Olmsted, 1998). These goals are parallel to the goals CRT encourages in the education curriculum: for students to tell their stories, to find their own voices, and to perceive the realness that others value. The act of finding one's voice is considered a way of naming one's own reality.

Casey (1995/1996) expressed, "Theories, methodologies, and politics of narrative research are in a process of being defined and redefined as particular researchers and groups of researchers struggle to make the various aspects of their work coherent and consistent" (p. 231). Scholars of color dominate this group of researchers struggling to make the various aspects of their work first reach the forefront in qualitative research. Ladson-Billings (2003) stated,

> Today, as I attempt to do my own work I am struck by the growing number of scholars of color who have chosen to go back into those fields, construction sites, and kitchens to give voices to their own people—their perspectives, worldviews, and epistemologies. These scholars, like James Gronniosaw, are attempting to have the lives of subordinated people "talk to them." Tired of bending their ears to hear the master's book talk, scholars of color are writing new texts from the lives and experiences of people much like themselves. (p. 420)

The burden is on the researcher to ensure clarity, coherence, and consistency of the research process. Casey (1995/1996) advocated for the importance of the relationship between the researcher and the subject of the research. It is also important to consider that learning to take respondents' storytelling seriously has had a number of unsettling effects on academic scholars, including having to suspend substantial portions of their academic training. According to Casey (1995/1996), "Whether implicit or elaborated, every study of narrative is based on a particular understanding of the speaker's self. At present, definitive features of narrative studies differ widely depending on their authors' deeply held beliefs about the nature of self " (p. 213). Based on this statement, there appears to be a thin line between the narrative process and the researcher. Collins (1990), a Black feminist, articulated an understanding about the thin line between the narrative process and the researcher.

> Finally, writing this book has convinced me of the need to reconcile subjectivity and objectivity in producing scholarship. Initially, I found the movement between my training as an "objectivity" social scientist and my daily experiences as an African American woman jarring. But reconciling what we have been trained to see as opposites, a reconciliation signaled by my inserting myself in the text by using, "I," "we," and "our" instead of the more distancing terms "they" and "one," was freeing for me. (p. xiv)

A major connection presented by Casey (1995/1996) to my inquiry is the following:

> In a world controlled by TV talk shows, tabloid exposés, and slogan T-shirts, telling one's story becomes exhibitionism, and listening to another's becomes voyeurism. Alternatively (or perhaps complementarily), story telling is the way to put shards of experiences together, to (re)construct identity, community, and tradition, if only temporarily. (p. 216)

African American males are often immersed into a world of voyeurism with massive images of the lives of the dominant group in our society. The stories they often see and hear bear little similarities to their own lives. Many of the reality TV shows and other sitcoms are shards of experiences that are far fetched from the everyday lives of African American males and are foreign to their identity, community, and tradition. African American males must move more in the direction of exhibitionism and less as voyeurism. This happens, as they become storytellers such as this experience of telling their stories about their experiences in reading.

Critical narrative is a way of characterizing the phenomena of human experience and its study, which is appropriate to many social science fields (Connelly & Clandinin, 1991). Another dimension that is important to me is the importance of a relationship between myself, the researcher and the participants, permitting a feeling of connectedness and a sense of equality. Hogan highlighted the research relationship as an important aspect of the narrative inquirer in the statement, "Empowering relationships feelings of 'connectedness' that are developed in situations of equality, caring and mutual purpose and intention" (as cited in Short, 1991, p. 126). Collins (1990) developed a theoretical rubric for explicating a

Black feminist standpoint that would be useful in evaluating the research relationship. Collins argues for concrete experiences as a criterion of meaning, the use of dialogue in the assessment of knowledge claims, an ethic of caring, and an ethic of personal accountability. As far as relationships, Collins affirmed the importance of being connected:

> In terms of Black women's relationships with one another, African American women may find it easier than others to recognize connectedness as a primary way of knowing, simply because we are encouraged to do so by a Black women's tradition of sisterhood. (p. 212)

In beginning the process of critical narrative inquiry, it is particularly important that all participants have voice within the relationship. Britzman (as cited in Short, 1991) explain about voice in the narrative sense:

> Voice is meaning that resides in the individual and enables that individual and to participate in a community.... The struggle for voice begins when a person attempts to communicate meaning to someone else. Finding the words, speaking for oneself, and feeling heard by others are all a part of this process. Voice suggests relationships: the individual's relationship to the meaning of her/his experience and hence, to language, and the individual's relationship to the other, since understanding is a social process. (p. 127)

Connelly and Clandinin (1991) validated these sentiments with the statement, "In beginning the process of narrative inquiry it is particularly important that all participants have voice within the relationship" (p. 127). This is the voice I am seeking from the African American males in this study to help understand their personal relationship with the subject area of reading and their motivation to read. Important to consider is the problem, after all, is not with the voices that speak but with the ears that do not hear (Casey, 1995/1996, p. 223). The greatest challenge before me is to present the stories of the selected African American males in an enticing manner with integrity, which will create listening ears.

VOICES OF QUE, JERMAINE, RICO, KOBE, TAY, AND TRAE

In the following sections you are going to hear the voices of six African American males, Que, Jermaine, Rico, Kobe, Tay, and Trae, with two from each grade level—sixth grade, seventh grade, and eighth grade. The six student participants were enrolled at Martin Luther King Jr. Middle School, an inner city school in The Atlanta Public School System. Martin Luther King Jr. Middle School (King Middle School) is an interesting school serving sixth grade through eighth grade students. King

Middle School is the first middle school in the state of Georgia offering single gender specific learning academies at the sixth grade and seventh grade levels, while eighth grade students are served in a coed environment. The student population at King Middle School is approximately 615 students. The enrollment distribution by race/ethnicity is as follows: White (4%), Black (86.7%), Hispanic (8%), and other (.13%) (Standard & Poor's, 2003-2004). King is located approximately 2–3 miles from the Martin Luther King, Jr. Center for Social Change in the downtown Atlanta area. King Middle School is a Title I school with an economically disadvantaged population of 86.7% (Standard & Poor's, 2003-2004).

The CRCT is designed to measure how well students acquire the skills and knowledge described in the Quality Core Curriculum (QCC) and the Georgia Performance Standards (GPS). The assessments yield information on academic achievement at the student, class, school, system, and state levels. This information is used to diagnose individual student strengths and weaknesses as related to the instruction of the QCC and GPS, and to gauge the quality of education throughout Georgia (Georgia Department of Education, 2004).

The CRCT results from 2003/2004 for students in reading who scored at or above proficient levels are sixth grade—all students (71.4%), Whites (70%), Blacks (71%), Female (83.5), and Male (62.2%); eighth grade—all students (60.4%), Whites (too few to report), Blacks (58.4%), Female (67.7%), and Male (53.5%) (Standard & Poor's, 2003-2004). Noticeably, students scored higher at each level in the sixth grade and declined for all subgroups at the eighth grade.

The six student participants, Que, Jermaine, Rico, Kobe, Tay, and Trae, qualify for low social economic challenges status as determined by free or reduced school lunch enrollment and the following characteristics: three students, one from each grade level (sixth-eighth) with Georgia CRCT scores in the 349 or higher range representing the 60th percentile or higher, and three students, one from each grade level (sixth-eighth) with scores in the lower range of 299 or less, representing the 30th percentile or lower on the total reading test. The CRCT for Georgia reports student achievement in terms of performance levels (1–3): (1) Level 1 does not meet standard score 299 and below, (2) Level 2 meets the standard with score range of 300–349, and (3) Level 3 exceeds the standard with a score of 350 and above (Millicans, 2005).

Que, Jermaine, Rico, Kobe, Tay, and Trae, completed a preestablished reading interest inventory assessment, an online learning-styles inventory, and a one-on-one interview. As I listen to and hear the stories from Que, Jermaine, Rico, Kobe, Tay, and Trae, I kept asking the following two major questions: (1) What cultural influences that facilitate or diminish personal reading motivation are revealed in the stories of middle-grade African American males' experiences in reading? (2) How is the motivation to read revealed in personal stories of high- and low-achieving African American middle grade males?

These questions help understand possible motivational differences and similarities in African American high- and low-level readers. How are the high- and low-level readers motivated similarly and differently? Why are the high-level readers more successful than the low-level readers? These stories provide directions to actions for educators in meeting the needs of both groups of African American males in an effort to develop a culturally congruent reading curriculum.

I was enlightened by my experience of working with Que, Jermaine, Rico, Kobe, Tay, and Trae, and hearing their voices. They responded to many questions with honesty and they often spoke frankly without hesitation. I want to make sure that the students are humanized. Meet these students and listen to their stories (Taylor, 2005).

Que

Que is a sixth grade student born June 27, 1993 (11 years of age). He has two brothers and one sister. Que does not pay for breakfast or lunch, which indicates the free and reduced lunch status of this student. He scored 350 in reading on the Spring 2004 Georgia CRCT, putting him in the exceed category of 60% and above. As Que stated,

> In elementary school I was excellent in reading. In middle school I did all right. My grades dropped from C–D to a D back to a C. I begin to start playing. I like most about reading is I like to read adventurous stories. Sometimes it will have adventure in it or be funny. The pictures—they are creative. The least thing I like least about reading—I don't like it when I get stuck on words. When story be boring—when it doesn't have excitement in it.

Jermaine

Jermaine, a 12-year-old sixth grader, was born May 8, 1993. He has two sisters and does not pay for breakfast or lunch. He indicated that he is rarely late to school or absent from school. Jermaine's estimated grade point average is a B (83–90) and on the Spring 2004 Georgia CRCT he scored 285 in reading. This score puts him in the 35% range and indicates that he did not meet the standard for reading. Jermaine has never failed a grade or skipped a grade. He does not routinely engage in extracurricular activities. His future plans include attending college. Jermaine said:

In elementary school I did well. I made Bs and in middle school I made Cs. For reading I like the most, the authors, the design on the covers, the characters how they are dressed, dancing on the pictures, make books funny by putting jokes in the books. The most I like about reading is reading teaches you stuff—learn drawing and about your life. I like least about reading when they have long pages.

Rico

Rico is 13 years old in the seventh grade and was born August 9, 1991. He has two sisters and is the youngest in his family. His goal is to complete high school. Rico is never late to school; however; he is absent from school a few times a week. His estimated grade point average is a C, a range of 74%–82%, with a score of 282 in reading on the Spring 2004 Georgia CRCT. This score on the CRCT puts Rico in the 35% group for the state reference test confirming that he did not meet the standard in reading. Rico elaborated:

> What I like most about reading is that you never know what can happen and what I like least is having to do a book report after reading. I am good at reading because I was practicing on it a lot by reading comic books and newspapers and stuff. I don't read at home that much, but I read at school a lot because I want to. I comprehend what I read. I enjoy reading books about sports and cars, but I dislike reading poetry and mysteries.

Kobe

Kobe is a 13-year-old seventh grader soon to be eighth grader born November 11, 1991. Kobe is one of five children; he has three sisters and one brother. Not only does he plan to complete high school; he plans to attend college and graduate. He has never been absent from school and rarely arrived late. He has never failed a grade or skipped a grade. He routinely plays basketball as an extracurricular activity. He receives free lunch. Kobe estimates his grade point average as a B in the 83% to 90% range. He scored 371 in reading on the Spring 2004 Georgia CRCT. His score on the CRCT puts him in the 60% group across the state with other seventh graders taking this test. Kobe reflected:

> In elementary school I had a higher reading level than actual grade level all the way during elementary. In middle school, I did well I always made A's. I like reading because you learn more things about history and things that you don't know. Reading builds vocabulary. What I like least about reading is I don't like to finish the book especially if it is boring, but I will complete

if required. It is cool to be a good reader. My friends don't mind that I am a good reader—they respect the fact that I am a good reader.

Tay

Tay is an eighth grade student. He turned fourteen on April 17, 1991. He has two brothers and one sister. His goal is to complete college. He is rarely absent or late to school. His grade point average is a C in the range of 74% to 82%, and he has never failed a grade or skipped a grade. He routinely engages in extracurricular activities. He receives free lunch. He scored 372 in reading on the Spring 2004 Georgia CRCT. Tay shared:

> Elementary, it was real good. I did the best I could do. My scores were high-—I made C's, B's, and A's. I did well in middle school also. What I like most about reading is how interesting the book is. If the book is interesting, I can picture it in my head. It helps to understand it more. The thing I like least about reading is that books sometimes start off boring or end boring, and it makes me not want to read it anymore. I am good at reading because I read a lot. I read in my spare time. I read a lot, every day at home and at school. I will read at different places if I see a book.

Trae

Trae is another eighth grade student. He is 13 years old, born August 22, 1991. Currently, his plans are to complete high school. He has two brothers and three sisters. He is rarely late to school, and he has been absent only a few times a year. His grade point average is a C in the 74% to 82% range. He has never failed a grade or skipped a grade. He receives free lunch His reading score on the Spring 2004 Georgia CRCT is 282, putting him in the 35%. He did not meet the standard based on this score. Trae said:

> During my whole elementary school, I got nothing but As and Bs. Really math and reading are my favorite subjects, I always do well. I just received my report card and made an A by Ms. C, my language arts teacher. Reading is the class I do the best in and it is the easiest. I like reading because you get to explore new things and learn new words. If you sit down with reading, it will take you places you never thought you would go until you are an adult. You learn so many new things. What I don't like about reading is that it is like long books, boring books, and stuff that is too hard for me to understand.

INQUIRY OUTCOMES

Several cultural influences emerged in the stories of these six African American males based on their experiences with reading and education. Cultural influences are important to consider as motivators of or impediments to reading for African American males. Noble (1995) suggested that cultures are reflected in the content and influence the development of curricula. According to Noble, culturally consistent educational practice is a systematic process of developing and stimulating the knowledge, skill, ability, attitude and character necessary for students to undertake socially-defined, goal oriented and culturally-meaningful activities. This process of becoming culturally consistent is important for African American males to become literate in reading.

The stories of these six students revealed positive self-perceptions as African American male readers. The strength of these positive self-perceptions was revealed, for example, in Jermaine's comments, "If I could write a book to motivate other African American males to read. I would write a book about life, how people should look, stop people from doing violence, and stop them that do drugs and stuff." Also, Que expressed somewhat similar thoughts on how to motivate other African American males to read, "I would write a book about people who don't have many things, people unfortunate, people who are ungrateful for what they have when other people don't have nothing at all." Rico wanted to share his personal experience as an African American male, "I would write a life story about me, about my past, about how hard it was growing up as a young Black male." The desire to change what is happening in their community and the world as they saw it by learning to read for these three students, remind me of when I was growing up during the Civil Rights period. Education was not an option, but a must to change our destiny, give us hope for a future, and to do so, reading was the way out for us as Black people and a community. These students assumed their stories would motivate their peers to read something that was relevant to their culture; and that, others would be motivated to read similar stories.

Jermaine shared a story written in one of his textbooks about the "Candy Stand". This story inspired him as it reminded him of the importance of work as an escape from poverty, homelessness, and laziness. Jermaine had witnessed many of these conditions within his community daily; the story reminded him of how a candy stand could change your destiny. For many African American males, employment is a major concern as a means of survival and being self-sufficient. Perry, Steele, and Hilliard (2003) explored the idea of freedom for literacy and literacy for freedom as representation of early struggles of African Americans encounters with literacy and education in the United States.

It is important for teachers to be aware of the many writings that relate to the culture of the students. Many aspects of interest in popular culture emerged in the stories of the African American males. Several of the students expressed interest in sports, music, computers, watching television, art, video games, comic books, movies, shopping, cars, and magazines. Day in and day out as I watch students in classrooms and walking hallways at the middle school where I work, I observe many commonalities shared by male students in the single gender male academies. Many of these Black males can often be observed rapping the words of one of the latest rap songs or "free styling" using their own words. I am constantly telling these students "pull your pants up over your bottom and tuck in your shirt so that your underwear is not exposed." Another common scene is a group of students playing football with a make-believe football, running and tackling each other in the hallways and classrooms. Also, students share video games and baseball cards routinely at school.

For many African American males, popular culture is an area that is easily communicated and expressed in many forums. I make this statement based on my own personal observations and experiences with African American males' exposure to rap/hip-hop music, video games, "urban-wear," BET/MTV videos, and other aspects of popular culture infiltrating their daily lives. It is present in the way students dress daily in and out of the school setting, the strong interest for most of them in the type of music they listen to and can be heard singing in classrooms and hallways around the school, and conversations about video games. The infusion of popular culture is important because it plays a dominant role in the ways in which people and especially young people construct, sustain, and maintain notions of self, history, and community (Dimitriadis, 2001).

My inquiry suggests that cultural influences are important to consider in the reading curriculum and instructional practices of African American males. Many educational leaders remain hesitant today in the area of curriculum studies to consider race as a variable in curriculum design and understanding, despite the necessity of seeking more clarity in realizing the connection between identity and the curriculum. Pinar (1993) identified the fragmented self as a way to help understand curriculum and identity:

> We are what we know. We are, however, also what we do not know. If what we know about ourselves—our history, our culture, our national identity—is deformed by absences, denials, and incompleteness, then our identity--both as individuals and as Americans—is fragmented. This fragmented self is a repressed self, that is, it "contains" repressed elements. Such a self lacks access both to itself and to the world. Repressed, the self's capacity for intelligence, for informed action, even for simple functional competence is

impaired; its sense of history, gender, and politics is incomplete and distorted. (p. 61)

Que, Jermaine, Rico, Kobe, Tay, and Trae claimed to being good readers, but they had not developed critical thinking skills or a real understanding of reading comprehension. Que stated, "Yes, I am good at reading, when I keep on going without stopping. When I don't get stuck on a word reading. Sometimes I ask questions what is this word? I try to sound it out—It may come out the wrong way." Similarly, Jermaine responded, "Yes, I am good at reading. I will practice reading sometime-practice reading hard words. I read every night at home before I go to bed. I read at break time at school and when we go to the library. To comprehend what I am reading, I continue going over words until I get it right. I comprehend some of the things that I read."

To me, that represents a fragmented self with repressed self-capacity of intelligence as identified by Pinar (1993). Despite the three students being identified as low-achievers in the area of reading, they did not admit to having any weaknesses in that area, but proclaimed to read regularly. Their functional competence is impaired due to a loss of identity from a loss of history, culture, and national identity. To consider curriculum as a racial text is important in moving ahead in curriculum studies, but there is no denying that race as a form of identity has consequences.

EDUCATIONAL AND SOCIAL CHANGES ENGENDERED BY THE INQUIRY

Fifty-years after *Brown v. Board of Education*, African Americans continue to experience inequities in education. As the nation commemorated the 50th anniversary of the Brown decision, it is important to recognize that Brown was only the beginning. African American students still attend the worst schools and have the worst academic performance (McNeil, 2004). Black youth continue to have the lowest test scores, are disproportionately placed in special education classes, and have the highest rate of expulsion and suspension (Ware, 2004).

Delgado and Stefancic (2001) proposed, "Many in the field of education consider themselves critical race theorists who use CRT's ideas to understand issues of school discipline and hierarchy, tracking, controversies over curriculum and history, and IQ and achievement testing" (p. 3). Again, this explains my stance as a CRT, as an educator and as a Black woman determined to make a difference inside and outside of classrooms.

Concerns about education and race were noted by Woodson (1990), "The thought of the inferiority of the Negro is drilled into him in almost every class he enters and in almost every book he studies" (p. 2). Schools were used to continue the exploitation of Black people after slavery by providing inferior and third-rate education. The current challenge is to change the oppressive aspects of life that silence and marginalize some while privileging others. There must be a new way of thinking, asking new questions, and making new commitments. Critical race theorists (Delpit, 1995; Gay, 2000; Hale, 2001; hooks, 1994; Irvine, 2003; and Ladson-Billings, 1992, 1998, 2003; Ladson-Billings & Tate, 1995; Tate, 1997) have continued the conversation about educating African Americans and other minorities. As stated earlier, I have always advocated for those less fortunate. For me, graduating from college was a sign that God was giving more to me so that I can give and do more for others. God continued giving me degree (master's)—after degree (specialists)—after degree (doctorate)—so that I can make a difference in the lives of others. As an assistant principal, my responsibility was to make sure that teachers provided quality and equitable instruction for all students. That did not happen. I was often in a tug of war against many of the White teachers as I advocated for the rights of children of color and more so, for Black males. The students were victimized with an incongruent curriculum that did not consider their cultural identity that led to mislabeling and inequitable discipline. This was disheartening for me and it hurt me to the core. I have since left that position because it was evident that my values did not match the values that were in place.

Currently, my position as an instructional specialist in an urban middle school serving single gender academies (sixth & seventh grades) provides many opportunities for me to share and influence curriculum and instruction. This position has provided me with many opportunities for input on how to address the different learning styles of Black males as well as all children. I have had an opportunity to present the voices of the students participating in this inquiry during professional development with teachers to give them insight into how to approach the learning process. Additionally, I provide gender specific learning strategies to the teachers to help meet the needs of the learner. Also, I am responsible for providing instructional resources for the learning process. This responsibility ensures that students will receive culturally relevant reading materials. The teachers value my input and often seek advice on how to improve teaching and learning with their students.

I continue to strive to impact social change in education on a broader level professionally. It is a difficult task and I often get frustrated. Despite how hard I try to make a difference, I feel as if I am taking baby steps. I can not seem to wrap my arms around this monster of education accountability. I am looking forward to a career move that will eventually allow me to reach more educators to change mindsets, instructional practices, and educational opportunities that will benefit all students. The struggle is not over. In addition to my professional commitments, I dedicate numerous hours working in my community to improve academic achievement and education for students of color. As a leader in my church and sorority, I facilitate parent workshops; assist in test preparation workshops for students for state testing; serve on a scholarship committee to provide funding for college for Black females; and coordinate recognition programs for students graduating from high school in the top 5%–10% of their class. These are some of the things to which I am committed to foster social justice in education.

The challenge is for my research to be viewed seriously and with the same merit as others conducting research in this area. Often times, those around you would rather seek research from those they consider to be more "accredited." Most importantly, this research must be extended to elementary schools. It is important to capture and maintain the desire students exhibited at the elementary level to the middle school level.

Many school districts and schools are seeking solutions on how to improve education for African American males. The discussion and implementation of single gender education is on the rise. Presently Atlanta Public Schools (APS), the school district where I am employed, is piloting two single-gender academies at Benjamin S. Carson Honors Preparatory School. The district selected Carson based on the challenging demographics of the community and the need to improve student performance. At Carson, APS will establish two single-gender secondary schools serving Grades 6–12, phased-in over time in the northwest corridor of Atlanta (APS, 2007). I begin to share my research with policy makers, community members, parents, teachers, and principals with the intent to create a culturally congruent reading curriculum for African American males and other minority students, while making changes in curriculum design, the instructional process, and the educational process with a wider audience.

The success of African American males should be a priority for all of us. I return to the concern about how reading/education relates to identity formation of African American males. I feel the statements by Hale (2001) accurately address the concern:

> The boy is father to the man. It is my opinion that we ignore the needs of African American boys in early childhood, the time when the foundation for later achievement is laid. By the time alarming problems arise, in adolescence, prospects are more difficult to reverse…. Academic failure is not an accident. Academic failure, incarceration, and unemployment are outcomes of public schooling for African American boys. More African American

males between the ages of eighteen and twenty-two are in prison today than enrolled in college.... African American males have the lowest grade point average and the lowest scores on standardized tests. Twenty-three million Americans are functionally illiterate, and the largest proportions of these are African American males. Unemployment for African American males between the ages of fifteen and thirty-five is fifty percent.... Most African American children, particularly African American males, do not like school. Many drop out intellectually by the time they are in the fifth grade and make it legal at the age of sixteen. (pp. 41–43)

There is no doubt in my mind that if this snapshot were representative of White males, there would be a declaration of a national epidemic. As a result, major changes would be forced to take place in curriculum design, the instructional process, and the educational process. To advance the education of students of color, it should be mandatory for teacher education programs to develop some format to open similar dialogues about racism. The subject is important in breaking down barriers for self-examinations for all parties, especially for teachers in diverse school settings.

REFERENCES

Atlanta Public Schools. (2007). *Single gender academies.* Retrieved on August 20, 2007, from http://www.atlanta.k12.ga.us/content/single_gender.aspx

Brown v. Board of Education. No. 347 U.S. 483 (1954). Retrieved July 20, 2008, from http://caselaw.lp.findlaw.com/scripts/ getcase.pl?court=US&vol=347&invol=483

Carbo, M. (1995). Educating everybody's children. In R. W. Cole (Eds.), *Educating everybody's children: Diverse Teaching Strategies for Diverse Learners* (pp. 1–18). Alexandra, VA: Association for Supervision and Curriculum Development.

Casey, K. (1996). Casey-New narrative research in education. *Review of research in education, 21,* 211-253. (Original work published 1995)

Chubb, J., & Loveless, T (Eds.). (2002). *Bridging the achievement gap.* Washington, DC: The Brookings Institution.

Clandinin, D., & Connelly, F. (2000). *Narrative inquiry: Experience and story in qualitative research.* San Francisco: Jossey-Bass.

Collins, P. (1990). *Black feminist thought: Knowledge, consciousness, and the politics of empowerment.* New York: Routledge.

Connelly, M., & Clandinin, D. (1991). Narrative inquiry: Storied experience. In E. C. Short (Ed.), *Forms of curriculum inquiry* (pp. 121–154). Albany, NY: State University of New York Press.

Crenshaw, K., Gotanda, N., Peller, G., & Thomas, K. (Eds.). (1995). *Critical race theory: Curriculum.* New York: Peter Lang.

Delgado, R., & Stefancic, J. (2001). *Critical race theory: An introduction.* New York: New York University Press.

Delpit, L. (1995). *Other people's children: Cultural conflict in the classroom.* New York: The New Press.

Dimitriadis, G. (2001). *Performing identity/Performing culture: Hip hop as text, pedagogy, and lived practice.* New York: Peter Lang.

Donahue, P., Daane, M., & Grigg, W. (2003). The nation's report card: Reading highlights 2003. *Education Statistics Quarterly, 5*(4), 40–53.

Flesch, R. (1955). *Why Johnny can't read.* New York: Harper & Row.

Gause, C. (2000). *The social construction of Black masculinity: (Re) presentations in the American pop culture.* Retrieved March 29, 2004, from http://www.gradnet.de/papers/pomo2.archives/pomo2.papers/gause00.htm

Gay, G. (2000). *Culturally responsive teaching: Theory, research, and practice.* New York: Teachers College Press.

Georgia Department of Education. (2004). *State of Georgia: Consolidated state application accountability workbook.* Retrieved June 27, 2005, from http://www.doe.k12.ga.us/_documents/support/plan/ayp_plan_workbook.pdf

Georgia School Council Institute. (2004). *School report card.* Retrieved October 17, 2004, from http://www.gsci.org/Report Center

Gordon, B. (1990). The necessity of African American epistemology for educational theory and practice. *Journal of Education, 172*(3), 88–106.

Hale, J. (2001). *Learning while Black: Creating educational excellence for African American children.* Baltimore: The Johns Hopkins University Press.

Harrison, L., & Harrison, C. (2002). African American racial identity: Theory and application to education, race and sports in America [Electronic version]. *Perspectives.* Retrieved March 29, 2004, from http://www.rcgd.isr.umich.edu/prba/perspectives/springsummer2002/harrison.pdf

Hilliard, A. (2003). No, mystery: Closing the achievement gap between Africans and excellence. In T. Perry, C. Steele, & A. Hilliard III. (Eds.), *Young, gifted, and Black* (pp. 131–165). Boston: Bacon Press.

Hilliard, A., Payton-Stewart, L., & Williams, L. (Eds.). (1995). *Infusion of African and African American content in the school curriculum* (2nd ed.). Morristown, NJ: Aaron Press.

hooks, b. (1994). *Teaching to transgress: Education as the practice of freedom.* New York: Routledge.

Irvine, J. (2003). *Educating teachers for diversity: Seeing with a cultural eye.* New York: Teachers College Press.

Kincheloe, J., & McLaren, P. (2003). Rethinking critical theory and qualitative research. In N. Denzin & Y. Lincoln (Eds.), *The landscape of qualitative research: Theories and issues* (2nd ed, pp. 433–488). San Francisco: SAGE.

Kunjufu, J. (1990). *The conspiracy to destroy Black boys* (Vol. III). Chicago: African American Images.

Kunjufu, J. (1995). *Countering the conspiracy to destroy Black boys* (pp. vii, 28–29). Chicago: African American Images.

Ladson-Billings, G. (1992). Reading between the lines and beyond the pages: A culturally relevant approach to literacy teaching. *Theory into Practice, 31*(4), 312–320.

Ladson-Billing, G. (1998). Just what is critical race theory and what is it doing in a "nice field like education?" *Qualitative Studies in Education, 11*(1), 7–24.

Ladson-Billings, G. (2003). Racialized discourses and ethnic epistemologies. In N. Denzin & Y. Lincoln (Eds.), *The landscape of qualitative research: Theories and issues* (2nd ed., pp. 398– 432). Thousand Oaks, CA: SAGE.

Ladson-Billings, G. (Ed.). (2003). Lies my teacher still tells. In G. Ladson-Billings (Ed.), *Critical race theory perspectives on social studies: The profession, policies, and curriculum*. Greenwich, CT: Information Age.

Ladson-Billings, G., & Tate, W. F., IV. (1995). Toward a critical race theory of education. *Teachers College Record, 97*(1), 22–47.

Lewis, M. (2006). *Teen's 10 year term for consensual sex draws attention to Georgia Law.* Retrieved August 10, 2007 from, http://www.Blackamericaweb.com/site.aspx/bawnews/wilson0111

McNeil, G. (2004, May/June). Laying the groundwork. *The Crisis, 111*(3), 21–23.

Millicans, S. (2005). *Georgia's Criterion-Referenced Competency Tests.* Georgia Department of Education. Retrieved August 27, 2005, from www.doe.k12.ga.us

Marshall, C., & Rossman, G. (1999). *Designing qualitative research* (3rd ed.). Thousand Oaks, CA: SAGE.

Moss, G. (2001). *Cultural exchange: Critical narratives of bilingual teacher experiences in the Texas-Spain visiting teachers program.* Retrieved on March 26, 2005, from http://proquest.umi.com/dissertaions/preview_pickup/41/78/394178/1/00003.gif

Noble, W. (1995). The infusion of African and African American content: A question of content and intent. In A. Hilliard, L. Payton-Stewart, & L. Williams (Eds.), *Infusion of African and African American content in the school curriculum* (2nd ed.). Chicago: Third World Press.

Olmsted, A. P. (1998). Words are acts: Critical race theory as a rhetorical construct. *The Howard Journal of Communications, 9*, 323–331.

Perry, T., Steele, C., & Hilliard, A. (2003). *Young, gifted, and Black: Promoting high achievement among African American students.* Boston: Beacon Press.

Pinar, W. (1993). Notes on understanding curriculum as a racial text. In C. McCarthy & W. Crichlow (Eds.), *Race, identity, and representation in education* (p. 61). New York: Routledge.

Short, E. C. (Ed). (1991). *Forms of curriculum inquiry.* New York: State University of New York Press.

Sirotnik, K. (1991). Critical inquiry: A paradigm for praxis. In E. C. Short. (Ed.), *Forms of curriculum inquiry* (pp. 243–258). New York: State University of New York Press.

Sowell, E. J. (2000). *Curriculum: An integrative introduction* (2nd ed.). Upper Saddle River, NJ: Prentice Hall.

Standard & Poor's (2003-2004). *No Child Left Behind.* Retrieved on October 17, 2004, from http://www.schoolresults.org

Stewart, S. (2007). *Supporters of the Jena Six Gather 43,000 signatures for petition, rally calling for equal justice.* Retrieved August 18, 2007 from, http://www.Blackamericaweb.com/site.aspx/bawnews/jenasix731

Tate, W. (1997). Critical race theory and education: History, theory, and implications. *Review of Research in Education, 22*, 195–247.

Taylor, C. (2005). *Reading through brown eyes: Toward developing a culturally congru-ent reading curriculum*. Unpublished doctoral dissertation, Georgia Southern University.

Ware, L. (2004, May/June). The unfulfilled promise of Brown. *The Crisis, 111*(3), 40–44.

Woodson, C. G. (1990). *The mis-education of the Negro* (6th ed.). Trenton, NJ: Africa World Press.

CHAPTER 12

DALTON'S SUICIDE

Dealing With Student Death in Education

Teresa J. Rishel

THE PERSONAL JOURNEY

Black and cream marble chess pieces are aligned perfectly with their corresponding squares, creating a harmonious symmetry on the checkered background. Needing to be polished, they gather dust in the corner of a room that I rarely use. Pictures are the same, scattered at various places throughout my home—visible, yet not intrusive in the monotony of life. The chess pieces, the pictures, and an assortment of other memorabilia serve as remnants of the pleasures and pains of life—and of my son, Tony, who committed suicide nearly thirteen years ago. Time's passing has not lessened their appeal to me but has more likely elevated them to monuments of remembrance. With so *little* to hold onto, and yet needing a connection to him, they remind me that he existed. All of us, I suppose, learn when, where, and how to bridge the past moments of our lives to

Personal~Passionate~Participatory Inquiry Into Social Justice in Education, pp. 199–216
Copyright © 2008 by Information Age Publishing

the present and eventually, envision ways to incorporate them into the future.

Memories that linger as a mixture of guilt, regret, and anger still have the capacity to hurt. In reflecting on Tony's life, I find that the adolescent years significantly impacted the choices and decisions that he eventually made. His quest for identity, the constant challenging and asking the "why" questions seemed unimportant, yet they were much more significant than I had realized. Being a young and inexperienced parent, as well as an unaware educator, I held the common belief that adolescence is "just a stage," and therefore, I did not take his journey seriously enough. I lacked perspective and failed to recognize the crucial development of decision-making and problem solving skills; that which appeared "normal" in terms of growth and development, would, in retrospect, become his albatross. While Tony challenged and questioned, he was also passive; while he displayed strength and perseverance, he lacked confidence and a positive sense of self-worth. Thus, when finally faced with a situation beyond his experience and abilities, the end of his teenage years also brought about his impromptu decision to die.

Personal experiences—particularly those which are serious, severe, or life-changing—are often reflected in life choices made thereafter. For many, the most painful experiences are buried in the recesses of our hearts and lend themselves minimally to the routines and requirements of daily life. In other words, we protect ourselves from the realities that are foundational to who we are, deciding instead to "deal with" them at pre-determined times and places. However, as I waded through the pain and recovery of losing a son to suicide, I found that the protection of relinquishing it to my private life was not enough. Instead, I sought action to forge a path to recovery.

Throughout the grieving process, I immersed myself in suicide literature and regularly attended a suicide survivor's support group. This eased much of the emotional pressure but also increased my knowledge and understandings of suicide. I learned about the adolescent grief process from watching my youngest son, Scott, navigate the rough terrain of healing in the school environment. School can be an alienating place to students who are struggling. Later, his journey would serve as a reminder to me that school personnel have a great deal of power over the emotional lives of students—a power that has the capacity to influence the life and death decisions that students make. Thus, as I drifted from the intense and immediate emotions of Tony's suicide, grieving and learning became intertwined as I found myself positioned on a more leveled perspective of understanding and acceptance.

As a way to bury the hurt and avoid dealing with suicide, after Scott left for college, I gave up my teaching job and become a school principal in a location away from my home community. My desire was not to advance my professional career but to find a way to escape; surely, I thought, a new beginning would help. However, weeks after my arrival at the school, the topic of suicide reemerged, and my leveled perspective abruptly changed. Entrenched in a specific understanding of suicide as a mother, my experiences deepened when Dalton, a student with whom I had worked closely in my role as his elementary principal, often expressed his desire to kill himself. Two years later, he committed suicide. Combined, these deaths offered a vivid picture of the importance of attending to the emotional and social needs of students and their decision-making abilities when facing life's challenges. It was through working with Dalton that I began to understand the adolescent years, particularly in terms of schooling. Dalton entered my life and eventually shattered my escape route as attempts to get away from the topic of suicide were undone as Dalton's issues surfaced.

Ironically, the methods and ways that I dealt with Dalton's problems and suicide ideation became part of my healing process. Through him—and because of him—I was forced to confront my loss. Without the experience of Tony's death, I would have been ill-equipped to comprehend Dalton or the despair of his life. Sadly, as in most cases where we cannot control the actions of others, even my experience, knowledge, and caring did little to alter the course that Dalton eventually chose. However, I believe—and I have to believe—that he lived a few years longer because of Tony's death and the impact it had on my professional knowledge.

Research has shown that adolescence is a stage charged with turmoil and confusion, identity-seeking, and self-analysis (Beane, 1990; Beane & Lipka, 2000; and Schlosser, 1992). During this time, adolescents are highly influenced by their peer groups, yet are also greatly affected by the overt *and* covert actions, reactions, and interactions with teachers and in school situations. Dalton was caught in a cycle of adolescent angst and confusion, trapped by the boundaries that the school environment placed around his already troubled life. I imagine that Dalton felt as though he had nowhere to feel safe, to breathe deeply, and to know that he was loved.

Dalton was a student who suffered a serious disconnect between home and school. Through the foggy glaze of my broken heart, Dalton's stories about home pierced a path of great compassion and the realization that I needed to use my experience to understand and embrace his. Coming from a family of extreme poverty, he dealt with the daily responsibility of caring for his two younger siblings while his mother worked at night. At the time, Dalton's home did not have running water, permanent flooring, or adequate lighting or ventilation; the refrigerator and cupboards were usually bare. For Dalton, the end of the school day was the beginning of a long evening of caretaking. The journey from home to school and back again only changed the scenery of his day, but not the way that he felt within. Homework and school responsibilities faded into the background—both in possibility and importance—as he shifted his attention to mere survival at the young age of 11.

Within a few short months of my arrival as principal, Dalton became a regular visitor to my office, sometimes as a result of misbehavior, sometimes because he just needed to talk. An academically talented young man, Dalton was known as one of the most intelligent students in the school. Yet, his daily homework and classroom work reflected otherwise. Dalton did not care about school or schooling; he had little regard for the *need* to do homework, often stating that it was too easy, too boring, or had little to do with life. Dalton was a deep thinker, proficient in national and global issues. He could debate with the skill of an adult and make significant contributions to most conversations. Homework only required that he memorize, fill in the blanks, or some other mundane task that he felt served little purpose.

Dalton's classroom behavior was not much better than his grades. His role as the class clown prohibited him from being considered a "serious" student and often resulted in his expulsion from class. Other students liked him for his ability to entertain, yet had little to do with him otherwise. His clothes were shabby, disproportionately sized, and most often dirty. He had few friends—and the ones he did have were similar in background and status to him. School was not a place of acceptance for him or his crowd, in part a result of their attitudes and behaviors towards school, and partly due to school personnel's lack of ability to identify the unique needs and challenges of this "out" group.

One afternoon in particular, Dalton was highly frustrated about a classroom discussion over a recently passed welfare bill that required his mother, among others, to increase the number of hours she worked per week. Dalton's argument was that mothers needed to stay home to take care of their kids, which met with great resistance from his classmates who believed welfare mothers were lazy. An explosion from Dalton resulted in his being sent to my office. During our conversation, Dalton expressed the futility of trying to fit in at school while dealing with his home situation and still finding the strength to go on. "I would be better off dead. I have decided to kill myself before it goes on too long." Dalton continued, but I remained frozen on his words.

What does one do in a moment like that? Where do the words come from—or the understanding? With mixed emotions, I resisted the temptation to dismiss the seriousness of the situation. This job was my refuge from the realities of suicide, the place that was not linked with my past. Here, in the midst of an ordinary afternoon, unknown to him, the one student that I truly knew and appreciated was pushing the very core of my being with his words. The process of grieving and learning came down to this moment, one which I had never expected in my role as an elementary principal.

Working slowly through the next few hours with Dalton, we found a common place to land, neither really understanding the perspective of the other, yet knowing that we were working together to save *his* life, and yet in many ways, to also save a piece of mine. Eventually, the proper authorities and agencies were notified as well as his mother. Yet, the residual effects of the afternoon stayed with me into the months ahead as Dalton and I returned to this very topic time and time again. Over the 2 years that he and I worked together, my understandings of suicide increased more than I desired. Keeping Dalton focused on wanting to live was an extraordinary challenge and one that often made me feel profoundly alone.

Watching Dalton's actions and interactions within the school environment continued to be a challenge as well, as I witnessed the various ways that he did not fit in—and was disallowed from fitting in—yet wanting to so badly. He could not join sports teams or after-school activities because he had to care for his brothers. His personality caused rifts with other students, and some school personnel were unable to find ways to connect with him—or even accept him. However, even popular students commit suicide, which leads to the notion that if these aspects of schooling were more humane, students may see that they have other options besides death. Dalton's demise was like watching a sad movie where you know that in spite of the hope that you hold, the ending would probably be exactly as you expected. Changing others' perceptions and ways of dealing with students such as Dalton was not an easy task, nor one which met with much success. The foundations of schooling—too cemented in tradition, routine, and expectation—prevent change meaningful enough to affect students such as Dalton. At the age of 15, Dalton committed suicide by pouring gasoline over himself and lighting a match. Life had finally gone on "too long" for him. My journey had returned full circle as I ran from my son's suicide to a new job, wanting to extinguish as much of it from my daily life as I could. What I received, instead, was another suicide and a broader focus—mother *and* principal.

THE PASSIONATE JOURNEY

A Research Study Emerges

To best understand Dalton's suicide, I explored the remnants left behind of his school life. Using a phenomenological research approach

(Patton, 1990), I constructed a case study of the impact of Dalton's death on school personnel who worked closely with him (Marshall & Rossman, 1999; McMillan & Schumacher, 2001; Merriam, 1988). Prior to interviewing the participants, however, I had to face my own story of Dalton and subject myself to answering the same types of questions that I would pose to them. Specifically seeking to know what aspects of school life contributed to his apathy, depression, and alienation, I alternated between the perspectives of mother, principal and researcher, constantly negotiating the story as it unfolded. Realities often emerged that tested my will as it became obvious that our life stories are fluid and changing. Phillion (2002) stated that what we write and know is "conditional, temporal, situated, fragmented, in transition, in process, in the midst" (p. 146) because we are "always in the midst of the story of our life and the stories of others' lives" (p. 146).

The study took place in an elementary and junior high school in a small, Midwestern school district. School personnel were selected as participants, using purposeful criterion sampling based on the extent to which they had interacted regularly and consistently with Dalton (McMillan & Schumacher, 2001). This resulted in 13 participants, 12 of whom were educators and one health care worker, who responded to guiding questions about Dalton's death through a series of structured and unstructured interviews.

Acceptance in the School Environment

Since school is the social mechanism for developing relationships and learning to work in group situations, relationships with peers are essential. The bonds that are forged, considered the "the litmus paper of life" (Beane & Lipka, 2000, p. 13), have the potential to be more influential on teenagers than their parents. Nina, a participant, reflected on how difficult fitting in was for many students, particularly as peers assess them:

> There's a lot of pressure to be accepted. It's the stigma put on kids, to be the popular one. Students are striving to just be accepted. You can look at a group of students and the way they're dressed and the way they conduct themselves. That is how they look at each other in class. They judge each other, especially when the teacher treats some students worse than others. (personal communication, July 26, 2002)

Nina makes a significant point that how students are treated in the classroom is a key factor in the level of peer acceptance that occurs. Teachers have control over the extent to which students suffer humiliation, alienation and stress in the school environment (Eccles & Roeser,

1999; Elkind, 1988, 1989; Wassef & Ingham, 1995). Teachers who have poor attitudes towards students or weak disciplinary and classroom management skills use punishment to communicate authority and control (Schlosser, 1992). This exercise of authority also teaches that if students are obedient and cooperative, they deserve to be treated better. An administrative participant concurred: "I would say that there is a tendency by adults to respond to each of them differently on how willing that kid was to get along in school" (September 9, 2002).

Teacher control, then, assumes the position that teachers respond positively only to those students who have "earned" it by acquiescing "self" to authority. This is not to say that students should not respect and listen to authority figures, but within the boundaries of being treated equitably and fairly. Connelly and Clandinin (1988) described how over a period of years, teacher control negates student autonomy. "The hidden message is that these children are not as worthwhile as others, and they learn to value themselves less, to have a lower self-image, to defer to others" (p. 155).

Dalton, however, was quite the opposite, resisting the notion that he should comply with teachers merely because they held "power" over him. Instead, he saw their power as something unearned and undeserved simply because they could hold students as captives *because of* their title as teachers. In addressing ways that Dalton was alienated in the classroom, one participant (Brin) stated, "Some [teachers] get into that attitude too, 'By God, I'll show you and you're not gonna pull shit on me and that's it and no other choices' " (September 9, 2002). To teachers such as this, teacher power was a "winning" stance in a pre-determined way of dealing with the student.

In much the same manner, Lila noted that teachers who use a linear approach are those who *cause* the most difficulties in teaching and disciplining students: "A teacher who is rigid and doesn't understand and doesn't take time with kids and doesn't accommodate differences is going to make problems *for* children" (September 11, 2002). The problem, according to Lila, is not with the student, but in how the teacher reacts. For students such as Dalton, winning stances and rigid, linear approaches may only further fuel resistance. Unfortunately, with the traditional methods of exercising teacher power and control, Dalton was often seen as an intruder in a system that worked for most others. Rarely were his actions viewed as appropriate responses to the teacher's lack of effective classroom management, affect, and interactions.

When teachers intentionally subjected him to their shallow judgments, Dalton retaliated through misbehavior and disrespect. Imagine the way that Dalton must have felt as a student in Jane's classroom: "There were negative feelings toward him. Maybe because they're disgusted with the mom for some reason. Some teachers resent kids that are on free lunches" (July 24, 2002). Jane's "hidden" agenda toward students like Dalton is obvious as you read between the lines. She described how "some teachers" viewed him and avoided directly including herself. It is interesting, though, that she failed to disguise her own feelings about him. During the same interview, Jane once again refers to the "free lunch" in describing Dalton:

> When he started in my class, he had not had a haircut; his hair was about down to his shoulders. He did not have new clothes to start the school year. He, of course, was on free lunches and was given school supplies by our office. (July 24, 2002)

Martha also made statements that indicated her frustration with—and lack of acceptance of—Dalton. For example, while her "heart went out to him," she had "no skills in dealing with, helping him with these problems that I knew he had" (July 26, 2002). Martha recognized Dalton's nonacademic problems but avoided dealing with them. Although she raved about his academic abilities and intelligence, giving him full credit for being well ahead of the rest of the students, she blamed him and did not find alternative ways for him to succeed in school, instead she focused more on his deficits:

> And he was so smart. If he wanted to have done his work, he could've done it in two minutes time and you know, had umpteen amount of hours of time to do things that he'd wanted to have done. (July 26, 2002)

It was important to Martha that free time was allowed only after the work was completed. Wanting Dalton to conform to the traditional ways of "doing school," such as completing all assignments, Martha overlooked *her* role in his failure at school. It did not seem to matter that the work was so easy that it could be completed in two minutes, but only that it had to be completed. This disservice to Dalton's academic abilities continued throughout his years of schooling in a variety of ways and in a number of classrooms.

On the other hand, Dalton loved those teachers who accepted and understood him, or at least gave him a chance in their classrooms without judging him. Reggie, one such teacher, felt that getting to know Dalton personally was the best method of understanding him and preventing further apathy. Reggie accepted Dalton as he was and avoided discipline as a way to control him:

> It just took a lot of strategies on my part, of getting to know him personally, and it helped because once I got to know him, I could relate something on

his level. If I didn't get to know him personally and viewed it as a discipline problem, then it would have been different, we would've battled … everyday. (July 30, 2002)

While most participants felt that the structure of schooling did little to provide hope for Dalton, Debbie found him to be an "interesting kid that had a lot of stuff that was going on in his head" (November 4, 2002). While she had no difficulties with Dalton, she felt other teachers could not accommodate to his needs and made his situation worse. "He respected me because I let him be who he wanted to be. He had freedom with boundaries. I felt it was boundaries and he felt it was freedom" (November 4, 2002). Similarly, Brin felt that some teachers were to blame because they held a grudge against him and never allowed him to get past it. Brin shared:

It's, you know, they're [Dalton and others] on their list for the rest of the year. They're picked on; they're put upon. They never feel like they do anything right. They're yelled at. If something goes wrong, they're the ones that get in trouble. (July 22, 2002)

Although Brin blamed other teachers, she also felt that "*everybody* let him down and this just kinda led to the cause, everybody … his mom, teachers, the school, the community, and certainly the welfare system" (July 22, 2002).

Part of Dalton's difficulty being accepted in the school community also stemmed from an aspect of his life which was totally beyond his control—his socioeconomic status. Because he was a "poor kid," he was not only subjected to the "free lunch" way of grouping students but also carried the additional burden of lacking familial support and involvement in his school life. These factors combined set the stage for him to be almost automatically distanced from his peers and unfortunately, from some school personnel. Dalton lacked the "cultural capital" (Apple, 1995) needed to gain full access to the same treatment, interactions, and caring that most other students were afforded unconditionally; he was valued less. In commenting on Bourdieu's theory of cultural capital, Aronowitz and Giroux (1993), make this overlap clear:

The culture of the elite is so near that of the school that children from the lower middle class can acquire only with great effort something which is given to the children of the cultivated class—style, taste, wit—in short, those aptitudes which seem natural in members of the cultivated classes and naturally expected of them precisely because they are the culture of that class. (p. 76)

In attempting to understand how some students can be so overtly alienated in an environment that is (supposedly) designed to be inclusive and student-centered, it seems that the burden of responsibility is still placed upon the students. *They* alone must overcome obstacles placed in their paths to success, over which they have little or no control. To be poor should not be grounds for punishment; to be intelligent, yet not subjected to rigor, should not result in further alienation. To be Dalton should not have been a bad thing:

> Still, the disparities between the elites and the poorer families were clear cut in the classroom and school. Children whose parents lacked financial clout faced serious roadblocks to educational success. They lacked school materials and supplies, had no access to technology, and were unable to participate in and benefit from extracurricular clubs and activities. (Rishel, 2008, p. 101)

Educators' Moral Decision Making

What did Dalton need if he was so intelligent? Did he need more schoolwork and homework? Did he need to learn to acquiesce to traditional schooling and ignore his own sense of self preservation? Was it even possible to find a "fit" for him within the school environment? What he needed most—and would have best served his needs—was an environment that would accept him as he was, support and encourage him, and essentially, just allow him (Martha's) "free time" to simply be a child. Differentiating Dalton's instruction could have been a starting place for encouraging his completion of assignments as well as complementing his academic talents. Decisions made about Dalton often came down to school life as described by Jackson (1990) in *Life in Classrooms*. Jackson asserted that how a classroom is conducted has little to do with the subject matter or the material but is based on the personality and demeanor of the teacher. Teachers who engage students through their abilities to "make even the dullest subject exciting" (p. 108) become the teachers that students love. Reggie and Debbie were Dalton's favorite teachers in junior high; they were teachers who displayed charisma, patience, and care for students, even while teaching what students considered boring subjects.

These moral aspects of schooling, where the actions and interactions of educators greatly affect students, must be recognized as significant factors in how a young person views himself within—and assimilates to—the school environment. Educators often fail to realize the impact or importance of their roles in these moral decision-making moments. Thus, teachers must learn as much as possible "about their own potency as moral agents and about the moral potency of the schools and classrooms in which they work" (Jackson, Boostrom, & Hansen, 1993, p. 293). Note Jane's emphasis on caring about Dalton as a way to keep him involved, a basic tenet of teacher moral decision making:

> If you're gonna nag him, nag him, nag him, nag him and constantly make him feel like he's never gonna, and its only to nag, not because you care about him, then he wasn't going to do anything for you. (July 24, 2002)

A further example of moral decision making that stifled Dalton's involvement at school was the decision not to allow him to participate as a comedian in the annual talent contest. Dalton's aptitude for telling jokes and stories was his legacy—nearly all of the 12 participants commented on his ability to entertain his classmates, and that he was not shy about causing laughter among the staff either. In a rather poignant story told by Jack, it was clear that Dalton's magic was rooted in humor even in the midst of discipline:

> In the course of our conversations when I'm giving him hell ... and he's just not letting anything bother him, kind of letting it go and I'm ranting and raving a little bit. And I stop. He's laughing and then I start laughing ... in the middle of the conversation! I said to him, "You're missing your calling; you need to be a comedian." (September 9, 2002)

Allen also felt that Dalton's humor was one of his greatest assets, particularly during moments that would have normally been serious and "threatening" to most students. Alan described how Dalton's "great sense of humor could make you laugh when you were trying to get after him and correct him" (July 30, 2002) and how humor eventually calmed the situation down. Still, in spite of the overall feeling of the participants that humor was Dalton's forte, he was denied the most appropriate venue for showcasing this gift—the school talent show—because, as Nina put it, "Dalton could not be trusted" (reference) in front of the student body to deliver appropriate jokes and stories. Without ever getting the opportunity to prove his trustworthiness—and gain some true admiration and respect from his peers and the staff—his reputation in the school pre-empted any other possible routes to disarming and changing these viewpoints. Nina was clearly opposed to his performing because it "was a little scary to let him in" (July 26, 2002).

In general, Dalton was prohibited from full inclusion in school, sometimes inadvertently but often intentionally. However, in either case, it seemed that those who alienated him the most and, even those who did so only occasionally, did so out of lack of knowledge rather than malicious intent. Many who worked with Dalton were trapped in their perception of "the" correct way to do school. With a lack of understanding and perhaps a lack of motivation, they did what they had always done without regard for more contemporary inclusive instructional and methodological strategies. Unfortunately, this did not help to improve Dalton's situation. Nina expressed how this must have felt to Dalton: "He had personal issues that he was never able to overcome that were deep inside him. But he *wanted* to be happy" (July 29, 2002).

THE PARTICIPATORY JOURNEY

Suicide: the Reality

Unfortunately, the suicides of Tony and Dalton are not atypical for this age group. Although suicide rates fluctuate, an alarming number still occur within the population that schools serve, particularly in adolescents. Suicide is the third leading cause of death in 15- to 24-year-olds, preceded only by accidental death and homicides (American Foundation for Suicide Prevention [AFSP], 2007; McIntosh, 2002). AFSP (2007) reports that the suicide rate has doubled over the last 20 years for those aged 10 to 14 years. Eccles and Roeser (1999) reported that adolescents become suicidal as problems increase with "family, friends, boyfriends or girlfriends, and school" (p. 504). Young people become caught in relationship and family problems, resulting in humiliation, depression, and inappropriate behavior. They become socially isolated, their self-esteem plummets, and they experience further depression (Butler & Novy, 1994; Elkind, 1989; King, Price, Telljohann, & Wahl, 1999). As educators, it is imperative that in the least, we are aware of the phenomenon of suicide through not only recognizing the behaviors and characteristics common to many suicidal students but also in knowing how to respond. Closely related adolescent issues include self-cutting, depression, and eating disorders, which have been linked to self-punishing or suicidal teenagers (Beane & Lipka, 2000).

Some students get to the point that they feel that life is unbearable. Without adequate decision-making and problem-solving abilities, the world becomes a lonely place. Elkind (1989) describes young people who are caught in a web of alienation, depression, and low self esteem as feeling that there is "no way out ... they are helpless, hapless, and hopeless" (p. 172). Lacking coping skills, they are prone to commit suicide as a result of their "unbearable anguish" (Hewett, 1980, p. 29). Combined, this should give us a clear indication that our young people are stressed, distressed, and unhappy. With the current focus on academic achievement and standardization, it would serve us well to understand that self-worth and self-care preempts students' desire or capability to perform well academically. As educators, we must surely see the importance of making ourselves available to students, watching closely, and listening intently.

A host of suicide prevention organizations support and strongly recommend that depression and suicide prevention become integrated into the educational system (AFSP, 2007; Kirchner, Yoder, Kramer, Lindsey, & Thrush, 2000; United States Public Health Service, 1999). An average class of high school students is likely to have at least one boy and two girls who have attempted suicide in the past year (American Association of Suicidology [AAS], 2007). The fact that every 16 minutes a suicide is committed in the United States leaves little room to wonder about the intensity of this issue (AFSP, 2007). Further, student suicides predominately occur in the home during the hours after school, falling directly between their school and home lives (AAS, 2007). It is clear that educators play a critical role in dealing with suicide.

However, according to a study on teacher knowledge about suicide, it was found that less than 50% of schools educate their teachers on even warning signs of suicide (King, Price, Telljohann, & Wahl, 1999). Opalewski (2001) stated that while most teachers of adolescents are aware of the problem of suicide, they are unprepared to deal with it effectively. The fact that they could make grievous mistakes due to their lack of knowledge is a serious consideration. In the same study, less than 66% of school counselors were found to be cognizant of the warning signs of suicide (King et al., 1999).

EDUCATIONAL AND SOCIAL CHANGE

Educators may recognize the present emotional and mental instability of many students, yet feel unqualified to handle the depth of emotional trauma that students suffer. Dalton was caught in this situation, where although school personnel recognized and sympathized with his life situation, they were ill-equipped in knowing what to do. As well, there was a general feeling that in order to change Dalton's school life, his home life would have to change first. Falling outside of an educator's realm of expertise and responsibility, it was simply an overlooked aspect of Dalton's life.

The deaths of Tony and Dalton—along with the emotional pain incurred by Scott—ignited in me the passion, the power, and the purpose toward researching suicide and its relevance to schools, teachers, and curriculum. I felt compelled to examine the roles, influences, and circumstances that the climate and culture of schooling play in a student's perception of self, life, and death. I began to question my lived experiences with suicide—and outside the parameters of autobiography—began asking "what is the story behind the story?" Kerdeman (1998), in discussing how we make meaning from life experiences, states that "it is necessary to live through a range of experiences that both affirm and shake up our orientation, such that understanding and self-understanding are not distorted or denied but clarified and furthered" (p. 10). As I continued my research into student suicide and the conditions of schooling that exacerbate this phenomenon, I felt compelled to understand it from the viewpoint of an adolescent—to "see" life through their eyes. In my attempts to do so, I soon realized that talking about or learning about suicide had never been a part of my education. It was not discussed while I was a student (although I had a schoolmate commit suicide while in high school), was not mentioned in my teacher education programs, and never surfaced as I worked toward administrative licensing. Suicide was always something that happened to someone else.

I now understand that suicide is a part of education and should be considered a required addition to school curriculums. Thinking about suicide, attempting suicide, or dealing with the deaths of loved ones to suicide *is* the lived experience of many students. It cannot be relegated to life outside of school and dismissed as unimportant in the educational arena. It affects how they think, act, and respond in the school environment; it affects their academic success. And it is with them regardless of what else occurs during the school day.

Establishing a professional and long-term commitment to suicide and the school community, the inclusion of teenage and young adult suicide became the participatory context for refining my approach to teacher education. In teaching my preservice teachers—particularly as we talk about adolescent development—I am drawn back into my experiences. Using a variety of methods that focus specifically on issues of adolescent anxiety and feelings of emotional abandonment, I include a foundation of affective education in my teacher education curriculum. As a result, my students no longer focus solely on the "nuts and bolts" of instructional methods, but are equipped with knowing how to ask the "why" questions instead of using the deficit approach in determining "what" the student did or did not do. They are armed with knowing to investigate negative student attitudes, lack of class and school participation, and low academic achievement instead of passively accepting these as common to some students.

The stories of Dalton serve to ignite the educator's understanding that their words, actions, and reactions—the hidden curriculum—are more powerful than lesson plans and methodology. I encourage teachers to know their students, and I require that lesson plans are supplemented with differentiation, choice, and a focus on social justice.

Additionally, as a method of furthering teacher knowledge, my suicide research is presented at teacher education classes and workshops throughout the Midwest. I instruct preservice and in-service teachers about student affect, school culture, and their role in guiding students whose lives are in turmoil. In particular, one workshop, *The Dance of Diversity*, addressed problems incurred by White beginning teachers in an African American school. The teachers struggled with discipline, behavior, and motivation, most often blaming the students and disregarding their own propensity to change the situation. Using Dalton's story, I drew from them the compassion that was needed not only to understand their students' lives more deeply, but also how a lack of understanding their role as the "White" teacher could cause further damage.

At the beginning of the workshop, one participant described her angst in consistently having to deal with two fourth grade boys who fought over pencils, stealing them from one another on a regular basis. She usually resolved the issue by making both boys miss recess. What she failed to see was how the underlying dynamic of poverty played a key role in her students' actions, further fueled by the fact that she did not truly understand. The boys did not have school supplies, especially at home, so obtaining them at school was important. To her, pencils were insignificant; to her students, they were objects of desire—and need. Instead of understanding her responsibility in finding a permanent resolution to the problem, she punished them further by taking away their much needed free time. After hearing about Dalton's struggles, she returned to her dilemma with a resolution: to make certain that school supplies were always available for the students and that the focus would be on learning, not discipline.

In discussing suicide with educators and teacher education students, the realities of suicide continue to emerge *because* each interaction provides new ways of knowing and eliciting the hidden meanings behind the audience's subtle words, actions, and assertions. In writing about suicide, I experience what van Manen (1990) said about how "writing separates the knower from the known, but it also allows us to reclaim this knowledge and make it our own in a new and more intimate manner" (p. 127). I have reclaimed what I know about suicide, no longer running from it, but making it available to those who have the greatest impact on students who are at the edge of life and death. If we want better schools, higher scores, and more academically prepared students, then we must reach into the undesirable pit of despair and deal with the issues we find there. We can no longer consume our time with concerns that are typical to any school, but must realize that real and human problems are the most prevalent aspect of the journey called life.

Discovering how the alienating effects of traditional schooling practices on youth were the result of educators' lack of awareness and knowledge and stigmatizing points of view, my passions became centered on the tenets of social justice, where the inclusion of students and their real-life stories had a place in the curriculum. I have realized that even the most stable students are vulnerable and their sense of balance can quickly be disrupted as a result of treatment by adults around them. Sadly, this awareness came many years after my youngest son suffered the aloneness of the school environment.

CONCLUSION

Centered on the components of school life that have the propensity to affect students' perceptions self, I have sought to understand the various roles of school personnel, the influence of the school environment, and the traditions of schooling. What I discovered was that the importance lies first in *knowing* that each has a profound effect on how students view themselves and are accepted in the school environment. Understanding is key, but more importantly, the aim must be to create positive educational change that supports the needs of the students. Outcomes must support students' experiences and problems as part of the learning environment. This is a matter of life and death for some students, and to a lesser degree, but nonetheless also important, in dealing with depression, at-risk behaviors, and student alienation.

Educators must be aware that when students feel they have little support or understanding, those who consider suicide have few other places to seek assistance. Reaching out is difficult for those contemplating suicide, but knowing that their words, actions, or emotions will not fall on deaf ears can be the best possible route to saving them. Accepting all students, regardless of their circumstances, behaviors, and attitudes will provide a forum where they trust and are trusted. It is important to note that those who have suicidal thoughts do not want to die as much as they fear—or dread—living. To them, facing the harshness and challenges of life, whether temporary or long-term, is more difficult than coming to terms with dying. Despite our inclination to assume which students are more likely to commit suicide than others, there is no specific "type;" suicide encompasses every class, race, gender, intelligence level, socioeconomic status, and sexual orientation. Sadly, I learned this the hard way.

My participation in suicide research is my heartfelt contribution to the memories of my son, Tony, to my student, Dalton, and to my surviving son, Scott. Through reflecting on their stories, their journeys, and their displacement at various times in the educational setting, I have been given a gift—albeit a sad and strange one—to help improve the school lives of present and future students. In the end, academic success is simply a sidebar to students' emotional, physical, and social success.

Education is about life, the future, and the quest for career attainment and success. Suicide is a curricular issue hidden among the integration of technology, test scores, standards, and honor rolls. It lies between layers of social interaction in clubs, sports, choir, band, and other activities. Suicide, masked within the ambiguity of the hidden curriculum and ostracized from the overt curriculum, is hidden among the students. It is lived experience (Rishel, 2007, pp. 297–322).

The chess pieces loom in the background as I gaze from my patio into the afternoon sun. They seem to beckon me, demanding that I *see* them as they really are, dusty and superficially neglected, yet ever prominent in my life. As I learn to bridge the past to the present and envision their role in my future, I realize that the chess set, as well as the other mementos, are incorporated in my journey toward suicide awareness for educators. With so *much* to hold onto, I find a connection to my son—which serves as my reminder that he existed.

REFERENCES

American Association of Suicidology. (2007). *Youth suicide fact sheet*. Retrieved June 23, 2007, from http://www.suicidology.org/associations/1045/files/Youth2004.pdf

American Foundation for Suicide Prevention. (2007). *Facts and figures: National statistics*. Retrieved June 23, 2007, from http://www.afsp.org/index.cfm?fuseaction=home.viewPage&page_id=050FEA9F-B064-4092-B1135C3A70DE1FDA

Apple, M. W. (1995). Cultural capital and official knowledge. In M. Berube & C. Nelson (Eds.), *Higher education under fire* (pp. 91–106). New York: Routledge.

Aronowitz, S., & Giroux, H. (1993). *Education still under siege: Critical studies in education and culture* (2nd ed.). Westport, CT: Bergin & Garvey.

Beane, J. A. (1990). *Affect in the curriculum: Toward democracy, dignity, and diversity*. New York: Teachers College Press.

Beane, J. A., & Lipka, R. P. (2000). *When the kids come first: Enhancing self-esteem*. New York: Educator's International Press.

Butler, J. W., & Novy, D. (1994). An investigation of differences in attitudes between suicidal and nonsuicidal student ideators. *Adolescence, 29*, 623–639.

Connelly, M. F., & Clandinin, D. J. (1988). *Teachers as curriculum planners: Narratives of experience*. New York: Teachers College Press.

Eccles, J. S., & Roeser, R. W. (1999). School and community influences on human development. In M. H. Borstein & M. E. Lamb (Eds.), *Developmental psychology: An advanced textbook*, (4th ed., pp. 503–546). Mahwah, NJ: Erlbaum.

Elkind, D. (1988). *The hurried child: Growing up too fast too soon*. New York: Addison-Wesley.

Elkind, D. (1989). *All grown up & no place to go: Teenagers in crisis*. New York: Addison-Wesley.

Hewett, J. H. (1980). After suicide. Philadelphia: Westminster Press.

Jackson, P. W. (1990). Life in classrooms. New York: Teachers College Press.

Jackson, P. W., Boostrom, R. E., & Hansen, D. T. (1993). The moral life of schools. San Francisco: Jossey-Bass.

Kerdeman, D. (1998). Hermeneutics and education: Understanding, control, and agency. Educational Theory, 48(2), 241–267.

King, K. A., Price, J. H., Telljohann, S. K., & Wahl, J. (1999). High school health teachers' perceived self-efficacy in identifying students at risk for suicide. Journal of School Health, 69(5), 202–207.

Kirchner, J. E., Yoder, M. C., Kramer, T. L., Lindsey, M. S., & Thrush, C. R. (2000). Development of an educational program to increase school personnel's awareness about child and adolescent depression. Education, 121, 235–247.

Marshall, C., & Rossman, G. B. (1999). Designing qualitative research (3rd ed.). Thousand Oaks, CA: McGraw-Hill.

McIntosh, J. (2002). U.S.A. suicide 2000 official data. American Association of Suicidology. Retrieved August 3, 2007, from http:www.suicidology.org

McMillan, J. H., & Schumacher, S. (2001). Research in education (5th ed.). New York: Longman.

Merriam, S. B. (1988). Case study research in education: A qualitative approach. San Francisco: Jossey-Bass.

Opalewski, D. (2001, Summer). Root issues of adolescent suicide. Performance Resource Press, Inc. Retrieved May 15, 2004, from http://www.prponline.net/SchoolSAJ/Articles/root_issues_of_adolescent_suicide htm

Patton, M. Q. (1990). Qualitative evaluation and research method (2nd ed.). Newbury Park, CA: SAGE.

Phillion, J. (2002). Narrative inquiry in a multicultural landscape: Multicultural teaching and learning. Westport, CT: Ablex.

Rishel, T. (2008). From the principal's desk: Making the school environment more inclusive. In T. Turner-Vorbeck & M. Miller Marsh (Eds.), Other kinds of families: Diversity in school and culture (pp. 92–131). New York: Teachers College Press.

Rishel, T. (2007). Suicide, schools, and the young adolescent. In S. Mertens, M. Caskey, & V. Anfara (Eds.), The young adolescent and the middle school (Vol. 6, pp. 297–322). Handbook of research in middle level education Series. Charlotte, NC: Information Age.

Schlosser, L. K. (1992). Teacher distance and student disengagement: School lives on the margin. Journal of Teacher Education, 43(2), 128–140.

United States Public Health Service. (1999). The surgeon general's call to action to prevent suicide. Mental Health: A report of the surgeon general, Washington, DC: Author. Retrieved June 20, 2007, from http://www.surgeongeneral.gov/library/mentalhealth/home.html

van Manen, M. (1990). Researching lived experience: Human science for an action sensitive pedagogy. New York: The State University of New York Press.

Wassef, A., & Ingham, D. (1995). In search of effective programs to address students' emotional distress and behavioral problems, part 1: Defining the problem. Adolescence, 30, 523–539.

CHAPTER 13

FOSTERING JUSTICE IN AN UNJUST WORLD

Stories Of Native American Women Professors

Angela M. Jaime

HERSTORY

I have been a part of the academic world as a student and professor for 17 years. During that time, I have had several mentors who have guided me through the successes and perils of my education. Of those mentors, only one has been a Native American woman.[1] Even though my interests have been the experiences of Native women in academia, I have had few Native women to draw on for leadership, support, and a source of energy. I have reflected on and studied the importance of mentors from within the cultural community to which a student belongs. I have realized that the mentorship provided by ethnic people to ethnic students is vital to their development as scholars and professionals. For those who believe

Personal~Passionate~Participatory Inquiry Into Social Justice in Education, pp. 217–232

that a mentor of any race, ethnicity, or gender could be as effective a mentor as a Native woman (for instance, in my case), I would have to disagree.

While working toward my bachelor's and master's degrees, I searched for advice from Native faculty for a number of reasons. I sought the approval of people in academia who have connections to Native communities. It was, and still is, important that I strengthen my ties with the people I want to help or with those whom I hope will benefit from my accomplishments. I also sought the guidance of Native professors to provide me with direction in my academic career. I felt they had unique insight into my past experiences since theirs were similar, and that they would guide me in a positive way. I am not implying that the non-Native people who advised me throughout my education have not also had my best interests in mind, but rather that the connection of shared experiences bonded the Native professor or instructor and me in a way that did not happen with other mentors.

My story is not a new story of Native students in higher education. I intend to tell my story so others can feel affirmed that they are not alone. It is vitally important to me to mentor other Native students as well as provide them avenues to seek and find their dreams. Currently, as a professor, my Native students top the list of my priorities. Without them I feel I have less purpose in my career. It is because of them that I work hard to meet and even exceed their needs. It is for them that I build upon my experiences in academia and offer myself as a mentor.

Betty Parent, a Native woman professor at San Francisco State University, was my major advisor throughout my master's program. While she raised three children, she received her bachelor's degree from the University of Alaska, her master's from Harvard University, and her doctorate from Stanford University. Betty treated me like one of her family. Her experiences in academia and her success are still influential in my life today. The relationship I share with Betty has mirrored the relationships I have had with other Native professors. Betty prepared me and continues to prepare me for a life in two academic worlds: Native and non-Native.

The assumption that individuals are measured and weighed equally on merit and accomplishments within the context of the academic world is a popular perception. We (especially those of us in the academy) know this to be untrue. We know, for example, that there are few Native American faculty members in universities in the United States. We also know there are even fewer Native American women on faculty; statistics reported by the U.S. Department of Education (2000) show lower numbers of Native women in academic positions and even lower numbers of tenured Native women professors as compared with their Native male counterparts. In addition, these statistics fail to illustrate the experiences of Native women while completing the degree process and when they are in academia. It is my contention that it is imperative that the academy recognize the low numbers of Native women professors and work toward addressing this injustice. My personal experiences as a Native American woman and my growing understanding of this injustice led me to explore these issues by closely examining the experiences of Native women in the academy.

RESEARCH AS PARTICIPATORY

Early in my doctoral work, I recognized the importance of examining the lives of other Native women in academia. The commitment I have to this topic reaches beyond this chapter. I believe that the lessons I learned from the women in my inquiry, and the information that I gathered, will aid me and other Native women in understanding our common experiences. Furthermore, as the experiences of Native women become documented for all to read, there is a greater chance of other Native women believing that they too can achieve their goals.

In the process of conducting my inquiry I sought out, interviewed, and fostered close relationships with two Native women professors who also experienced challenges and struggles as well as achievements and successes in institutions of higher education (Jaime, 2005). Through the process of getting to know them, my feelings regarding the importance of sharing their stories were reaffirmed. While I listened to the women tell about their lives over the course of one face-to-face interview lasting two to three hours and many communications thereafter, themes of decolonization and transcendence emerged. The stories the women told me reiterated the importance of sharing personal experiences from a Native woman's perspective. I went into the project looking for stories about "Western" success and found affirmation of my own academic plight as well as what success in life can mean.

Learning about the lack of Native women in the academy and the lack of their voices about their academic experiences in the literature led me to ask my Native women participants: What experiences did you have that discouraged you from pursuing a career in higher education? What experiences did you have that motivated and/or supported you in pursuing a career in the academy? These questions arose from within me, from my passions and from my challenges. I wanted to express my experiences and struggles for others to read. Sharing my story has not been the easiest thing to do; but anytime I feel it would help another, I would not hesitate to do so. Through the journey I have taken with the Native women, partially represented in this chapter, I have come to realize how important it is to understand the passions and personal stories of others, particularly those of Native women.

In the process of envisioning this inquiry, I became and continue to be adamant about the voices of Native women. The stories of the women that I interviewed are rich with detail and emotion. For me, it is an absolute necessity that they be heard by the reader and that the reader have a sense of getting to know these women throughout the text. After having read vast amounts of literature that reflect the voices of non-Native people first and Native women second, I made it my mission to establish that the Native women in my research are the storytellers of their own lives. They collaborated with me to narrate portraits of their lives. They feel that the portrait we created together is an accurate representation of them.

To meet the goals of reflecting the voices of the Native women and accurately representing them, I utilized a method called portraiture (Lawrence-Lightfoot & Hoffman-Davis, 1997) to paint a picture of the Native women in collaboration with them for the reader to experience. Through genuine dialogue and communication with the Native women, *we* constructed a written picture of their stories and experiences. I also asked my participant/collaborators to embrace a non-Western version of storytelling and to feel free to use this as a vehicle for describing their journeys through life. Through this process of participatory inquiry, I began to feel close to my cultural community again. Living in a world where Western thought is the "right way" to think had left me little leeway to feel whole. With the encouragement of my advisor and committee I was able to believe I could "be me" culturally in the inquiry and survive the institution built to challenge me daily.

As I began to feel comfortable with my methods of inquiry—personal, passionate and participatory—I built a case for their use in my research. The lack of research on Native American women and the ways in which much of the research was conducted, constructed, and presented made me realize the importance of the voices of researchers who are from the groups that they are studying (Smith, 1999; Wilson, 1998). I raise this point to shed light on the research about Native American women that has been written *about* them rather than *by* them. Non-Native researchers tend to essentialize a Native woman's experience. On the other hand, Native scholars, like Gretchen Bataille (1978), Angela Cavender Wilson (1998), Devon A. Mihesuah (1998), and Linda Tuhiwai Smith (1999), among others, speak as members of the communities and cultures in which they engage in research and with the permission of the Native people they are writing with and about. I drew on and continue to draw on the enormous strength of the women named above and their scholarship.

They were the mentors I needed then and still look to now during my academic endeavors.

Although there were many questions that I wanted to ask and topics that I wanted to address regarding the issues Native women face throughout their academic careers, I narrowed the scope of this research to the areas of negotiation in being Native as well as being academics and specifically, how they negotiate culture, traditions, communities, relationships, career, and identity within and outside the institutions to which they belong. In much of the material that I have read about Native people, Native women have been hidden or nonexistent in the paintings of Native communities as seen by non-Native people. This inquiry works to address this injustice. What was previously invisible about Native women is now the central focus in this work (Denzin & Lincoln, 2003). Through this lens, I now want readers to begin to listen to the stories of the Native women participants/collaborators as they share their lives and experiences. I, as well as my Native women participants, want readers to see us in the painting in which we were previously made invisible by the dominant society.

GETTING TO KNOW THE NATIVE WOMEN

My mother has always been a strong role model in my life. When I told her that I wanted to be a professor and that I would need to get my PhD, she was supportive. It seems only fitting that a woman who has survived domestic violence, poverty, and hardships beyond mention would be the one that I would think of first when writing my inquiry. Without her support and love, I would not have made it to this stage in my life. As I thought of my Native women participants and their influence upon me, I began to see a connection. The woman who raised me and sacrificed for me is the major reason I am here. The two women with whom I have been so fortunate to have crossed paths have also become mentors and role models.

I struggled with a way to communicate each woman's story to my readers. It came to me one day as I was writing my mom an e-mail in which I was explaining to her the stress that I was under and the events that had occurred over the past days. It was perfect. I would write letters to my mother telling her about the Native women that I had met, and I would tell her their stories. This method seemed so natural. I was already telling my mother about the women and their amazing lives each time I spoke with her on the phone, during visits at home, or over e-mail. In writing the letters I am retelling the story that each of the women has shared with me about herself. I have included descriptions of their work and passions. I have revisited my field notes and communications with my mother over the course of my writing to construct a full, lively, and loving picture based on my impressions of these women. I drew from notes and interviews from my first and subsequent meetings with each of these women and what I have learned from reading their academic work. I included parts of the transcripts from the interviews and correspondence that I have carried on with the two Native women. For the sake of narrative flow, I have removed my questions and edited portions of the women's responses. I have made every effort to retain original wording and to be true to what I thought each woman was trying to say. The date of each letter is marked with the day of the meeting or event. My intent was to allow the reader to experience the events as I experienced them. I have not included all the letters I wrote to my mother about the Native women, nor have I included all parts of the letters I include in this chapter. Rather, I have included a taste of those most significant to the understanding of my passion for this project and the participation of the Native women in this inquiry. In allowing the reader to experience the words of the women in a creative way, my hope is that the reader will connect with the Native women and hear their voices.

The letter vignettes are a true representation of the correspondence that I have had with my mother about my work. Some of the letters in the original text are long; my rationale for the length of each portrait can be traced to the methodology—portraiture and storytelling. I felt it important to allow the reader to explore the various dimensions of the women and their lives. The letters included their words in a way that not all readers may appreciate, yet traditionally in the Native communities that I have visited and belong to, storytelling is not a quick process or event. In some cultures and places, I have heard of stories told by elders and storytellers that can last many hours and sometimes can extend over the course of many days. I wanted the words of the women to appear within the letters to my mother as often as was appropriate. My mother hears not only my voice but theirs as well. For this chapter I have extracted vignettes of the original letters to give the reader an understanding of who my participant/collaborators were as well as the process of my participatory research. Context is given before and after each vignette to assist in situating the portrait for the reader.

LETTERS TO MOM

This first vignette conveys the feelings I had before I interviewed my first participant/collaborator, Paula (pseudonyms are used for participants), and my description of the setting. The excerpt also gives a brief introduction to some of Paula's cultural background.

May 12, 2003

Dear Mom,

Hi mom. I hope all is well and school is not getting too stressful for you. I wanted to tell you about my interview with Dr. Paula Fairfield. You know this was the first interview, so I was really nervous. I have read so much information about collecting data and doing research that I thought this would be no big deal; I was wrong. I was sweating while sitting in my office thinking about the interview only an hour before I went to meet with her. She was already in her office when I arrived, and I felt like I was late. She insisted that I call her Paula. I have known her for six or more years, but I always feel a little weird talking to professors without addressing them as Dr. so-and-so until I get to know them better and/or they have told me to call them by their first name.

Paula chose to have the interview in her office in the Women's Studies program. She was packing her things in the office to have them moved to her home department office, as her term as associate director in the Women's Studies program was ending. We spent some time talking about her stepping down from her position; she seemed very upset and said that this was not an easy decision. The up side to the coming weeks after this move is that she will be leaving to retreat back to her house in Atlantic City where she spends the summers; this is close to her reservations, her daughter, and her maternal family. Her daughter lives in New York City; she is 28 and works for an advertising company. She seemed excited about seeing her daughter and departing from Lafayette.

Paula is affiliated with the Powhatan-Renape Nation in southern New Jersey. They have a non-residential reservation called the Rankokus reservation; it was a state park before it was given to the tribe for educational and cultural purposes. She explained that originally her tribe lived in Virginia and in the early 1900s a group of her people migrated north to New Jersey. Her tribe is state recognized in New Jersey and Virginia. Paula gave some historical background to the situation.

The first reservation that we got in Virginia was due to a treaty with the British, not with the so-called American system. Historically the Powhatan Confederacy included what is now Washington DC, northern Maryland, part of the northern border of North Carolina, part of West Virginia, and all of what is now Virginia. That is why we are recognized by the state of Virginia and are not a federal tribe. It is the Pamunkey Reservation and across the river is the Mattaponi Reservation, also established in the 1600's. The Pamunkey and Mattaponi tribes are part of the Powhatan Nation or Confederation. We have the oldest reservation in America in Virginia, from the1600's. It is our original land—it's just less space, but it is in the same state; just a greatly reduced land mass. So nobody had to be relocated like to Oklahoma or to some other place. The New Jersey reservation was established in the 1980's for Powhatans who had migrated north since the early 1900s. The Powhatan Renape Nation which has a reservation called Rankokus, located in southern New Jersey, is composed of families who have ancestry from the Virginia based Powhatan tribes. (P. Fairfield, personal communication, May 6, 2003)

It is important to understand the story Paula provides in this introduction to her heritage. We all come from different places and times, and Paula contextualizes tribal history eloquently. Much like the letter introducing Paula, my next letter describing Lily also situates the warm person Lily is and her cultural background.

August 1, 2003

Dear Mom,

I drove to Woodland yesterday to interview Lily as my second participant/collaborator. I met Lily at the American Indian Studies Conference in February, where she gave a presentation on developing standards in American Indian Studies. She was very energetic and knowledgeable. When we exchanged emails a few weeks before I was set to arrive in Green Bay, Lily suggested that I stay on the reservation near her house. I stayed in the casino hotel on the Oneida reservation. It was really nice. The front desk made a mistake with my room request for non-smoking, and they didn't have any rooms at my rate left, so they upgraded me to a high-rollers room. It was fancy and big; I felt important.

On the day after I arrived, I met Lily in the restaurant across from the main casino entrance. There were a lot of White people there. But I did see more Native people in my visit than I had seen since the conference in Arizona last February. Most of the Native people were employees in some capacity; nevertheless, it was nice to see so many Native people. Lily brought me a huge bundle of sage wrapped in tissue. It was really thoughtful of her to bring me a gift when I was the one asking her to share her story with me. That is what Native people are all about: giving and honoring each other when they see someone doing something positive. I love that about our culture. I know not all Native people give without the expectation of receiving, but to me it happens more often in the Native community than in any other community that I have been a part of.

Lily was dressed in a cute black-and-white checkered sundress. It was a hot day outside even though it was only ten in the morning. We ate brunc,h and I talked about Esai, Luis, you, and what I have been doing with my life for the past thirty years. I wanted her to get to know me a little before I interviewed her so that she might feel more comfortable about sharing her life story with me. After brunch we decided to drive to her house, about a mile away, to conduct the interview. I was happy that she had suggested going to her house; I wanted the chance to see where she lived. Her three-year-old son, Skye, was visiting his grandparents who live about half a mile from her house.

When we arrived at her house, she took me on a tour. Everything was so clean, and each thing had its place. I was impressed that the house was so big and that the location was ideal for her and Skye: it is close to family and friends, within the reservation boundaries, and near the university.

We decided to sit at the kitchen table to conduct the interview. The windows were open, and I could hear the breeze rustle through the trees in the backyard. Lily had hung some chimes off the back deck. The sound of their soft ringing was soothing and made me feel at home. The chimes I have here at home help to put me to sleep at night when the wind is soft and the windows of my bedroom are open. This was only the second time that I had met Lily, and yet I felt so comfortable and relaxed with her. She has a caring way about her. It is hard to explain, but she seems concerned about so many things, yet when I talked I felt that she was truly listening. I liked her instantly, not only because she is so close to Myl, but because she was so willing to help me without even knowing me.

Lily is Ojibwa of Lac du Flambeau from Northern Wisconsin. Her father is half Ojibwa and part Shawnee. Lily's mother is "Anglo" of Polish and German decent. I found it interesting that she used the term Anglo rather than White or simply referred to the European heritage by name. I felt it showed respect to her mother and also showed her sensitivity toward others by not referring to their skin color. Lily was raised in Mill Town and refers to herself as an "urban Indian."

I asked Lily about her involvement with her own tribe and with those in the area where she resides. She expressed with some reservation that she votes during elections by absentee ballot. There are some real concerns that she has about visiting or spending time on her reservation. One of the more difficult times during our interview was the story she told of the abuse that she survived as a child. It brings tears to my eyes to think of the pain that she endured and still deals with today. She based her dissertation on the experiences that she had of sexual, physical, and emotional abuse. Lily's father was an abusive person to Lily. He assaulted her not only verbally and physically but also sexually. The first few pages of Lily's dissertation are a reflective piece on one of the many times that her father beat and raped her. It was hard to read the words that she wrote. The central tenet of her thesis concerns the oppression of marginalized groups that speak out against the White patriarchal power structure.

Not only do I describe Lily's cultural heritage, but also a bit about her life currently, and the dissertation she wrote to complete her doctorate. Lily is a remarkable woman. The barriers she has overcome and the strength she shows through her actions are incredible. Even having only just gotten to know her, I was overcome with emotion during her story.

Both women, Paula and Lily, struggled throughout their careers with obstacles placed in front of them by people in the academy. This may be true for many people; the significance in this inquiry and for these women is that they accomplished the seemingly impossible for so many women and minorities—they became two of less than one hundred Native women with tenure in institutions of higher education (U.S. Department of Education, 2000). The following letters describe their experience reaching and attaining tenure in their home institutions.

She(Paula) attributed the ease of tenure in her career to the location of her Mid-Western University; the rural area and lack of social activities afforded her the opportunity to do a great deal of work. She mentioned many times during the interview that her life in Mid-Western Town has been limited socially. While on sabbaticals and between semesters, she spends much of her time away from Mid-Western Town; her house in New Jersey makes for a great getaway and provides her the opportunity to be closer to her Native community, her daughter, her husband, and her mother. Paula also mentioned that with her Ph.D., she is sometimes treated differently by family members than she was before she earned the degree and began working at Mid-Western; some of her family members' actions reflect a lack of support.

Being a Native professor in a predominately Caucasian university plays a major role in the way Paula is perceived; she mentioned that she gets called for everything having to do with Native people. She claimed that since she has come to Mid-Western University, there have been some White faculty who have changed their identity to Native American. The university claims six or seven Native American faculty, but Paula says there are really only three: herself, a professor in the geology department, and one Native woman in the history department. Her students react differently toward her than they do to her White colleague counterparts; students are more resistant to her and are more defiant on her evaluations than they are on the evaluations of non-color faculty. She says this about her graduate students:

> *Now at the graduate level it is better, because the grad school has international students and students from other parts of the country who are used to the diversity. So I have a more positive rapport with the graduate students than I do my undergrad students. I encounter a lot of racism here at Mid-Western with the undergrads, I really do. (P. Fairfield, personal communication, May 6, 2003)*

Paula mentioned that her department asked to "count" her as an African American in order to provide the illusion that they were meeting the diversity concerns of external reviewers at the University. She declined the request and told them to hire an African American. She also mentioned that the men in the Native culture are sometimes more oppressed than the women. Paula continued to explain that the men in minority cultures are seen as more threatening than the women to the White power structure. She was very concerned that there were no "strong Black men" in positions of power at Mid-Western University. Paula explained that she felt support at Mid-Western, but it was support she sought out and created with colleagues and family.

Paula's experience is unique in that she stood firmly on her ground and forced her colleagues to take responsibility for the lack of diversity in the department. Sadly not many professors would have done this, and even less minority women professors. Most colleagues and administrators would expect women of color to submit to their requests and follow the rules set for only us in the academy. Lily experienced a similar situation during her tenure review.

We also talked about the issues that Lily has faced as a woman in academia. During her graduate work as a doctoral student, she was harassed by a professor she worked with as a teaching assistant. When she complained to the university administration, they basically told her to keep quiet about the issue and continue with her work; she was treated horribly. I asked her about where she felt gender and race intersected within her experiences as a professor, and not just in thinking about harassment and issues of discrimination. Her answer came in the form of a very profound story regarding her tenure process.

When I was in my tenure review a year ago last spring, one of the members of the tenure committee asked me in my review, what would happen if tomorrow there weren't any American Indian studies at Woodland. What would I teach? What would I do? And I knew that my answer wasn't going to be the tenure friendly answer, but I gave it anyway. I said I would leave and I didn't give a reason why. And then I guess they prodded and asked me why, and I said because there wouldn't be anything here worth teaching anymore. And of course that was not the right thing to say, because none of them are in my discipline and these are all older guys too that had been there forever—older White men that have been there forever. So one of them said to me, "Oh but you're wrong, because if we did away with American Indian studies we would still have a justice studies emphasis in what is the equivalent to sociology and we would still have women's studies." And I said, "Oh, that's interesting to me that you make those distinctions that American Indian studies is over here by itself, because for me in my mind if you do away with American Indian studies then women's studies doesn't exist anymore because why would you devalue a program like American Indian studies and continue to value women's studies because they would probably go away at the same time in my mind. And the justice studies program that talks about these same issues, although maybe not focusing from a gender perspective or focusing on a racial perspective, justice studies would be gone as well." And so their question to me was all of that would go away because in my work and in my mind those disciplines, those programs of study, are so interconnected. If you look [in] my file [at] all the scholarship and the research that I've done, there is no boundary between them and they all flow together. And the same is true for my service. Not service to the institution but my outside-the-institution community service and my research are so connected that they can't really be separated. It's hard for me to say, well that goes in the scholarship box and that goes in the community service box because my scholarship comes out of it—it is my service. It's the same thing. And again in my mind, those things are so connected. (L. Paris, personal communication, July 21, 2004)

The committee was tickled by her answer; they told her that they had never considered the connection of different disciplines in the way that she had explained it. I respect Lily for taking a stand and not feeling intimidated in that situation to tell the committee how she felt. I appreciate the honesty that she shared.

It occurs to me now that the experiences these two women have described and their responses to their peers are profound; both women are so strong and cool about their answers. I have learned so much from their strength through this process.

In both interviews I asked questions about their ideas of success and what that looked like in their careers. The next vignette provides a taste of what Paula had to say about her accomplishments:

Success is feeling comfortable with our personal life, family, career, spirituality, etc. Success is an inner feeling and can not be defined by others. For me, success is feeling peaceful within myself even if there is external turmoil around me. One can still be successful internally while going through a divorce, coping with illness, tragedy, etc. On the other hand, one may seem "successful" to others [because of] superficial aspects or outward appearance but not feel successful internally. I feel successful internally and externally. My family grounds me when I feel stressed out from career demands. I find a comfort and solace interacting with my immediate family. I am also close to my extended family; especially the ones involved in the arts. And when my family, rather than my career, is stressing me, I try to find peace through spiritual beliefs and practice—especially those rooted in the Native American culture. No one's life is perfect. It is being able to deal with the inevitable ups and downs in a positive way that really indicates if a person is "successful." (P. Fairfield, personal communication, May 6, 2003)

Success is really an individual definition. It is reassuring to know that professors who have been in academia for ten plus years are so well grounded in their families. I felt closer to Paula at this moment than at any other time in our relationship. I am truly glad we were able to spend time together and to get to know each other better. She has been so supportive of me since we have met and has shared her thoughts with me on the topic of my research.

For Lily, it was never about an abstract idea of success but rather balancing her life and doing right by the ones she loves. In the following vignette, Lily explains the importance of balance:

Over the course of the interview, Lily explained to me both directly and indirectly that her position as a professor means a great deal to her; she also described the balance that she tries to keep in her life. When I asked her whether she feels that she is successful, she quoted an elder:

Well, I know the thing that my elders talk about is living a life that's balanced. I think that when I was younger, and I don't know, I think a lot of people in the dominant culture, you wonder, maybe they don't wonder, but some people wonder, what is the meaning of life. And the summer I was working in the Menomonee community at an American Indian studies institute with teachers, it's always an amusing experience, one of our elders was talking and she said, "In Indian communities we don't wonder— we didn't in the past wonder—what the meaning of life was. We knew. The meaning of life was to be good to each other. Be good to yourselves. Be good to other people and be good to all beings. Treat other beings kindly—not only humans, but all [living things]. And that's the meaning of life." And to me that's living a balanced life and if you're able to do that, to be kind to yourself and all the beings, that's all that matters; and that, to me, if I'm able to do that, then I have success at being human. And as I answer that question, I'm thinking about Skye, being a good parent [to him] but that's all, that's all a part of it. (L. Paris, Personal Communication, July 21, 2004)

Her words have resonated with me since that day. I hear her saying the words, and I think about my own life: Am I good to myself? Am I a good parent and life partner? Living a balanced life is important to me.

As stated before, I only included a few vignettes from the research to provide readers with an idea of my process through this inquiry. Of course, I am partial to the letters in their entirety simply because they paint a clear and beautiful portrait of these two Native women. However, for this chapter I included vignettes that I felt present a picture of their background, their strength of conviction, and their understanding of balance and success.

OUTCOMES RESULTING FROM THE INQUIRY

When I chose this area of research, I thought the first reason this information was valuable would be to help me on the road that I have chosen to follow—working as a professor. My choice of understanding the role of Native women professors was to learn through their personal experiences. It occurred to me that I was not the only one to benefit from this endeavor. It seemed likely that this research would favorably affect other Native people who might be seeking a graduate degree or a career as a professor. Through the experiences and advice of Native women professors, other Native people can learn from those who have gone before them. More importantly, the self-defining stories of Paula and Lily provide a positive perspective of Native women. The women in this inquiry have shared stories of their struggles and challenges. These stories provide me, and many others like me, an understanding of what we might expect in higher education. It is my true hope that this inquiry helps other Native women to face and overcome the challenges lying ahead of them if they choose to pursue a career in higher education.

EDUCATIONAL AND SOCIAL CHANGE
RESULTING FROM THE INQUIRY

This inquiry with Native women has changed me. I am hopeful about my career choice and look forward to each day as I enter my office. I feel that

I am able to do the kind of work and research that means something to me—work that entails personal meaning for me, work that I feel passionate about, work in which I feel proud to be actively involved, work that builds on the experiences and insights of my mother, my participants and other Native women. This research also benefits many players in the lives of Native women: counselors, teachers, mentors, administrators, parents, community members, and others in higher institutions in all capacities. If people take the time to hear the voices of the Native women, they will hear them say that there is a need for support systems to be put into place to help Native women achieve their goals and dreams. They will also hear that the institutions surrounding Native women, from the time they step foot in the public school system to the time they retire as a professor, are built to and continue to challenge the very existence of Native women. Hearing this message echoed through the Native women's voices has catapulted me to be constantly vigilant about the perpetuation of negative images surrounding Native culture and, more specifically, Native women in regards to their self-esteem and the way in which outsiders continue to treat them. It has also pushed me to be an advocate for Native women in higher education through my research, teaching, and above all, my mentoring.

The mentoring I do with Native students, especially the women, is my priority as a professor. I spend additional time with Native students, I fight harder with administration and colleagues for opportunities for Native students, and I raise critical questions no one else asks about injustices toward Native students and students of color. I have worked hard to achieve the position I now hold in my career. This privilege I possess is, and will be, used to help others like me achieve their goals. I have created opportunities for Native students to have access to a Native woman during advising in their academics and through student organizations. I am visible to my students and make sure they know I am watching in case they stumble and need a helping hand.

My teaching is based on the same philosophy as my mentoring of Native students. I ask hard questions; I stay visible and active in students' lives; and I teach from a critical perspective. My students are rarely faced with mundane material, but rather asked, and in some situations, pushed to think outside the box. My White students are provided opportunities to learn about Native culture and community through field observations and on-campus activities, a variety of media resources most professors fail to use, and me—a Native woman who knows her culture and is not afraid to face controversial issues. It is my goal to encourage students to dialogue about racism, sexism, and discrimination of Native students in present day classrooms. It is not my intention to befriend my students but rather to expose them to the areas of life in education which are not so beautiful. The Native women in my research have taught me to be strong and face adversity with pride and courage, to educate the naïve and the unaware.

I have strong feelings about the way in which this research process and final product have grown. Using the methods of inquiry I chose and telling the stories of the Native women through letters will hopefully lay a path for others to follow, and to envision research through a nontraditional lens. Blazing trials for others is never an easy task, yet, one I embrace and look forward to continuing through my future research. The work with Native women will never be over for me. I intend to continue to create and provide space for Native women to tell their stories. It is my hope that in reading this work others will find resonance in my stories and the stories of my Native women participants, feel the strength of our words, and join our struggle, and the struggles of all Native peoples, to foster social justice in an unjust world.

NOTE

1. Although it is certainly desirable to refer to Native people by their tribal names and to point out individual tribal traits, it is not feasible to do so when discussing the tribes in general. Therefore, unless noted otherwise, the term Native or Native American will be used to refer to all tribes.

REFERENCES

Bataille, G., (1978). *Transformation of tradition: Autobiographical works by Native American women* (Report No. EDC-RC-95-2). West Lafayette, IN: Purdue University. (ERIC Document Reproduction Service No. ED173002)

Denzin, N. K., & Lincoln, Y. S. (2003). Introduction: The discipline and practice of qualitative research. In D. K. Denzin & Y. S. Lincoln (Eds.), *Strategies of qualitative inquiry* (2nd ed., pp. 1–45). Thousand Oaks, CA: SAGE.

Jaime, A. M. (2005). *Narrated portraits: The lived experience of Native women in academia.* Unpublished doctoral dissertation, Purdue University.

Lawrence-Lightfoot, S., & Hoffman Davis, J. (1997). *The art and science of portraiture.* San Francisco: Jossey-Bass.

Mihesuah, D. A. (1998). Commonality of difference: American Indian women and history. In *Natives and academics: Researching and writing about American Indians* (pp. 37–54). Lincoln: University of Nebraska Press.

Smith, L. T. (1999). *Decolonizing methodologies; Research and Indigenous peoples.* New York: Zed Books.

U.S. Department of Education, *2000 Digest of Education Statistics,*. Retrieved November 4, 2002, from http://nces.ed.gov/fastfacts/display.asp?id=72

Wilson, A. C. (1998). American Indian history or non-Indian perceptions of American Indian history. In D. A. Mihesuah (Ed.), *Natives and academics: Researching and writing about American Indians* (pp. 23–26). Lincoln: University of Nebraska Press.

CHAPTER 14

IT STARTS AT HOME

The Familial Relationship of
Scholarship, Education, and Advocacy

Tammy A. Turner-Vorbeck

THE RELATIONSHIP OF INQUIRY AND ADVOCACY

Much of our research is born out of the personal or private realm of our lives and it takes place at an interesting intersection of the personal and the professional, the private and the public. Our research certainly represents questions we feel need to be answered; yet it also often originates from and leads us to positions of advocacy. This confluence necessitates a careful deconstruction and dismantling of the artificial dichotomy between the objective and the subjective, creating the space for authentic, passionate, participatory inquiry, such as that represented in this collection.

In my own life, like so many of us, I have multiple roles. In my professional life, I work in academe as a curriculum researcher and a teacher educator. In my personal life, as a mother of three children adopted as older children from the state of Indiana's foster care system, I find myself

Personal~Passionate~Participatory Inquiry Into Social Justice in Education, pp. 233–246

functioning as an advocate, striving to meet the unique educational challenges presented by my children's schooling experiences. My personal and professional lives have come to intersect through my research, where I bring my academic knowledge and my personal experiences to bear upon the dual questions: How *is* and how *should* the construct of family be represented within curriculum?

My focus upon these dual questions was a response to the real life situations of my three children who struggled in classrooms and schools that were insensitive to their unique experiences as adopted children. When faced year after year with tearful children fresh off the afternoon school bus with social studies (family tree activities), language arts (biographical family narratives), biology (genetic/dominate gene exercises) assignments requiring them to provide and utilize family background information that was non-existent for them, I knew there was a need to educate school personnel to replace the ignorance out of which these assumptive assignments were made. The negative impact of school curriculum involving the concept of *family* upon my three children was enormous and called for my direct intervention as a caring parent. Perhaps the most tragic aspect of this fact was that teachers and school personnel were often unaware of the damage they were imparting by asking for baby pictures that my children did not have, asking for the origins of their first names, which my children did not know, or requiring them to trace their biological roots, which was not only painful for my children but also impossible. It was the years of working with teachers to help foster their understanding of ways to address *family* in the curriculum that are more inclusive that led me to create a mission statement for myself.

My personal "mission statement" operationalizes my passions and goals for social justice, particularly focused upon the area of family structure diversity and equity, and serves as the foundation of my continuing inquiry. It reads as follows:

> Supporting the theoretical with the experiential, it is the intent of my writing and my teaching to provide others with an understanding of the complex relationship between the primary forms of curriculum on family at work in schools in order to fully illuminate the real-life consequences that various curricular messages about the concept of family create for students.

I use this statement to continually guide me and I highly recommend developing such a statement that is unique to you and your passions. It is something you can return to in order to continue to strive to reach the goals you have identified in your own efforts toward social justice, in whatever personal and professional realms you deem relevant.

Putting my own "mission statement" into practice, I have crafted a sphere of scholarship for myself that both *inquires about* and *advocates for* the expansion of multicultural education to include an often neglect yet common form of diversity, family structure diversity. In a related manner, I work to insure that I maintain a heavy focus upon issues of family diversity in all education foundations courses, child development and educational psychology courses, pedagogy seminars, and multicultural education courses that I teach. I also readily offer seminars to preservice and in-service teachers on family diversity awareness and curriculum sensitivity to *othered* forms of family. Reports from students and from teachers exposed to such ideas leads me to believe that this topic has a profound effect upon their teaching and that keeps my passion and my determination alive!

As evidence of how it is possible to successfully combine inquiry and advocacy, an article published in the journal of *Multicultural Education* (Turner-Vorbeck, 2005) contains research I did on the inclusion of a family diversity unit in an existing teacher education program's multicultural education course. What follows in this chapter are excerpts from that research study.

EXPANDING MULTICULTURAL EDUCATION TO INCLUDE FAMILY DIVERSITY

The composition of families is changing (Huston, 2001) and is readily apparent in the variety of families represented by students in today's classrooms. Advocates from the fields of social work and psychological counseling (Okun, 1996) as well as from adoptive, step, and gay family support networks (Geis-Rockwood, 1990) have stepped to the fore to call for changes in curriculum and for teacher education programs to recognize and address this often neglected form of diversity. Yet, the multicultural education and diversity issues discussed in today's teacher education courses at our major universities and colleges are often still restricted to their foundational concerns with discussions of race, ethnicity, class, and gender. Introducing the topic of family diversity provides another dimension of diversity for preservice teachers to consider and explore while they try to construct meanings for the monumental topics under discussion and critique in teacher education classrooms. The very notion of "family" offers most students some degree of ownership in the topic through their personal experiences of family; however, as they are asked to deconstruct narrow societal definitions of what constitutes a family, they begin a journey that often leads to discomfort, resistance, and challenges to what is defined as a normal and valued family in our society. The contentiousness of this sort of conversation mirrors and buttresses issues surrounding race, class, and gender across their multicultural education curriculum,

.uly allows uniquely personal access to powerful stereo-
., hidden deep within their conceptions of what constitutes
.as writing describes a research and teaching project that was
., and implemented to investigate the promise of the integration
.nily diversity issues into a pre-service teacher multicultural education
.arriculum to better prepare pre-service teachers to respond to the needs
of all students, regardless of their varied familial backgrounds.

RATIONALE

The overall purpose of this research project was to investigate the promise
of the exploration of family diversity issues through a multicultural education curriculum to heighten the awareness and sensitivity of pre-service
teachers to needs tied to students' differing family structures as well as to
overall issues of diversity in the classroom in order to better prepare these
teachers to meet the needs of an increasingly diverse student population.
Pre-service teachers were introduced to family diversity issues as a special
unit of instruction placed inside the existing curriculum in the undergraduate multicultural education course at a major Midwestern university's teacher education program. This research continues as a part of my
ongoing inquiry investigating how family diversity is addressed in both
teacher education programs and multicultural education as a whole,
including both theory and practice.

Issues of family diversity are becoming critically important as the
demographics of families in this country and indeed, the world change
(Huston, 2001); yet they are often an ignored part of broader diversity
discussions. Through the investigation of this project, participants' awareness of family diversity issues was identified and assessed in terms of participants' willingness to recognize and address such issues in their own
classrooms. In addition, it is believed that providing these pre-service
teachers with opportunities to explore issues of diversity through the specific subject area of family structure holds the potential to heighten their
overall sensitivity to broader diversity issues such as class, race, ethnicity,
and language and to further struggle to avoid generalizations which
sometimes accompany such concepts that have often either become
loaded with preconceived connotations or reduced to complete ambiguity
such as "multicultural" (Derman-Sparks, 1989).

There is little doubt that there exists a broad call for the inclusion of
diversity issues throughout teacher education discussions. Much of this
discussion takes place under the umbrella of multicultural studies. Scholars writing in the area of multiculturalism today emphasize the need for
pervasive antiracist education aimed at social justice (Nieto, 2000);

suggest content integration, knowledge construction, prejudice reduction, equity pedagogy, and the creation of an empowering school culture (Banks & Banks, 2001); argue for a *cultivation of humanity* (Nussbaum, 1997); call for *culturally responsive teaching* (Gay, 2000); and attempt to define genres of multiculturalism, each with their own definitions and goals (Bennett, 2001; Duarte & Smith, 2000). In university classrooms for pre-service teachers all over the United States, future educators are engaged in attempts to make meaning of these notions and imagine their application to real students in real classrooms. With areas such as race and ethnicity forming the foundation of these studies, there also exists a need for an examination of other aspects of diversity which represent the varied physical and social worlds within which today's schoolchildren live and learn, and family diversity represents a very important one.

PARTICIPATORY RESEARCH PROCESS

Phase one of this project involved the completion of a literature review of relevant writings in the areas of family diversity and curriculum and educational practices in the classroom. Building upon what was learned in phase one, phase two involved the design and creation of a unit of instruction tailored to meet the needs of a preservice teacher audience and also to provide for analysis of preservice teachers' attitudes toward nontraditional families and children from those families, as well as their abilities and willingness to work collaboratively to identify personal prejudices and how those might translate into classroom practice.

The participants were preservice teachers (predominantly White, European-American) within the teacher education program of a prominent Midwestern university which offers a reformed teacher education program redesigned in terms of research findings on best practices. This teacher education program includes a focus on traditional diversity issues such as race, gender, culture, and language. The family diversity curriculum unit was introduced to a total of three sections of the single, required multicultural education course within the teacher education curriculum across three semesters. Each section contained an average of twenty-six students. A summated, 5-point Likert scale questionnaire provided foundational data on student attitudes toward family diversity and curriculum issues (Miller, 1991) as well as a focal point for reflection when returned to participants during their journal writing activities at the conclusion of the lesson. A less formal survey discussion at the end of the lesson provided formative feedback on the overall success of the lesson (Smith & Ragan, 1993). In addition, guided discussions in which the participants were encouraged to actively encounter and answer questions of their own prej-

udices and belief systems provided a strong foundation for self-explora-
tion, which was also reflected upon and evident during the journaling
experience (Clandinin & Connelly,1994) as well as integrated into the
activities. The guided group activities included the construction of a K–5
classroom activity for a lesson on family. Such activities created an opportunity for the participants to bring to life antibias activities involving family diversity which could be used in their own future classrooms. All of
these activities were also reflected upon in the journal writing activity.

THE FAMILY DIVERSITY CURRICULUM UNIT

Syllabus space and time are precious within a multicultural education
course designed to function as the only class within a reformed teacher
education program dedicated to addressing issues of diversity and equity.
As such, the addition of this curriculum unit on the topic of family diversity was allotted two hours of class time. During the class session before
the Family Diversity Unit, a brief introduction to the unit was provided,
attitudinal questionnaires were administered and collected (anonymity
was maintained), and short, foundational readings by Derman-Sparks
(1989) and Okun (1996) were assigned and provided. The Family Diversity Unit was then taught during the next class period. A description of
the curriculum unit is provided in the section that follows.

Laying the Foundation

After spending a few minutes on introductions, the overarching
research question for the project was shared with students as a point of
orientation: "How can teachers help their classrooms to become more
inclusive and accepting environments for children from differing family
structures just as we know they should be sensitive to the gender, racial,
cultural, and language differences of students?" The opening query uni-
formly resulted in a majority of students admitting that they had not previously considered that family diversity would be a likely issue in their
classrooms or in their curricula. Following the brief discussion of the
introduction of the topic of family diversity, the objectives for the unit
were openly shared with students: (1) develop an awareness and an initial
understanding of the issue of family diversity; (2) discover our own opinions and biases on family diversity,; (3) create/explore some tools for use
in the classroom, and (4) reflect on our views of family diversity through
journaling.

Objective 1: Develop Awareness and Initial Understanding of Family Diversity

To accomplish the first objective of developing an initial understanding of the topic, a brief lecture was given to provide foundational information. The changing demographics of the U.S. school population were addressed, including the fact that less than fifty percent of children in schools in America are represented by a two biological, heterosexual parent family and that the trend away from traditional, nuclear families is increasing (Coontz, 1997). This demonstrates the necessity for teachers to contemplate how they will address and work with issues of family diversity in their classrooms. A few short narratives collected from people from non-traditional families, in which they shared some of their personal painful school experiences, were read to the students to help to put a human face on the real consequences of teacher ignorance or indifference toward family diversity. Various forms of families were introduced (e.g., foster, adopted, step, grandparent/relative, gay/lesbian, interracial, etc.) to expose students to a wide variety of forms of family with which they might not have been familiar. To compliment descriptions of difference, a discussion of the unifying themes across families was provided. This notion is based upon how families function with similar goals and purposes such as, providing basic needs, child rearing, socializing members, establishing and maintaining cultural traditions, and delegating responsibilities and roles.

Objective 2: Discover Student Opinions and Biases on Family Diversity

The second objective of uncovering student opinions and biases about family diversity was achieved through a guided discussion of the two assigned readings as well as discovery of the students' own ideas. The students were asked to write down their responses to this question:

> Being honest, what are some of the personal prejudices you hold or have previously held about nontraditional (single-parent, adoptive, gay/lesbian, step-parent, multiracial, etc.) families?

Students were then asked to move into pairs to share their responses with a partner and to work together to complete these two questions:

> How do you think those prejudices translate into the classroom environment?

> How, as a teacher, might you create a more positive, accepting environment for children from nontraditional families?

The class was reconvened as a whole group and answers to the question of biases held about differing forms of family were verbally volunteered, written on the board, and discussed. Responses to the second group of questions answered in pairs were then collected and discussed. Many students were amazed at the extent to which they and their classmates held strong prejudicial beliefs against nontraditional forms of family.

Objective 3: Create Activities for Use in the Classroom on Family Diversity

Having laid a foundational understanding of family diversity, followed by guided discovery of existing biases held by students, the third objective provided a positive and practical direction in which to turn by requiring some creative thinking about how to use classroom activities to be inclusive of many forms of family. The exercise began by first critiquing the traditional family activities in which seemingly innocuous assignments were exposed as having a negative impact on many children. Students from nontraditional family structures often feel awkward and excluded when asked to write an autobiography, bring baby photos to class, make a family tree, or do genealogy studies. If they are being raised by single parents, step-families, grandparents/relatives, gay parents, or in adoptive or foster families, there will likely be some background that is missing, complicated, or even kept secret. Well meaning teachers can be exclusionary by using such familiar activities without realizing it.

An example of an inclusive alternative to the traditional activities, called the ME Poem, was shared with the class. In this activity, students are encouraged to complete nine descriptive statements about themselves, their interests, and their lives, including family members:

1. MOLLY **(first name)**
2. smart, athletic, funny, crazy **(4 adjectives)**
3. sister of Maureen **(family)**
4. **who loves** Mom, Maureen, Dad, and Judy
5. **who needs** love, good friends, and loyalty
6. **who wonders about** other cultures, diseases, and other states
7. **who would like to see** Florida, Paris, and people being nice to everyone else
8. **resident of** Petaluma, California, on Ellis Street
9. REGIN **(last name)**

The class was then instructed to break into small groups of three or four students and work with markers and large sheets of paper to create a unique activity which could allow K–5 students to express information about themselves and their families in a freer and less restricted way. The excitement in the room surrounding this exercise was palpable and the ideas generated were enthusiastically shared in a lively "show and tell" session afterward. Students routinely expressed satisfaction with their ability to ideate a tangible solution to the challenge of using inclusive activities on family. Additional commercially available examples of such activities, materials, and lessons were then provided, such as the film and accompanying instructor's guide, *That's a Family!*

Objective 4: Reflect on Views of Family Diversity Through Journaling

Before giving students their reflective journaling assignment to be completed outside of class, the overall class totals for the attitudinal questionnaire were shared (maintaining individual confidentiality). Their individual completed questionnaires were then returned to them by use of a special labeling code. The journaling assignment sheet with the following questions was then given out:

Use your own paper, to thoughtfully answer the questions that follow. This should represent approximately 2 to 3 pages of written reflection. Return your assignment to your instructor.

- Thinking back over the readings on family diversity, what issue(s) intrigued you most or caused you to think about something you had not considered before?
- During the class discussions, many issues concerning family diversity surfaced. What made the biggest impression on you and why?
- How do you feel that these issues have impacted your ideas about teaching?
- Do you see any of these ideas translating into your own teaching practice? How?
- Do you have any personal experiences which you can relate to this discussion?

Revisit the answers you gave on the questionnaire. How would you answer these questions now?

- Describe what FAMILY DIVERSITY means to you.
- What types of families do you expect to see represented by the students you will teach?

OUTCOMES RESULTING FROM THE INQUIRY

In the course of participating in this project, participants were exposed to readings on family diversity written from the perspectives of people living these experiences. Bringing these family situations to life was an important part of the experience. Through the attitudinal questionnaire and subsequent discussions, participants were asked to search into their own histories and to explore their own biases against particular family structures and how they thought those biases might or might not impact upon their teaching. In addition to discussing the affective elements involved in the teaching of students from nontraditional families, participants were also able to "deconstruct" traditional classroom activities on the topic of family, often thought of nostalgically (such as the "family tree" activity) but shown to be detrimental to children who have hidden histories or simply lack that information. Participants were then able to work together in small groups to create new and innovative activities that would be inclusive of all students. Tying this together and mirroring the theory-into-practice notion, participants reflected again upon their original answers to the questionnaire on attitudes toward differing family structures, their experiential readings and discussions, traditional exclusionary activities and improvements upon those, and their new perspectives on family diversity and how to address it in the classroom environment.

Attitudinal Questionnaire

The attitudinal questionnaire consisted of 10 Likert-type questions and two open-ended questions. It was designed to provide a baseline for locating the beliefs about families held by each participant and for participant reflection upon their responses after the unit's completion. The closed-ended questions asked for degrees of agreement or disagreement: (5 = Strongly Agree, 4 = Agree, 3 = Undecided, 2 = Disagree, 1 = Strongly Disagree). The results are provided in the section that follows.

Questions: (1) As a teacher, you would worry about children in your class whose parents were divorced. (64% Agreed or Strongly Agreed); (2) The definition of a family is a group of people in which there are two married, biological parents who are both living at home and caring for their children. (16% Agreed or Strongly Agreed); (3) You plan to use a "family tree" exercise to talk about family genealogy and help children to be proud of their "roots". (68% Agreed or Strongly Agreed); (4)Talking openly in the classroom about gay and/or lesbian relationships is a form of supporting those types of relationships. (12% Agreed or Strongly Agreed); (5) You plan to hold a "bring your grandparents to school day".

(64% Agreed or Strongly Agreed); (6) You feel sorry for the children of single mothers because they do not receive the amount of attention and support they need at home to be successful at school. (36% Agreed or Strongly Agreed); (7) Not mentioning types of families other than traditional, two-parent families can cause a student from a nontraditional family to suffer self-esteem troubles. (63% Agreed or Strongly Agreed); (8) You plan to practice an antibias curriculum. (68% Agreed or Strongly Agreed); (9) You often think to yourself, "Why can't we just let children be?" or "Children don't have any prejudices." (16% Agreed or Strongly Agreed); (10) Children who were adopted are no different than other children in terms of their development and their needs at school (60% Agreed or Strongly Agreed).

The open-ended questions produced a variety of responses as participants were asked to consider: (1) Describe what family diversity means to you. and (2) What types of families do you expect to see represented by the students you will teach? Some students revealed inclusive definitions of families that went beyond the traditional, nuclear family. A larger number demonstrated an understanding that a significant number of the students in their future classrooms would not be from traditional, nuclear family structures. Overall, the results of the attitudinal questionnaire indicated and provided some illumination of the biases that existed prior to the family diversity unit.

Reflective Journals

Since time spent with the students was limited, it was from the reflective journals that evidence of growth among participants became apparent. Below are three excerpts from student participant reflective journals:

> The biggest impression made on me was what my fellow classmates seemed to think about family diversity. Some of them seemed quick to judge others simply on what choices they had made. I think this attitude may impair them when it comes to teaching kids because it is hard to judge parents and not judge their children as well. My religion tells me not to believe in homosexuality but after discussing these issues in this unit, I also believe that you cannot judge children negatively because you personally disagree with decisions their parents have made. I want to make all of the kids in my class feel like they belong. —*Susan*

> Family diversity is a concept that was never previously discussed during my education. Our class discussion really made me think about it. I cannot understand how in one sentence a person can say that a child needs two loving parents in a home and then also go on to say that homosexual parents

cannot provide that. This issue has really opened my mind and eyes personally and also in thinking about how to handle the topic of "different" families when I become a teacher myself. —*Joy*

What made the biggest impression on me was when we listed our biases on the board. I felt so overwhelmed by these biases. I know that I am guilty of having some of these negative thoughts but I hadn't even realized before that I even held them. I don't know exactly how to remove these biases but the unit on family diversity has gotten my attention and I will take some of these new ideas with me when I teach. I now think it is important for me to remember to be as aware as possible of the backgrounds of all of my students and to also be aware of my own biases toward those backgrounds.— *Sarah*

EDUCATIONAL AND SOCIAL CHANGE RESULTING FROM THE INQUIRY

Overall, this research project indicates that expanding the definition and scope of multicultural education curriculum holds the potential to prepare new teachers to practice diverse family inclusion in several ways: (1) by broadening preservice teacher awareness of diversity to include family structure diversity since the composition of the American family has changed drastically and continues to evolve; (2) by assisting preservice teachers in discovering and examining their own prejudices concerning children from diverse family backgrounds and providing them with ways to address those biases; and (3) by exposing pre-service teachers to ways to reflect upon their own thoughts and practices as well as ways to work collaboratively with others to raise awareness and solve problems.

Additionally, as a teacher educator and a mother of three children adopted at older ages from the state foster care system, I find the necessity of empowering teachers to confidently and proactively address family diversity in curriculum and in the classroom to be of critical importance. Curricular conceptual representations of family must be reshaped to accurately reflect and honor the many and varied ways in which people form caring groups that support and honor their members. Curriculum, widely conceived, refers to both formal forms of curriculum such as lessons, textbooks, and activities as well as informal forms of curriculum such as school culture (teacher speech, school functions, and paperwork) and popular culture (movies, television, and books) (Turner-Vorbeck, 2006).

Teachers need to be made aware that commercially prepared lessons and textbook depictions of families and family life remain focused upon a traditional, nuclear family with a few ethnic variations of this theme presented in the more progressive versions. These limited depictions of family represent a standard of family against which we are all to measure our own. Perhaps less obvious are aspects of school culture which contribute to a lack of inclusiveness of varied forms of family. School paperwork forms that are sent home with students to be completed by adults at home are still designed to identify and designate a responsible parent and are usually not flexible enough to allow for the accurate reflection of the complex caretaking networks formed by many current family conditions. Classroom assistance is still most often sought under the moniker of "Room Mothers." Teacher talk about concerns for children from single parent (read: dysfunctional) homes is rampant and thinly disguised, if at all. Parents are sometimes even directly subjected to teacher prejudice on the psychological soundness of family forms with remarks given such as "I'll be watching for abandonment issues to surface in your child" when the child is identified as adopted. In conservative climates, even in public (as opposed to parochial) schools, students are openly, but off-the-record, told that a gay, lesbian, and/or transgender lifestyle is immoral (Turner-Vorbeck, 2006).

Mimicking the narrow and limited images of family portrayed through formal curriculum and school culture are those created and perpetuated through mass media and popular culture.

> Informal curriculum in the form of popular culture has become heavily influential due to the amount of exposure students receive to various forms of media such as movies, television, and books and it serves to buttress what students are learning about families in schools. Most popular, top-selling children's books and related television series and movies such as the *Berenstain Bears* books (Berenstain & Berenstain, 1962), the *Arthur* books (Brown, 1976), the *American Girl* doll stories (Tripp, 1991) and even the *Harry Potter* books (Rowling, 1997) continue to feature portrayals of families in the literary and visual images of American child culture that still consist largely of traditional, two parent households with the mother fulfilling the role of primary nurturer and caregiver. (Turner-Vorbeck, 2006, p. 165)

As discussed, limited attempts on the part of classroom materials and textbook publishers to broaden conceptions and discussions of family, damaging talk, procedures, policies, and negative biases largely held and commonly practiced in school culture, and the predominance of traditional images and portrayals of exclusively nuclear family forms in curriculum and popular culture should leave teachers and parents alarmed at the chronic incongruence of the curricular representations of family to the actual, living, everyday families of our students. Yet, there still exists the possibility of representations and discussions of family becoming more inclusive through continued research, education, and dialogue and through personal, passionate, participatory inquiry.

REFERENCES

Banks, J., & Banks, C. (2001). *Multicultural education: Issues & perspectives* (4th ed.). New York: Wiley.

Bennett, C. (2001). Genres of research in multicultural education. *Review of Educational Research, 71*(2), 171–217.

Berenstain, S., & Berenstain, J. (1962). *The big honey hunt.* New York: Beginner Books.

Brown, M. (1976). *Arthur's nose.* Boston: Little, Brown and Company.

Clandinin, D. J., & Connelly, F. M. (1994). Personal experience methods. In N. K. Denzin & Y. S. Lincoln (Eds.), *Handbook of qualitative research* (pp. 413–427). Thousand Oaks, CA: SAGE.

Coontz, S. (1997). *The way we really are: Coming to terms with America's changing families.* New York: Basic Books.

Derman-Sparks, L. (1989). *Anti-bias curriculum.* Washington, DC: NAEYC.

Duarte, E., & Smith, S. (2000). *Foundational perspectives in multicultural education.* New York: Addison Wesley Longman.

Gay, G. (2000). *Culturally responsive teaching: Theory, research, & practice.* New York: Teachers College Press.

Geis-Rockwood, W. (1990). *Shapes: Families of today* (2nd ed.). Santa Barbara, CA: Stepfamily Association of America.

Huston, P. (2001). *Families as we are: Conversations from around the world.* New York: The Feminist Press.

Miller, D. (1991). *Handbook of research design and social measurement* (5th ed.). Newbury Park, CA: SAGE.

Nieto, S. (2000). *Affirming diversity: The sociopolitical context of multiculturalEducation* (3rd ed.). New York: Longman.

Nussbaum, M. (1997). *Cultivating humanity.* Cambridge, MA: Harvard University Press.

Okun, B. (1996). *Understanding diverse families: What practitioners need to know.* New York: The Guilford Press.

Rowling, J. (1997). *Harry Potter and the sorcerer's stone.* New York: Scholastic.

Smith, P., & Ragan, T. (1993). *Instructional design.* Upper Saddle River, NJ: Prentice-Hall.

Tripp, V. (1991). *Meet Felicity.* Middleton, WI: Pleasant Company.

Turner-Vorbeck, T. (Winter, 2005). Expanding multicultural education to include family diversity. *Multicultural Education, 13*(2), 6–10.

Turner-Vorbeck, T. (2006). Representations of family in curriculum: A post-structural analysis. In C. Cherryholmes, E. Heilman, & A. Segall (Eds.), *Social studies—The next generation: Researching social studies in the postmodern* (pp. 153-169). New York: Peter Lang.

CHAPTER 15

BECOMING AN
AGENT OF SOCIAL CHANGE

Stories of Sweatshops,
Sweetshops, and Women's Social Activism

Betty Christine Eng

AUTOBIOGRAPHICAL ORIGINS OF THE INQUIRY

Aiieeeee! Juk sing, juk sing! my mother cried out in despair. "Juk sing" or
"hollow bamboo" is how I was often criticized by my mother as I grew
up Chinese in America. Like bamboo, my outside appearance suggested Chinese or Asian features and origins. And, like bamboo, my
mother thought me empty and hollow inside, devoid of the honored
traditional Chinese values and beliefs. "Don't you know better than to
tell the Chinese father of Mona, your high school classmate, that he has
lost weight? Though you are a daughter of China, you are just like a
juk sing," my mother scolded me. At the time, I was puzzled and
shaken by my mother's scolding and did not realize until much later
that my mother's reaction meant so much more. This episode, which

more than a few minutes, left an indelible impression that
social activism and this personal, passionate, and participa-
ographical inquiry.

about 16 years old, and we were at the community Chinese
store in Sacramento, the valley city that is California's state cap-
here I grew up. I had thought my remark part of a friendly and
polite conversation intended to compliment and please. Being slim and
trim, I thought, was a desirable sign of beauty and well-being, American standards I had been socialized to achieve. While I was born in
China and in a sense was, and am, a "daughter of China," my mother
thought my behavior was like that of the Chinese who were born and
raised in the United States, who did not know any better. My mother
was afraid that these "juk sing" Chinese were so absorbed into American culture that they did not have any more Chinese left in them. My
mother's lecture to me continued,

> His loss of weight is not a flattery! It may be a sign of a serious illness,
> that he is worried about his children or his finances. In my days in China,
> only those who were poor and did not have enough to eat were thin.
> Being 'fat' is a sign of prosperity and good fortune. Besides, don't you
> know that Mona's father has just gone out of business and is no longer
> the boss of his own grocery store? He is now forced to become a hired
> clerk behind the counter. Your loud greeting in recognition of him prob-
> ably embarrassed him. It would have been better for you to have just
> looked the other way.

I had not known of the recent change of employment status or the
complicated and intricate meanings, as understood by my mother, in his
thinness. I had thought my greeting a simple and well-intentioned
remark. Growing up in the United States, my understanding of a compliment and social etiquette often jarred with that of my mother and caused
her much distress. Our different understandings became a persistent
source of tension between us.

My mother's lament continued, "Ai ya! Have I not been a good mother
and teacher for you to become so twisted? The ignorance you show
shames me in our community. What has our coming to 'Gold Mountain,'
America, the land of opportunity and promises, done, and what have you
become?" Indeed, what had growing up Chinese in America *done*, and
what had I become? My mother's criticism of me in my teens left me feeling
shame for her "loss of face" in our community. I was confused about who
I thought I was and who I was supposed to be. The exchange in this particular scene was played out on numerous other occasions as I grew up
Chinese in America. Many others like her, I later learned, shared my
mother's lament. Reflecting on this episode decades later, I have a better

understanding of about what exactly my mother was worried. While I recall being stunned by her criticism at the time, I now realize that my mother was expressing deep concern and care for me. She was worried that I was becoming someone other than the good daughter she expected. Reflecting back, this lament was also, I believe, an expression of my mother's fear of failure in not being the good mother she was supposed to be. As I reflect on these experiences, I begin to realize that the way I feel about myself affects my identity.

I am a Chinese American woman, born in the People's Republic of China and raised in the United States. For 18 years, I have been working in Hong Kong, first as a counselor, then a teacher eduator, and now a professor in the discipline of pyschology. My inquiry takes me to the soils of three landscapes: China, the United States, and Hong Kong. Through my journey, I learn that my identity, culture, and sense of belonging are situated in what Ming Fang He (2003) has termed the "in-betweenness" of cross-cultural lives. He, a teacher educator from China who later studied in Canada, writes:

> The strangeness we experienced in China, in Canada, and back in China made us feel dislocated as if trapped in an "in-between" culture, a place that felt neither Chinese nor Canadian, a place where the world passed us by. It was as if we were caught up in a backwater as the rivers flowed past us. Where can we stand? Who are we? What have our identities and cross-cultural experiences got to do with teacher education and curriculum making in the field of contemporary education? How can we verify our invisible education in the turbulent waters.... Is it possible for us to transform our cross-cultural experience into a curriculum for our personal and professional lives? (p. 2)

I find that I am not a Chinese, nor an American, but a rich and complex blend of multiple identities that are evolving, improvised, and contested. "In-betweenness," I learn, is a fluid place for tensions, challenges, discoveries, and transformations. Embedded in my autobiography are experiences that provided the beginnings of my quest to understand my identity, culture, and sense of belonging which are the focus of this inquiry.

I have realized that by retelling my stories, I engage in acts of reclaiming my personal identity and that of my community. As my autobiographical narratives are shared, resonated, and intertwined with others in the community, the *private becomes public* and the *personal becomes political*. It is not possible to separate what happens to me personally from what is happening in the world. By giving voice to the personal and asserting its place in the public space, it reframes a community's history and invites a new way of understanding others and ourselves as members of a global commuity.

My social activism has arisen and flourished from the stories of my family, particularly those of my mother. These stories have inspired my participation in the formation of Asian American studies and, later, journeys to China and Hong Kong. As these stories of experience unfold, they become intertwined to shape an evolving social activism, to understand how women become agents of social change. These stories are personal, passionate, and participatory. Through my autobiographical writings, I am retelling stories that, for reasons discussed later in this chapter, have been systematically silenced in classrooms. Elaine Kim and Norma Alarcn (1994) contend that writing self is also an act of writing nation. Kim, a Korean American, describes her writings about herself as *lifetime* stories that are integral to her understanding of Asian culture. Kim views her writing as a struggle to "define and claim a Korean American identity that could protect me from erasure or further marginalization in my American life" (p. 3). Kim and Alarcn strongly believe that through writing personal histories, a sense of nationalism is developed that provides a binding source of strength for the community.

The retelling of stories is an act of defiance and self-determination that challenges a community that has been made invisible. Janice Mirikitani (2000), a writer and one of the early Asian American "cultural workers" echoes this view: "My work as an activist … is inextricable from what I write" (p. 127). Collectively, they are stories that resonate with others and that connect a family or a community. Leila Fu, the heroine in Fae Myenne Ng's (1993) book, *Bone*, says: "Family exists only because somebody has a story and knowing the story connects us to a history" (p. 36). These stories are not a part of a narrative to be inserted into mainstream literature but are a distinct narrative that Wendy Ho (1999) states are in the "process of being lived, contested and constructed in the flux of U.S. culture and society" (p. 211).

My autobiographical writings also convey my hopes for the future of the communities I live and work in, what Carolyn Heilbrun (1988) describes as writing "in advance of living" (p. 11) that invites us to imagine the possibilities of an alternative life. My hopes for the future are embedded in my participation in social activism and community organizing that struggle for a fair and just society. These struggles, extended to the classroom, strive to democratize the classroom by giving voice to learners and teachers in curriculum deliberations that engage us in conversations about what is to be taught, who our teachers are, and how subjects are taught. It is the narratives of experience that shape and are shaped by the life histories to provide knowing and illumination that I explore in this chapter. The personal, passionate, and participatory qual-

ity of my inquiry permeates my life and becomes a
social activism. My autobiography is a journey of ᵜ
crosses identities and cultures over a period of four deca᷍
ence of growing up listening and contesting the narratives
and community becomes embedded in my classroom curric᷍
pedagogy.

RETELLING STORIES AND
RECLAIMING IDENTITIES WITH NARRATIVE INQUIRY

I use narrative inquiry methods (Clandinin & Connelly, 2000) and the
Chinese tradition of story telling (Eng, 2005b) in recounting my
experiences to explore how experience inspires and shapes our lives.
Narrative is a process of reflection to make meaning of experience (Alter,
1993; Clandinin & Connelly, 2000; Crites, 1971). This exploration is
grounded in John Dewey's (1938) belief that to study education and life is
to study experience. For Dewey, experience is the starting point for all
social science inquiry. Dewey encouraged teachers to respect all sources of
experience, urging teachers to recognize experience as both means and
the goal in education. For Michael Connelly and Jean Clandinin, teacher
educators and researchers, experience is best represented and
understood through narratives or stories. I found that narrative inquiry
provided the academic platform and the entrée for me to position the
retelling of stories and reclaiming of identities. My personal stories about
growing up Chinese in the United States flourished into a community
narrative that in turn formed a life-long inquiry. I also turned to the
growing body of literature among Asian American Studies scholars and
activists such as Pat Sumi (Tachiki, Wong, & Odo, 1971) and Elaine Kim
(Kim & Alarcn, 1994), historian Judy Yung (1995), and poets Janice
Mirikitani (1995) and Nellie Wong (1977) to understand the narratives of
my community. Each of these women was a social activist who engaged in
redefining their identities as acts of empowerment that challenged the
prevailing power structure. In the early years of the Asian American
movement, in the late 1960s and early 1970s, writings by social activists
were groundbreaking and original, not necessarily intended for the
academic community, nor published by the conventional press. Pat Sumi,
in particular, was instrumental in shaping my thinking and wrote a
number of position papers on women, that were circulated among
community activists but never formally published. Pat was responsible for
leading and coordinating a network of women across the United States
who taught Asian women courses. Many of the women who taught these

ses were still students at the time and were on the faculty of niversities such as the University of California at Berkeley, San Francisco State, Stanford, and Yale. Together, we led study groups on women and engaged in discourse about power and oppression, writing new curriculum in the pioneering programs of Asian American Studies. In our curriculum, the classroom texts were our embodied experiences conveyed in life histories and expressed in assignments such as "What Made Me the Person I am Today" and "Interviews with My Mother."

Reflecting on this period, I realize how momentous and influential it was in instilling and sustaining a sense of social justice in my life. Glenn Omatsu (1994) describes the impact of this period this way:

> For Asian Americans, these struggles profoundly changed our communities. They spawned numerous grassroots organizations. They created an extensive network of student organizations and Asian American Studies classes. They recovered buried cultural traditions as well as produced a new generation of writers, poets, and artists. But most importantly, the struggles deeply affected Asian American consciousness. They redefined racial and ethnic identity, promoted new ways of thinking about communities, and challenged prevailing notions of power and authority. (p. 20)

The following narratives of experiences trace my developing awareness of social justice through hearing the stories of my family, particularly those of my mother, and the voices of women in a community center that became the curriculum for my classroom.

OF SWEATSHOPS AND SWEETSHOPS

Growing up and experiencing the life of my mother, who worked in the sweatshop or garment industry of California, influenced me profoundly. My mother labored, with many others like herself, long hours under harsh conditions as seasonal and temporary workers. This was an educative experience.

Sweatshops are sewing factories where women, primarily immigrant women who possess little education or job skills, are forced to secure jobs that are paid below the minimum wage for working 12 hour days in crowded, poorly lit rooms with little ventilation. At the time my mother worked in these sweatshops in the early 1970s, a long sleeve, button-down collared blouse might take half a day to complete and earned her 80 cents apiece. A more elaborate garment, such as a dress, could bring up to $2.00 but required more time. My mother describes her experience this way:

I was not the fastest or most skillful of seamstresses. Sometimes I would earn only $8.00 in a week after completing a dozen garments. Other women who were more clever than I could make their industrial size sewing machines roar like a train with fierce speed. The owners of the shops encouraged us to continue working into the night and arranged for a sewing machine for our use at home. (Eng, 2001)

The labels of the garments represented some of the most exclusive designer brands that were, in turn, sold to consumers at a markup of 200%–500% more than my mother was paid. My mother labored in these sweatshops during the months when she was not working in the canneries. The wages she earned supplemented the family income, and she labored in these types of work until her retirement. With less than a high school education in China, limited English language skills, and no job training, she was grateful for the work. I am deeply beholden to my mother's labor but outraged by the exploitation to which she was subjected. For my mother, the sewing factories were her *sweetshop*, a source of much needed income, not the sweatshops I protested as a community activist. My anger at the exploitation of my mother and other women like her found expression in community organizing that took me to the very sweatshop my mother worked, picketing, and calling for a boycott of the labels of the companies the sweatshop served. Needless to say, this competing view of sweatshop and *sweetshop* between my mother and I represented the growing tensions in our relationship. I was discovering and claiming a new understanding of the experiences of our immigrant community. These experiences developed my awareness and understanding of systematic discrimination toward a community. I sought answers to the questions: Whose interest does it serve to exploit my mother in the sweatshops? Who benefits from my mother's labor? How did such use of labor come about? How can I participate in making fundamental social changes to prevent such exploitation?

My mother's gratitude for the income from her *sweetshops* bound her, as I saw it, in servitude to exploitation. For my mother, my actions must have alarmed, terrified and caused her to lose face in the community. She was probably shocked and bewildered by what had become of her normally reticent and obedient daughter. Looking back, I realize my mother's story taught me enduring lessons about courage, resilience, duty, loyalty, and responsibility. These qualities were extended to serving my community and created a social activist spirit that guides my work today. My mother's story is not an isolated one for it is shared and reverberates throughout communities across the United States. It is the story of shared experiences of women, of daughters and mothers, of minorities, of new immigrants, of the working class.

PARTICIPA
COMMUNITY IS CURRICULUM

The story of my mother working
instance of how stories of experien
my knowledge of what it means to
by my mother, a story that I exper
being, and that I, in turn, retold to
lum. My mother's story is one that
instills and nurtures a sense of soci.. justice and shapes the way I teach.
The act of retelling stories and reclaiming identities resonated with others like me and formed an Asian American movement that led to the formation of Asian American Studies programs across the United States in the late 1960s.

Through Asian American studies, I came to a growing awareness and realization that, throughout my schooling, I had been taught a curriculum that excluded the lives and experiences of my Chinese community. Through rediscovering and reclaiming my history, I learned of the systematic exploitation of Chinese laborers who died working on the railroads as a result of the hazardous dynamiting work in mountainous terrains, and of murders of Chinese miners and burning of Chinatown campsites by racist prospectors, who felt threatened by the growing presence of the Chinese during the gold rush in the 1800s (Sung, 1967; Wu, 1972). I learned through our research that Chinese were not allowed to purchase property like European immigrants, but could only work as laborers, on farms, in laundries and in saloons. These were meager paying and labor-intensive jobs that other immigrants did not want, according to such scholars as Chen (1980) Takaki (1979) and Wong (1982). I had been thoroughly ignorant of this part of my history.

I had been taught, instead, to praise the American "melting pot" that welcomed its people and provided opportunities and success for all who were diligent, responsible, and willing to work. I came to perceive my school experience as one that taught me to fit in and adapt. I was fulfilling the expectations of Asians as a model minority ("Success story of one," 1966), who, despite racism and economic hardships, served as exemplars to other minorities of how to be successful. The message was that if one worked diligently, persevered, and obeyed the rules, one could succeed in the melting pot of America. America, I was taught, was a land of opportunity for all, and only those who were lazy and irresponsible were not successful. When I discovered the fallacy of the "American dream" and of Asians as a model minority during the Asian American movement, I felt deceived, betrayed, and exploited. I also discovered my voice, and learned to express my outrage and anger through teaching Asian American studies.

My students shared similar stories of experience. They were stories of parents working in the laundries that were later documented by Paul Siu in his book, *The Chinese Laundryman* (1987), of "paper sons" who established false family relationships to circumvent the Chinese Exclusion Act and to gain passage to the United States. Other stories told of arranged marriages and of family pressures to succeed that channeled us into professions such as business, engineering and teaching, rather than the social sciences, arts and humanities. By telling and retelling these stories of experience, we were developing a clearer, fuller, and deeper understanding of who we were and of our place in the curriculum. As learners and teachers, we were collectively rediscovering and reclaiming our past, present and future to develop our identity, culture and sense of belonging; the experiences of the community became curriculum; and the curriculum became community.

ASIAN AMERICAN STUDIES: STRUGGLES AND NEOPHTES

Teaching Asian American Studies for about 10 years, I witnessed the connection of one's experience and its potential to empower us to become agents of social change. The self-awareness that one develops through sharing common experiences with others eliminates the isolation we experience in our lives. This isolation is often the source of a sense of helplessness and powerlessness. By sharing our stories of experience, we connect to each other, and we begin to place our experiences in a larger social context. As a social activist, I participated in making visible our stories of experience in the curriculum and making radical and fundamental changes in the educational system. Lane Ryo Hirabayashi and Marilyn Alquizola (1998) write of this period:

> What some may not know, and many may have forgotten, is that the administration of the two earliest Asian American Studies was original and radical, if not revolutionary, in intent and practice. In the late 1960s and early 1970s, a coalition of students, lecturers, and community activists organized and ran the Asian American Studies programs at San Francisco State and at the University of California at Berkeley. They collectively controlled all aspects of the Studies, from the courses to the overall curriculum, to the hiring and firing of professors and even administrators. (p. 354)

As neophytes in the academy, all we had were our experiences. I had lived out my life as a young Chinese woman in the Chinese community, within one of the embodied experiences that were the subject of the new curriculum. I was one of the few Asian Americans who participated alongside Black, Chicano, and Native American student activists, who negotiated with the university administrators to establish the Ethnic Studies Program. I do not believe there was anything exceptional about me that I was chosen to be one of the program's first lecturers. Honed by the experiential lessons from my mother's lament of being a "juk sing," or a "hollow bamboo," I happened to be present at a pivotal moment that demanded an Asian voice. When I began teaching Asian American studies at Sacramento State College, I was just completing the final year of course work in teacher education there, only slightly more "qualified" than my fellow Asian American student activists who followed. My teaching there, and for a time at the University of California at Davis as a teacher and counselor, continued for a period of over 10 years. Looking back, I would characterize myself as a rather ordinary person, unworldly and shy, who found herself in extraordinary circumstances in a remarkable time.

We were students in our early to mid-20s who sat at the same table with university presidents and renowned scholars in established disciplines. While we found voice and claimed authority from our student movements, we were seldom taken seriously or welcomed at the table (Hirabayahi, & Alquizola, 1994; Liem, 1998). We were seen as intimidating and confrontational militants, who would graduate and, they hoped, would eventually go away. I viewed the administration's establishment of the Ethnic Studies Program as an experimental and temporary appeasement of the liberalism of the 1960s and 1970s civil rights and student movements.

I also participated in the formation of services for alternative counseling for the Asian community, especially targeting recent immigrants who had little education or job skills. My community's stories of experience served as a source of inspiration and a catalyst for social change. Women's personal experiences of domestic violence, assault, and rape led to the formation of shelters and counseling services for battered women. Their experiences, shared and re-told, provided a collective unity that galvanized us to make fundamental social change. Here, the realization of the personal being political unfolds to empower women to become agents of social change.

I came to my university teaching positions with great reluctance. I thought the real action was happening in the community and not within the ivory towers of academia. I envied my fellow Asian Americans who pioneered alternative community service centers for young immigrant teens to support their cultural adjustments and language skills, and those who established culturally appropriate counseling services for Asian Americans, day care centers for low-income families, or Asian law and health clinics. They were in the midst of communities where I yearned to be and where the real action and real life were unfolding. It was in community work that our ideals could be tested and put to practical, useful purposes to serve the community. My teaching at the universities was only a "day job" intended to be a temporary way for me to serve the community. This "day job" continued for about ten years, primarily at California State University, Sacramento, and later as a teacher and counselor at the University of California, Davis. I stayed on in the universities because I came to view my classroom as my community and my teaching as a means for social change through education. My teaching in Asian American studies became, for me, the community located or housed on campus. For class assignments, our students interviewed members of the community, beginning with their mothers and fathers to explore their family history, wrote autobiographies, and served as interns in community-based organizations. My students' experiences took place in context, for though experiences are individual and personal, they are played out in a *milieu* and not in isolation. Personal experiences, I believe, are best understood when placed in a context that explores the whole of a life within a community. I discovered that my curriculum is the community and the community is the curriculum.

I experienced personal rage and anger and sought explanations, understanding, and resolution through social change. Together with others who shared common experiences and views, we established alternative ways not only to improve the status of the people in our community, but also to make fundamental, constructive changes in the social system. While the location of my teaching and the direction of my career have changed over the years, the experiences of this period have left an indelible and enduring mark that have shaped and informed my social activism.

Looking back, I realize how the establishment of Asian American studies was a momentous and historical movement in redefining the educational landscape across the country. For Asian Americans, this movement profoundly changed our communities by pioneering community-based services. Asian American studies raised our consciousness redefined our identities as we retold our stories, promoted new ways of thinking about communities, and challenged the prevailing notions of power and authority.

LOOKING BACK AT SITTING IN FRONT

When teaching in Asian American Studies at the time, and as I still do now, I arranged the students' desks or chairs to form a circle in the classroom. I believe that this circular formation of seating enhances the reciprocal and collaborative roles we play as learners and teacher in a shared conversational dialogue that recognizes, values, and respects the voice of everyone in the class. It is my belief that the teacher is not the sole source of knowledge and that the learners' knowledge should be not only invited and welcomed, but also seen as a requisite for the curriculum. The circular seating is not only representational of that relationship, but serves to make everyone "equal" and visually accessible to each other.

On the first day of class one semester, I found I was assigned to a large lecture theatre to teach my class, "Asian Women in America," a course I had developed. The desks were bolted to the floor, looking down onto the podium intended for the lecturer. I managed to find a freestanding chair, placed it in front of the podium, and sat down looking upward into the lecture theatre. It was in this position that the students entering the room first saw me, and when it was time to begin the class, I introduced myself as the teacher. I had come to anticipate the gasps of surprise, gleeful laughter, and sometimes bewilderment, when students discovered that I was to be their teacher. Not much older than they, with my hair worn long and straight, and dressed casually enough to pass for a student myself, I probably confounded their image and expectations of a university professor. Except for a few Asian American teachers in the departments of science, mathematics, and engineering, it was rare to see Asian Americans in other academic disciplines. Rarer still were Asian American women teachers on university campuses during that era. Even though the course was about Asian American women, my students were still surprised to find an Asian American woman teaching the course. For the most part, the teachers in Asian American studies were the youngest among the university faculty during that period.

What I had not anticipated, however, was an initial sense of ambivalence on the part of some of the Asian American students, along with mixed acceptance of another Asian American who so closely resembled themselves. One such student confided to me later that when she first saw me sitting in front of the class, she had not realized that I was the teacher. She had thought me another student and felt offended and somewhat disturbed that I dare sit in the position reserved for the professor.

Indeed, how dare I, and others like me, sit in that position, for all I had were my experiences. How presumptuous and impertinent I must have appeared to displace and turn upside down the expected image and role of the university professor, to redefine the relationship between learners and teachers and the process of learning and teaching. I was not only rearranging the classroom furniture, I was rearranging and challenging fundamental assumptions about curriculum and the role and relationship of learners and teachers. Asian American studies extended an open and empowering invitation to learners and teachers to a journey dedicated to exploring our Asian American experience never before accessible to us in academia. Asian American studies provided us the opportunity to reflect on our personal experiences and to rethink and transform our understanding of who we were, our experiential histories and our place in the curriculum.

A QUEST FOR IDENTITY, CULTURE, AND SENSE OF BELONGING

When I first came to live in Hong Kong in 1985, I thought this would be an opportunity to discover my culture, my identity, and the place where I belonged. The journey to Hong Kong was, I felt, a response to rectify my mother's criticism of me as a "juk sing" or hollow bamboo. Choosing to live in Hong Kong meant, I thought, to live as a member of the majority culture. This invitation to work and live in a predominantly Chinese society seemed an exhilarating and meaningful opportunity to immerse myself in what I believed to be an authentic Chinese culture and to explore and discover the answers I had been seeking. My decision to live in Hong Kong seemed a continuation and extension of the Asian American movement and Asian American studies to dig more deeply into my understanding of my Chinese American identity and culture.

Currently, I am on the faculty of a university in Hong Kong teaching courses in counseling and psychology, but for over 10 years, I was a teacher educator with the Hong Kong Institute of Education (HKIEd), the leading institute in Hong Kong whose sole purpose is teacher education. Integral to my journey has been my commitment to community organizing as a way of making meaningful social change. I see an interactive and reciprocal exchange between the community and the curriculum (Eng, 2005a).

NEW TERRITORIES: THE HONG KONG INSTITUTE OF EDUCATION

HKIEd was established in April 1994 by a government ordinance to upgrade teacher education and professional development through an amalgamation of its Colleges of Education. HKIEd's new campus was to be located in a district of Hong Kong called the New Territories. The name of its location, in many ways, reflected the new territory into which I was venturing. HKIEd presented an opportunity for my becoming a teacher educator in 1995. Again, this was an opportunity to translate my social activism to the classroom as I continued to view education as a powerful means for social change. Here, I thought, was an opportunity to instill the values of social justice and equity, to cultivate a new generation of social activists. During this period, HKIEd actively recruited academic staff, particularly those who had international experience or were from overseas, to teach in their newly developed programs. As a result, I came to teach in what is now the Department of Educational Psychology, Counselling and Learning Needs, where my primary areas of teaching were in school guidance and counseling, child and adolescent development, personal and social education, and inclusive education. Becoming a teacher educator at HKIEd seemed to be a unifying synthesis of my professional experiences as a teacher and counselor and enabled me to turn the educational space inside and outside my classroom into a space for cultivating social activism.

However, what I found most exciting and meaningful about being a teacher educator at HKIEd was the prospect of being in the midst of the Hong Kong Chinese community. The student body and teaching staff were almost all ethnic Chinese, primarily Hong Kong-born. The campus was another world from the mostly non-Chinese expatriate community that I had grown to know in my former position as a counselor at an international school. Since HKIEd was in the early stages of its development, it would, I thought, offer exciting opportunities to participate in creating a curriculum that reflected Hong Kong's recent educational reforms aimed at upgrading teacher education programs. I was to propose and develop new courses and participate in the successful validation of a number of HKIEd's degree programs. Given the direction my research methodology was taking me, I wanted to explore ways in which narrative inquiry could be reflected in our curriculum and as a new way of doing scholarly research in the Hong Kong milieu. I was embarking on new territories in such a variety of capacities.

THE HONG KONG FEDERATION OF WOMEN'S CENTRES

I felt it was imperative that I connect with community when I arrived in Hong Kong in the mid-1980s. Connecting with the Hong Kong women's community was an extension and continuation of my work in the California community and a way to inform my teaching. My belief that there is a reciprocal relationship between the community and the curriculum meant that I needed to be in the midst of the Hong Kong milieu.

When invited to join a women's organization in Hong Kong, I quickly became a member. The Hong Kong Federation of Women's Centres (HKFWC) became a forum to participate in social change for women in Hong Kong. I was introduced to the HKFWC through a network of women friends I formed in the mid-1980s. These women were community activists and friends with whom I shared a common bond of understanding and commitment to making social change.

I remember that I was licking stamps and addressing envelopes, along with other women volunteers, for 5,000 invitations to a film gala fundraiser to maintain one of the centers. I was the honorary secretary of the executive committee of the HKFWC and chair of the committee responsible for invitations and program materials. I volunteered for this task to get to know the grass roots women at the heart of the work for which the HKCWC is intended. I was a newly elected member of the Executive Committee, composed of about eight other women, educated professionals, mothers of well-established economic status. Executive members represented but one level of involvement at the HKFWC.

The HKFWC came into existence in 1981 with a mission to assist women to develop their potentials, to improve the rights and status of women, and to offer recommendations to the Hong Kong government concerning women's issues and policies (HKFWC, 1999). Violence against women, spousal abuse, divorce, extra marital relations, health care, and job retraining are some of the issues that the Centres have addressed through supportive services and programs.

I wanted to get to know the grassroots women and to understand what brought them to the center. These women, who first came to the center seeking its services, became volunteers assisting other women. This reciprocal exchange of roles and relationships of women serving women is at the heart of a woman-centered organization that is for women and run by women. In conversation there, the following exchange occurred (Eng, 1997):

> "How is it that you came to the HKFWC?" I ask of them. Siu Ping[1] tells me that she was introduced by a friend and found the company and friendship of the Centre a good way to spend her time now that her only child is in school. She has volunteered for the Centre's hotline service for almost three years. "But why not another organization in which to volunteer your time? Other organizations such as child abuse services, saving the environment, or services for new immigrants are also in great need of volunteers," I inquired. Siu Ping replies, "Well, it could very well be that I could have participated in these organizations, but I am at the Centre because it is conveniently close by to my home and I feel comfortable here."

Chow Po King, a full time homemaker with three young children, is also a member of HKFWC. Her experience with the HKFWC, and what she learned and gained from her participation, is a story of personal empowerment to become an agent of social change. She says:

> Through participating in various activities of the Centre, such as small groups, health talks, stress management classes.... I have come to know other women with similar interests. Apart from widening my social circle, I

have also gained an increase in awareness of women issues....In helping others in my volunteer work, I have benefited myself also,—I have increased my knowledge and widened my experience. I have also learned about building self-confidence and about fostering personal growth.... The Centre is really like a home to us. We really feel a sense of belonging to it. (HKFWC, 1996–1997, p. 41)

Through brief conversations with two grass-roots members of the HKFWC, I found that they did not come to the center because of political beliefs or visions. For them, becoming agents of social change through participation and volunteer work in the centers's services developed from their personal stories of experience as Chinese Hong Kong women. The women in the community did not need to share the mission of the center. Nevertheless, it was essential for Siu Ping and Po King to feel a sense of belonging there, to find friendship and feel at "home." What can we learn about their stories to inform our classrooms? One lesson we can draw is that our classrooms and schools should provide a safe place where students feel welcomed, valued, and at home. Creating such spaces in our classrooms is an essential part of curriculum making.

EPILOGUE: A SUMPTUOUS FEAST

My mother lost herself in the journey from China to Gold Mountain. She lost her identity, culture, and sense of belonging. She lost China and lost me as the Chinese daughter she wished me to be. I feel she has suffered in many of the same ways as I did in our move. She did not know what to teach or ask of me, wanting me to be American but also wanting me to remain Chinese. I am aware that my journey has been guided by a persistent debate with my mother, who was herself divided and splintered, although she desperately wanted me not to be lost and always held dreams and hopes for me.

There is a contradictory and ironic relationship between what my mother wanted for me and what I chose. My mother wanted me to live in the United States and remain Chinese. However, I left the United States in an attempt to become *more* Chinese by moving to Hong Kong. I discovered along the way that there are a multitude of ways to be Chinese, and that identity is fluid, contested and forever changing.

Perhaps I took my mother's *juk sing* criticism as a challenge and answered it in a way that she did not anticipate, by moving to the other side of the world. I stunned and surprised her by expressing and using my American-ness in ways she did not foresee, by asserting my independence and seeking to understand the hollowness of my inner core. I feel I have resolved the inconsistency and contradictions by coming back to my

Chinese roots and choosing to live in international and multilingual Hong Kong, where I can be both English-speaking and the "Chinese" I have become and am forever seeking to be.

For my mother, I will always be "going the wrong way," for we have a different understanding of how to achieve the quest for ourselves. I have had the opportunity to explore and reflect upon my quest through this personal, passionate and participatory autobiographical inquiry. My mother will never imagine that along this journey she has been a loyal companion and one of the most influential women who have nurtured and cultivated the social activist spirit in my teaching, learning, life and work.

"Eat a sumptuous feast in my place," my mother would instruct me as she pressed a *lai see*, a red packet filled with lucky money, into the palm of my hand whenever I ventured from home. She would tell me this whether my travels took me to Shanghai, Paris, Sydney, Moscow, or just to San Francisco, a couple of hours from our Sacramento home. My journey has been in her place, and on her behalf, as if she were I and I were she. In this respect, I often feel that my mother is at least curious or perhaps even a little in awe of my quest. She seems to want to journey with me, but is too restrained or cautious to follow the call. Still, *in her own place*, through this inquiry, my mother has participated in the journey, through her retelling of our family narratives that inspired my activist spirit. Through this journey, she too, I believe, has gained an understanding of her displacement and loss in our move from China to Gold Mountain, and of how she became the person she has become. Through this research inquiry, my mother and I have shared a sumptuous feast together although she may will never find the words to articulate this experience. I can never fully articulate it either.

The experience of my mother and the experience of Asian American women I lived and worked with in the United States, the experience of women at the HKFWCs, and that of many other marginalized and suppressed women I have met and worked with have cultivated and sustained my social activism. Their stories counter the stereotype of Asian women as quiet, passive, and submissive. Their stories tell us that Asian women are willing to challenge convention, to take risks, and to rock the boat, to create waves, and to re-shape the landscapes in our quest for home. Each of their narratives lived experiences powerfully portrays a life-long, ongoing inquiry of social activism.

NOTE

1.   A pseudonym.

REFERENCES

Alter, G. (1993). Empowerment through narrative: Considerations for teaching, learning, and life. *Thresholds in Education, 19,* 3–5.

Chen, J. (1980). *The Chinese of America.* San Francisco: Harper & Row.

Clandinin, D. J., & Connelly, F. M. (2000). *Narrative inquiry: Experience and story in qualitative research.* San Francisco: Jossey-Bass.

Crites, S. (1971). The narrative quality of experience. *Journal of the American Academy of Religion, 39*(3), 291–311.

Dewey, J. (1938). *Experience and education.* New York: Simon & Schuster.

Eng, B. C. (1997). *Interviews with HKFWC members.* Unpublished manuscript. The Ontario Institute for Studies in Education/University of Toronto, Canada.

Eng, B. C. (2001). *Interviews with Mother.* Unpublished manuscript. The Ontario Institute for Studies in Education/University of Toronto, Canada.

Eng, B. C. (2005a). Hong Kong shifting classroom narrative. In Paul Chamness Miller (Ed). *Narratives from the classroom: An introduction to teaching* (pp. 89–107). Thousand Oaks, CA: SAGE.

Eng, B. C. (2005b). *Exploring teacher knowledge through personal narratives: Experiences of identity, culture and sense of belonging.* Unpublished doctoral thesis, The Ontario Institute for Studies in Education of the University of Toronto.

He, M. F. (2003). *A river forever flowing: Cross-cultural lives and identities in a multicultural landscape.* Greenwich, CT: Information Age.

Heilbrun, C. G. (1988). *Writing a woman's life.* New York: Ballantine Books.

Hirabayashi, L. R., & Alquizola, M. C. (1994). Asian American Studies: Reevaluating for the 1990s. In K. Aguilar-San Juan (Ed.), *The state of Asian America* (pp. 351–364). Boston, MA: South End.

Ho, W. (1999). *In her mother's house, the politics of Asian American mother-daughterwriting.* Walnut Creek, CA: AltaMira.

Hong Kong Federation of Women's Centres. (1997). *Hong Kong Federation of Women's Centres Annual Report, 1996–1997.* Hong Kong: Author.

Hong Kong Federation of Women's Centres. (2000). *Hong Kong Federation of Women's Centres Annual Report, 1999–2000.* Hong Kong: Author.

Kim, E. H., & Alarcn, N. (1994). *Writing self, writing nation.* Berkeley, CA: Third Woman Press.

Liem, R. (1998). Psychology and the teaching of Asian American studies. In L. R. Hirabayashi (Ed.), *Teaching Asian America* (pp. 151–159). Lanham, MD: Rowman & Littlefield.

Mirikitani, J. (1995). *We, the dangerous: New and selected poems.* London: Virago.

Mirikitani, J. (2000). Janice Mirikitani. In King-Kok Cheung (Ed.), *Words matter: Conversations with Asian American writers* (pp. 123–139). Honolulu, HI: University of Hawaii Press.

Ng, F. M. (1993). *Bones.* New York: Hyperion.

Omatsu, G. (1994). The "four prisons" and the movements of liberation. In K. Aguilar-San Juan (Ed.), *The state of Asian America activism and resistance in the 1990s* (pp. 19–69). Boston: South End.

Siu, P. C. P. (1987). *The Chinese laundryman.* New York: New York University Press.

Success story of one minority group in U.S. (1966, December 26). *U.S. News and World Report,* pp. 73-76.

Sung, B. L. (1967). *Mountain of gold: The story of the Chinese in America.* New York: MacMillan.

Tachiki, A., Wong, E., Odo, F. (with Wong, B.) (Eds.). (1971). An interview with Pat Sumi. *In Roots: An Asian American Reader.* Los Angeles: University of California.

Takaki, R. T. (1979). *Iron cages: Race and culture in 19th-century America.* New York: Knopf.

Wong, B. (1982). *Chinatown, economics, adaptation, and ethnic identity of the Chinese.* New York: Holt, Rhinehart and Winston.

Wong, N. (1977). *Dreams in Harrison Railroad Park: Poems.* Berkeley, CA: Kelsey St. Press.

Wu, C. T. (1972). *"Chink!": A documentary history of the anti-Chinese prejudice in America.* New York: World Publishing.

Yung, J. (1995). *Unbound feet: A social history of Chinese women in San Francisco.* Berkeley: University of California.

CHAPTER 16

CONCLUSION: PERSONAL~PASSIONATE~ PARTICIPATORY INQUIRY

Potentials, Contributions, Concerns, and Future Directions

JoAnn Phillion and Ming Fang He

SOCIAL JUSTICE ORIENTATION

In this concluding chapter we illuminate the potentials, contributions, concerns and future directions of *personal~passionate~participatory inquiry* by discussing the qualities of this form of inquiry demonstrated in the work featured in this book. We refer to the questions raised by Ayers (2006, p. 88) in his work on research in the public interest to illustrate these qualities. In chapter 1 as we reflect upon our discussion on the convergence of diversity on the educational landscape and this form of inquiry by tracing its historical origins and evolving development in education, we call for a form of social justice oriented inquiry with explicit

Personal~Passionate~Participatory Inquiry Into Social Justice in Education, pp. 267–273
Copyright © 2008 by Information Age Publishing
All rights of reproduction in any form reserved.

agendas that focus on equity, equality, and social justice, with *specific methodologies* that foster the participatory process, and with *focal outcomes* that enact social and educational change. We term this form of inquiry *research for social justice: personal~passionate~participatory inquiry.* An array of research on life in schools, families, and communities, done by a diverse group of practitioner researchers, educators, and scholars, with whom we have been working for years, is featured to illustrate some particular qualities of this form of inquiry.

Personal~passionate~participatory inquiry draws on diverse research traditions (see chapter 1). Many of these traditions promote social justice oriented work and the "Democratic Ideal" (Dewey, 1916, pp. 86–88) in education and life. The Deweyan, democratic, social justice oriented readings of the texts in this book lead us to share Dewey's (1938) belief that

> a democratic society repudiates the principle of external authority.... A democracy is more than a form of government; it is primarily a mode of associated living, of conjoint communicated experience ... individuals who participate in an interest so that each has to refer his own action to that of others, and to consider the actions of others to give point and direction to his own. (p. 87)

Paralleled with Dewey's Democratic Ideal, the work of Du Bois (1903/1994), Cooper (1892/1988), and Woodson (1933/1977) has also influenced social justice oriented research in terms of an emphasis on the emancipatory, participatory, and social action orientation of inquiry.

Social justice oriented work has strong connections to life in schools, communities and societies. Researchers engaged in this form of inquiry use stories to tell hidden and silenced narratives of suppressed and underrepresented groups to counter metanarratives that portray these groups as deficient and inferior (Gutierrez-Jones, 2001; Ladson-Billings, 1998, 2003; Parker, Deyhle, & Villenas, 1999). By telling counter stories, researchers recognize the importance of commitment to equity and social justice and their obligation to link inquiry to social and educational change. The explicit aim of democratic and social justice oriented work is to engage with oppressed groups and individuals and empower them to take effective action toward more just and humane conditions.

POTENTIALS AND CONTRIBUTIONS

Personal~passionate~participatory inquiry, as demonstrated in the chapters in this book, has distinct qualities. These qualities, woven throughout each chapter and highlighted in particular chapters, illuminate its potentials and contributions. Researchers establish explicit research agendas that focus on equity, equality, and social justice. They ask themselves questions about what is missing from the "official story" that will make the problems of the oppressed more understandable (Ayers, 2006, p. 88). These qualities are apparent in work aimed at the emancipation of teenage mothers in general and African American teenage mothers in particular (Dell Wilkerson); in work aimed at developing curriculum that is meaningful to African American males to promote success in schooling in general and in reading in particular (Clara Taylor and Margie Wiggins Sweatman); and in work aimed at recognizing the confines created by place and history, and the impact this has on young women in general and those in the Southern United States in particular (Angela Haynes).

Researchers working within this form of inquiry bring their personal, professional, and cultural experience to their inquiries to connect the personal with the political. They contextualize their inquiries within the historical, sociopolitical, and cultural struggles of under represented individuals and groups in order to understand and act upon these struggles. These researchers focus on inquiring into participants' own perspectives on their marginalization and ways they have developed to succeed, in their own terms, within mainstream societies. They make meaning of the inquiry in relationship with their participants with the intent to address inequality and injustice. They ask themselves questions about "policies [that] serve the privileged and the powerful, and how are they made to appear inevitable" (Ayers, 2006, p. 88)? The above mentioned qualities are demonstrated in the work on women as agents of social change in communities through an examination of the history of Asian American activism as exemplified through the author's story (Betty Christine Eng); in the work on Native American women's perspectives on their experiences in academia and their ideas of success in order to bring the education of Native Americans to the center of concerns in education (Angela Jaime); and in the work examining the school experiences of low income youth who commit suicide and implications for equitable education for all students (Teresa Rishel).

These researchers bring experience to inquiry, connect the personal with the political, and inquiry with life, and develop their inquiries grounded in theoretical foundations and research methodologies that foster participatory processes. The driving force, the passion that fuels the inquiry, is researcher and participant concerns (individual and community) and long term commitment aimed at rectifying inequality. This driving force generates a democratic, nonauthoritarian, and libratory orientation in which researchers listen to "issues that marginalized or disadvantaged people speak of with excitement, anger, fear, or hope" (Ayers, 2006, p. 88) and enter into a genuine dialogue in which they learn directly from individuals and communities about problems and obstacles they face. Researchers also explore possible solutions to problems and obstacles by drawing upon the experience and knowledge of participants. These qualities are highlighted in the work using critical race theory and Black feminism in an inquiry into the lives of four generations of Black women and its impact on the author's voice and vision as a principal (Sonya D. Jefferson); and in an examination of the impact of communal experience of African Americans on the success of African American women who participated in the desegregation of U.S. schooling (Wynnetta Scott-Simmons).

These researchers also connect the theoretical with the practical to enact positive social and educational change. This quality is prominent in the work on creating space for immigrant girls to succeed (Joanna Stoughton Cavan); and in the work on African American girls and the importance of developing positive self-images to counter negative stereotypes (Paula Booker Baker). Educational change is also envisioned as curriculum reform in many of the chapters. There are repeated calls to examine mainstream curriculum which negates the experience of students with diverse backgrounds and to develop curriculum which creates opportunities for all to achieve. These calls range from developing curriculum that focuses on imagination (Robert Lake); to developing multicultural education curriculum that recognizes and validates forms of diversity including that of family structure (Tammy Turner-Vorbeck); to a culturally responsive preservice teacher education curriculum that fosters an empathetic understanding of diverse students (Lyndall Muschell).

CONCERNS AND FUTURE DIRECTIONS

The particular qualities of *personal~passionate~participatory inquiry* that embody its strengths can also create concerns or dilemmas for researchers and participants. One such quality is the democratic and social justice orientation. Researchers engaged in this form of inquiry neither control the research setting nor determine in detail what steps are followed in pursuit of inquiry. They act as participants not as authorities. One of the dilemmas for personal~passionate~participatory researchers adopting a non-authoritarian stance in which they join the lives of their participants, is that the researcher, who feels deeply committed to her participants, may nonetheless be powerless to effect change in the life of participants and/or in the situation in general. As much as Rishel was an advocate for her student she was unable to prevent his suicide and unable to effect any long term change in the school. Cavan was able to implement programs for immigrant students in her school, but was unable to prevent the immigrant girls in her study from dropping out of college track classes.

Another dilemma for personal~passionate~participatory inquirers adopting a non-authoritarian stance in which they live in the midst of their participants' lives, is that the intimacy, closeness, and caring that may develop can create vulnerability (Behar, 1996) for the researcher and participants. The more intimately the inquirers become involved in their inquiries, the more they may come to care for their participants, their communities, and their concerns. With increased involvement of the inquirers, participants begin to develop trust. As the level of trust develops, participants may reveal "sacred and secret stories" (Crites, 1971) which may make inquirers and participants vulnerable. Haynes discusses how she grappled with this dilemma as she revealed stories of her family, which if judged by outsiders, might paint a picture of being a racist or sexist; if judged by her family, she might be perceived as a traitor. Jaime's Native American participants revealed stories of racism and sexism in academia; while the findings were presented with pseudonyms, there still could be repercussions for the researcher and the women who participated in the inquiry.

Personal~passionate~participatory inquirers may also be vulnerable within the academic community. From a scientific-based perspective, some of the work done by these authors could be judged to be inadequate for lack of academic rigor and/or validity. Different rationales could be used to bolster this idea. All authors link their inquiries to their personal stories as mothers, grandmothers, teachers, administrators, and community activists. They are deeply invested in their participants and the issues; some could say this kind of work is "subjective" and "biased". Most authors use stories to portray their findings; some could consider this work to be "soft" and "unscientific." They take an activist stance; this could be construed as "personal" and "non-academic."

The potential criticisms are also what make the work significant. Three key points make the work meaningful. First, data are presented in a life-like way; readers vicariously experience complexities, contradictions and dilemmas of people's lives. There is a sense of "being there" and a sense of urgency for change. Dell, herself an African American teenage mother, illustrates the complexity of her experience and details what is needed to provide support to allow these mothers to be successful in school and life. Second, researchers uncover hidden and untold stories of their participants to counter "the official story." This creates a sense that they know what they are confronting. The stories told challenge orthodoxy, awaken critical consciousness, and create possibilities for change. Scott-Simmons explores the lives of four African American women with a particular focus on the spirit of togetherness on which African American communities

thrive in spite of the challenges of segregation, integration, and resegregation. As a teacher educator, she works with pre-service students to
develop critical consciousness of their rights and responsibilities to preserve cultural and linguistic heritages and to work together as a community to foster social justice. Third, the researchers demonstrate strong
commitment to the plight of their participants and the injustice embedded in the larger society. This commitment can begin with some small
change and expand to a larger context. Cavan realizes that there are
things she can accomplish in her classroom and her department to fight
against injustice. They may be small steps; but they can bring about
change. Everyday she is challenged personally and professionally to make
change in her schools so that education brings about social change.

Personal~passionate~participatory inquiry thrives on the researcher's
passionate involvement, strong commitment, and unfaltering advocacy for
disenfranchised, underrepresented, and invisible individuals and groups.
This passion, commitment, and advocacy can not be cultivated in isolation.
Rather, it calls for a community of researchers with shared concerns to
work together as allies with schools and communities, to take to heart the
concerns of their participants and communities, and to develop strategies
to enact educational and social change that fosters equity, equality and
social justice. This community can only flourish when the efforts of
researchers join with the efforts of all educational stakeholders—
preservice and in-service teachers, educators, administrators, educational
policy makers, students, parents, and community members, particularly
those who advocate for people who are marginalized and those who are
committed to the enactment of social justice and positive educational and
social change. Our vision for the future is one in which this community
grows beyond authors in the book to include more people committed to
the ideals of this form of inquiry. This expanded community, for us,
embodies possibilities, and creates hope, for more fulfilling, more equitable, more humane lives in an increasingly diversifying world.

REFERENCES

Ayers, W. C. (2006). Trudge toward freedom: Educational research in the public
   interest. In G. Ladson-Billings, & W. F. Tate, (Eds.), *Education research in the
   public interest: Social justice, action and policy* (pp. 81–97). New York: Teachers
   College Press.
Behar, R. (1996). *The vulnerable observer: Anthropology that breaks your heart.* Boston:
   Beacon.
Cooper, A. (1988). *A voice from the South.* New York: Oxford University Press.
   (Original work published 1892)

Crites, S. (1971). The narrative quality of experience. *Journal of the American Academy of Religion, 39*(3), 291–311.

Dewey, J. (1916). *Democracy and education: An introduction to the philosophy of education.* New York: Free Press.

Dewey, J. (1938). *Experience and education.* New York: Collier Books.

Du Bois, W. E. B. (1994). *The souls of Black folks.* New York: Fine Creative Media. (Original work published 1903)

Gutierrez-Jones, C. (2001). *Critical race narratives: A study of race, rhetoric, and injury.* New York: New York University Press.

Ladson-Billings, G. (1998). Just what is critical race theory and what's it doing in a nice field like education? *International Journal of Qualitative Studies in Education, 11*(1), 7–24.

Ladson-Billings, G. (Ed.) (2003). *Critical race theory: Perspectives on the social studies—The Profession, policies, and curriculum.* Greenwich, CT: Information Age.

Parker, L., Deyhle, D., & Villenas, S. (1999). *Critical race theory and qualitative studies in education.* Boulder, CO: Westview.

Woodson, C. G. (1977). *The mis-education of the Negro.* Trenton, NJ: Africa World Press. (Original work published 1933)

EPILOGUE

A Love Letter to the Personal~ Passionate~Participatory Research Group

Bill Ayers

Goodbye to research that's arid, dry, self-referencing, and self-satisfied. Goodbye to inquiry as a theory of the mundane, a trivial pursuit of the obvious.

Welcome to an approach that is overflowing with life, crackling with the surprising and contradictory harmonies of love, stunning in its hope for a better world.

Personal~passionate~participatory—the rhythm is intentional, and every word counts. These engaged scholars have the courage to get close, to let compassion and yes, intimacy—not distance or some mythical objectivity—guide their every step. We see research that is proudly partisan—not neutral—and that is willing to challenge the status quo, which as everyone can see is itself an assault on the oppressed and the marginalized. We see researchers spending their intellectual and physical and emotional energy in solidarity with—rather than in service to—their

Personal~Passionate~Participatory Inquiry Into Social Justice in Education, pp. 275–276
Copyright © 2008 by Information Age Publishing

communities. We see a faith in people to name their own predicaments, to tell their own stories, to ask questions of the universe, fighting to make sense of it all as they construct their own lives. The best authority and the finest measure of anyone's hurt or hope—these scholars show us—is that individual herself; life as anyone has lived it must become part of the massive reservoir of knowledge and feeling that justice demands.

The operating instructions one can deduce form this exciting work echo Mary Oliver's "Instructions for living a life" from her poem "Sometimes":

> Pay attention
> Be astonished
> Tell about it. (p. 37)

Are you paying attention? Are you being astonished?

These public and engaged intellectuals are, and they are telling about it.

Goodbye to self-doubt and second-guessing. Goodbye to blacking out on life, sorrowful sex, and unfulfilled desire. Goodbye to "working on your relationship"—aren't we ever off the clock? Can't we give up control for just a minute? Can't we for once stop thinking and just enjoy?

Goodbye to negotiating who's to blame and what needs to change, breakups that never end, dog wars and inner wars. Goodbye to deference, didacticism, ego and the need to always be so damned right. Goodbye to complacency in a heartless world. Goodbye to being that kid in the box who never comes out. Goodbye to prisons and border guards and walls—whether in Palestine or in Texas—and goodbye to quarantines, deletions, and closures. Goodbye to all that.

Welcome to the unknown, to jumping off the edge, to the dance of the dialectic. Welcome to the new and the now, to endlessly learning how to live again and how to love anew. Embrace relentless curiosity, simple acts of kindness, the complexity of humanity, the wonder of it all. Embrace struggle and the poetics of resistance, history, and agency. Embrace world peace and inner peace. Each day in every way, vote for love—all kinds of love for all kinds of people in all kinds of circumstances and situations. Embrace a new world, and then dare to taste it with a kiss.

REFERENCE

Oliver, M. (2008). Sometimes. In *Red bird* (pp. 35–38). Boston: Beacon.

ABOUT THE AUTHORS

Ming Fang He is an associate professor of curriculum studies at Georgia Southern University. She advises doctoral students, directs doctoral dissertations, and teaches graduate courses in curriculum studies, multicultural education, and qualitative research methods. Her preservice teacher education courses are in foundations of education. Most of her recent published work is on cross-cultural narrative inquiry of language, culture, identity in multicultural contexts, cross-cultural teacher education, and curriculum studies which includes: *A River Forever Flowing: Cross-Cultural Lives and identities in the Multicultural Landscape* (2003); *Narrative and Experience in Multicultural Education* (Eds.) (2005); and *Handbook of Curriculum and Instruction* (Eds.) (2007). She coedits two book series: *Research for Social Justice: Personal-Passionate-participatory Inquiry* (with JoAnn Phillion; IAP); *Landscapes of Education* (with William Schubert; IAP). She was an editor of *Curriculum Inquiry* (2003–2005), an associate editor of *Multicultural Perspectives*, and a part editor of *International Handbook of Asian Education* (2008). Her current research has expanded to language, culture, identity in multicultural education with a particular focus on ethnic minority and immigrant education in the United States, Canada, Hong Kong, and Mainland China.

JoAnn Phillion is an associate professor in the Department of Curriculum and Instruction at Purdue University. She uses narrative inquiry in teaching graduate courses in curriculum theory and multicultural education, and in an undergraduate course in preservice teacher development. Her research interests are in narrative inquiry in immigrant student education, multicultural education, and teacher education. She has published extensively on her long-term narrative inquiry in an inner-city Canadian school. Her recent research is on minority students' experiences in Hong Kong schools and preservice teachers understanding of diversity issues in an international field experience. She is involved in teacher education in Hong Kong and directs a study abroad program in Honduras. She published *Narrative Inquiry in a Multicultural Landscape: Multicultural Teaching and Learning* (2002; Ablex). She coedited *Narrative and Experience in Multicultural Education* (2005; SAGE) and the *Handbook of Curriculum and Instruction* (2008; SAGE) with Ming Fang He and Michael Connelly.

Paula Booker Baker is an assistant principal at an elementary school in the metro-Atlanta, Georgia (2007–present). She has also worked on special assignment as the Title I and school improvement coordinator and teacher mentor in a North Georgia middle school. She has been working with students from prekindergarten through eighth grade in public schools. She received her EdD in curriculum studies from Georgia Southern University. She was the recipient of the *Bryan Deever Memorial Scholarship* (2004–2005). She was selected by her colleagues as *Teacher of the Year* (2002 and 2005) and was a nominee for *Disney's American Teacher Award* in 2002 and 2004. She obtained funding from the *Fulbright Memorial Fund Teacher Program* (2005) for travel to Japan to experience Japanese culture and education. Her research interests include narrative approaches to multicultural education, culturally relevant pedagogy, teacher education, resilience in African American women and students, and equity in schooling. Her research has been featured in *Current Issues in Education* and *Multicultural Perspectives*.

Joanna Cavan has been teaching French for over 20 years. She is a National Board Certified teacher of French. She is chairperson of the Department of World Languages at her school and has been working in this school for 12 years. She has served on the local community school counsel, presently serves on the school disciplinary committee, and sponsors the French National Honor Society. She is a teacher support specialist mentoring new teachers throughout the first year of teaching. For the past 10 years she has taught a reading strategies class for teachers K–12 through staff development. She is certified to teach online courses through Georgia Virtual School. She received BA in French and History at a southern university, MEd from Mercer University, EdD in curriculum studies from Georgia Southern University. She has presented her research findings to the faculty in her school to promote a deeper understanding of immigrant students, and has developed a system to mentor and counsel immigrant students and families. She organizes foreign language instruction workshops for her county schools and has established an afterschool club for immigrant students where they share their experiences. She also presents her research at GERA and AERA.

Betty C. Eng is an assistant professor at the City University of Hong Kong in the Department of Applied Social Studies. She was a teacher educator for over 10 years at The Hong Kong Institute of Education. She has also been a counselor at an international school in Hong Kong and universities in the United States where she focused on diverse learning needs of students. Prior to living in Hong Kong, she taught in the Faculty of Asian American Studies, Women Studies, and School of Education at California State University, Sacramento, and the University of California, Davis. She is a Chinese American who was born in China and raised and educated in the United States and has been working in Hong Kong for 18 years. She obtained her EdD at the Ontario Institute for Studies in Education of the University of Toronto. Her doctoral research was an exploration of teacher knowledge through personal narratives of identity, culture, and sense of belonging. Her current research interests include teacher knowledge, counseling, cross-culture studies, narrative inquiry, and inclusive education.

Angela Haynes is a media specialist at Altamaha Elementary School in Baxley, Georgia. As a former high school English teacher, she incorporates her love of language and literature in daily interaction with students and colleagues. Raised in the same rural area in which she now teaches, she seeks to challenge students through advocating dialogue and critical literacy. While acquiring her EdD in curriculum studies from Georgia Southern University, she recognized a need to challenge the cultural stereotypes wrought by the trappings of place—especially the South with which she was familiar. She continues to write and speak about her experience with place, class, and gender. She is a member of AERA and other professional organizations, and has presented her research at various conferences.

Angela M. Jaime is an assistant professor in the Department of Educational Studies of College of Education at Wyoming University. She is an enrolled member of the Pit River and Valley Maidu of Northern California. She earned BA in ethnic studies with a concentration in American Indian studies at California State University, Sacramento, MA in the College of Ethnic Studies with an American Indian studies focus at San Francisco State University, and PhD in curriculum studies at Purdue University. She specializes in American Indian education, the study of Native women and their experiences in higher education, multicultural education, and women studies.

Sonya D. Jefferson is a principal of Terrace Manor Elementary (Title I School) in Augusta, Georgia. She has been an educator for 25 years and has served as teacher and administrator at the elementary and middle school level. She advocates for children living in poverty and works with teachers and parents in the school community. Drawing on knowledge she has gained from her participants and her research inquiry, she has developed an ethic of care-and justice as a framework for transforming schools, such as the one she leads, into spaces where all children can reach their highest potential. She obtained her EdD in curriculum studies from Georgia Southern University. Her research interests include the history of Black education, school improvement, and leadership development. She has presented her work at AERA, NAME, and Georgia Reading First conferences.

Robert Lake is an assistant professor in the Department of Curriculum, Foundations and Reading at Georgia Southern University where he received EdD in curriculum studies. He has contributed to *Journal of the Imagination in Language Learning*, and is currently working as an assistant editor on a book titled: *Imagination, Cognition, and Language Acquisition*: (in press; Bastos). His research interests include curriculum of imagination, aesthetic education, postcolonial education, small schools, narrative inquiry, critical reading theory, alternative assessment, and problem-finding/solving education. He is currently teaching two courses: *Diversity in Educational Contexts* and *Investigating Critical and Contemporary Issues in Education.* He has also taught preservice reading courses and high school English as a second language.

Lyndall Muschell is an associate professor in the Department of Early Childhood and Middle Grades Education at Georgia College & State University. She obtained her EdD in curriculum studies from Georgia Southern University. In her research titled *Using Multicultural Literature to Develop Empathy and Compassion in Preservice Teachers: A First Step in Preparing Culturally Responsive Teachers,* she explores possibilities for using multicultural literature to develop empathy and compassion towards others as a first step in preparing culturally responsive teachers. This research interest grew from her 20 years of experience of working with preservice teachers. In addition to working with preservice teachers, she provides inservice and staff development workshops for inservice teachers in the public school systems within the middle Georgia area. She is an active member in professional organizations and presents her research at AERA, NAME, GAYC, NAEYC, Georgia Preschool Association, GERA, GCATE/GATE. She has been recognized frequently by her students as a Phi Kappa Phi Honor Professor.

Teresa Rishel is an assistant professor in the Department of Teaching, Leadership and Curriculum Studies at Kent State University. She teaches graduate and undergraduate courses in middle childhood, curriculum, and multicultural education. She received her PhD from Purdue University in 2003 and was the recipient of the Curriculum and Instruction Department's *Outstanding Dissertation Award* in 2004. Her research interests are adolescent suicide in exploring teacher-student relationships, school culture, and the hidden curriculum. Her work is published in *Handbook of Research in Middle Level Education Series, Handbook of Critical Media Literacy,* and *Other Kinds of Families: Exploring Diversity in School and Culture.*

Wynnetta Scott-Simmons is an assistant professor in the Tift College of Education at Mercer University. She obtained EdD in curriculum studies from Georgia Southern University. She teaches preservice and graduate level courses in reading instruction, reading theory, reading action research, language arts, and literature. As a preservice teacher educator, she works with African American and other minority students to raise their awareness of the importance of self-definition, culture, community, and educational access. She is currently an elected board member of the Georgia affiliate of AERA and has presented her research at AERA, NAME, GERA, GCATE/GATE. She taught English as a second or foreign language to native Thai and Chinese speakers in Thailand and Singapore.

Margie Wiggins Sweatman is an assistant professor at the Tift College of Education of Mercer University. She obtained her EdD in curriculum studies from Georgia Southern University. In her research, she uses critical race theory as a theoretical framework and critical narrative inquiry as research methodology to explore ways in which race can be used as a lens for examining issues of literacy for minority students and the interconnectedness of race and socioeconomics in student outcomes. She conducted her research in a metro Atlanta middle school which serves a predominantly African American population. She has found the cultural incongruence in the reading curriculum and how grade level textbooks perpetuate low academic achievement among African American students with reading disabilities. She works with teachers, administrators, and African American parents to develop a culturally responsive pedagogy that meets the needs of all students, particularly those who learn differently. Her current research and teaching interests focus on meeting multicultural needs in education by developing culturally responsive pedagogy that addresses race, class, and ability.

Clara Taylor has worked in many settings within the private sector, corporate sector, and education. She has worked as a middle grades educator, school counselor, assistant principal, and currently an instructional specialist in the Atlanta public school system. She received BS from Jacksonville State University, MA in school counseling from Clark Atlanta University, EdS in school counseling from State University of West GA along with her educational leadership certification, and her EdD in curriculum studies from Georgia Southern University. Her research interests include closing the achievement gap, reading achievement, cultural diversity, and motivational studies to improve student achievement. She conducted research on the influence of intrinsic and extrinsic motivational factors on reading achievement of middle grade students and the relationship of the teaching styles on the academic achievement and self-esteem of cultural diverse students. She has presented research at regional and national conferences such as NAME and GERA, and at local and regional communities such as leadership and teacher development workshops.

Tammy Turner-Vorbeck, PhD, is a visiting professor of teacher education at Wabash College whose focus includes multiculturalism/diversity, curriculum theory, and sociology of teaching. Her research explores relationships among schooling, culture, and identity, particularly family structure diversity and equity issues. As the mother of three older children adopted from state foster care, she combines the personal and the professional through continued advocacy for "othered" forms of family. She is coeditor of a book titled: *Other Kinds of Families: Embracing Diversity in Schools* (2007; Teachers College Press). Her work has also appeared in *Curriculum Inquiry* and *Multicultural Education*, and she is the author of several book chapters. She speaks at educational conferences on issues of family diversity and representations of family in school curricula, and she provides workshops to preservice teachers and teachers on addressing family diversity in curricula and classrooms.

Dell Wilkerson is an eighth year business education teacher for Fulton County Schools in Atlanta, Georgia. Certified in business education (6–12) and educational leadership (P–12), she has taught an array of business courses. Currently, she is teaching computer applications, business management, and accounting I and II. She received EdD in curriculum studies from Georgia Southern University. She is a recipient of Page's H. M. and Norma Fulbright Scholarship (2004) for pursuing an advanced degree. Her research interests are in narrative approaches to women and feminist studies, particularly the education of Black women in the U.S. South. In her research, she uses feminist thought and autobiography to examine her experience as a Black teenage mother and how she has become successful in spite of difficult circumstances such as poverty, racism, and other adversities. She currently works with policymakers, social service agencies, school administrators, educators, teachers, and parents to promote a strong focal point of Black feminist education as a means to secure quality jobs, housing, and healthcare for teenage mothers and their children in Black communities.